CRICKET WORLD CUP

CRICKET WORLD CUP

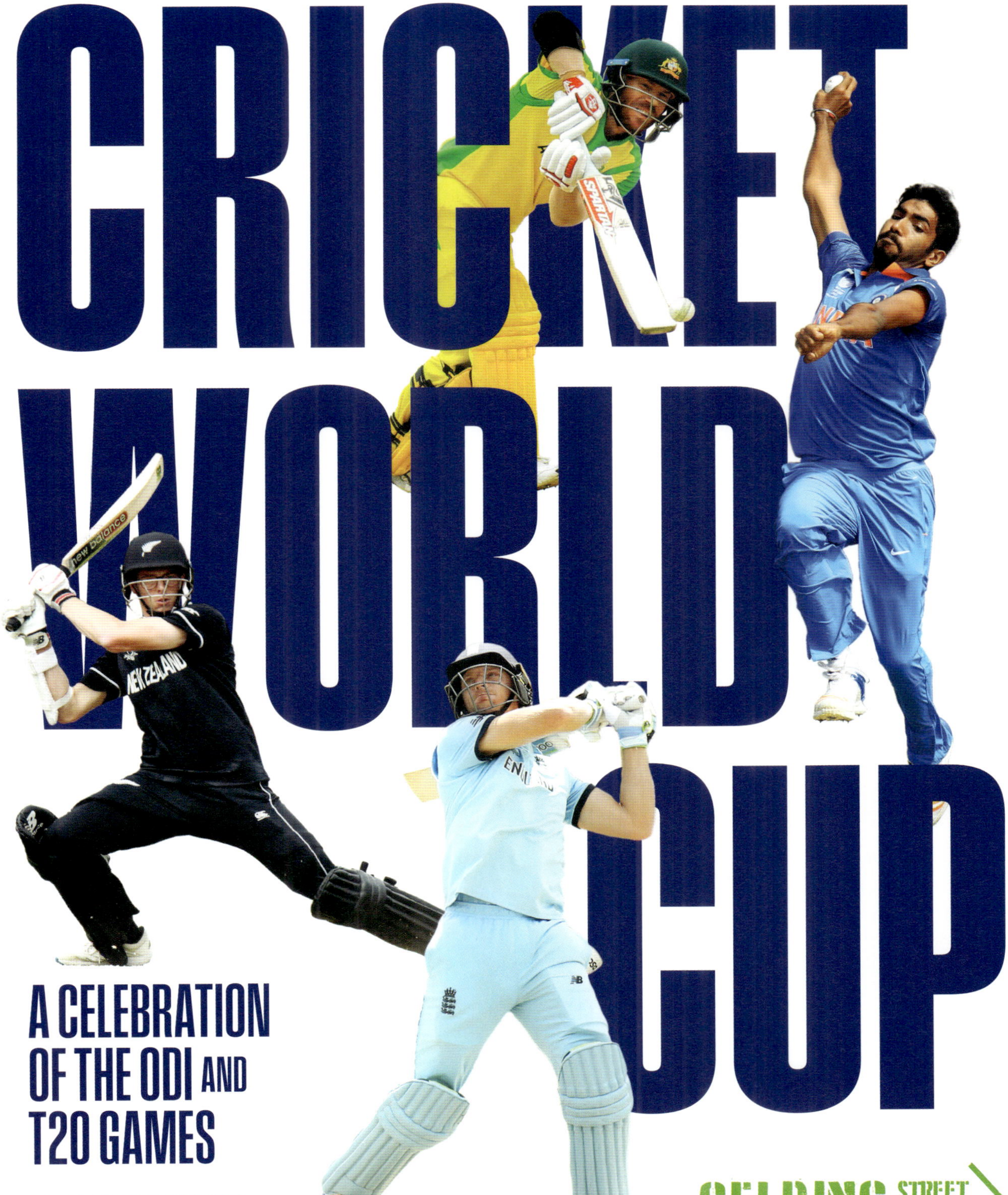

A CELEBRATION OF THE ODI AND T20 GAMES

LIAM HAUSER

GELDING STREET PRESS

A Gelding Street Press book
An imprint of Rockpool Publishing
PO Box 252
Summer Hill
NSW 2130 Australia

geldingstreetpress.com
Follow us! @ geldingstreet_press
Published in 2025 by Gelding Street Press

ISBN: 9781922662071

Design and typesetting by
Christine Armstrong, Rockpool Publishing
Edited by Brooke Halliwell

NATIONAL LIBRARY OF AUSTRALIA

A catalogue record for this book is available from the National Library of Australia

Printed and bound in China
10 9 8 7 6 5 4 3 2 1

Marlon Samuels in action during his half-century for West Indies against Pakistan in a 2007 World Cup contest at Sabina Park in the Caribbean. The wicketkeeper is Kamran Akmal.

LG
PEPSI

CONTENTS

Introduction 1

ODI World Cup (60 and 50 overs per side) 5

1975: Windies defy gallant Aussies in first World Cup decider 6

1979: King for one day; Richards on fire as Windies go back-to-back 18

1983: Indians stun Windies 28

1987: The Aussie revolution 38

1992: Cornered Tigers come from out of the blue 50

1996: Green and Gold no match for de Silva 62

1999: Aussies reign supreme after early setbacks 74

2003: No Warne, no Waughs, no worries for Aussies as Ponting's team finishes unbeaten 86

2007: Another undefeated tournament as Aussies achieve three-peat 98

2011: Tendulkar's glorious swansong 108

2015: Battle of the Trans-Tasman rivals 120

2019: Stoking the fire as finalists can't be separated 132

2023: Final ambush foils Indian surge 144

T20 World Cup 157

2007: India pips arch-rival in inaugural T20 World Cup decider 158

2009: Pakis prevail in another all-Asian decider 166

2010: World Cup glory for England at last 174

2012: Watto wins battle but Windies win the war.....182

2014: Indians fire until Sri Lanka steals the glory.....190

2016: Breathtaking Brathwaite onslaught seals deal for Windies.....198

2021: Déjà vu as Aussies dismantle Kiwis 206

2022: England completes the double.....214

2024: World Cup cricket hits the United States 222

Statistics 233

Bibliography 247

About the Author 248

INTRODUCTION

While Test cricket remains the highest level of attainment for any cricketer, the limited overs World Cup has become another vital component of the cricketing landscape. Due to the World Cup not having first-class status, purists and traditionalists could debate its worthiness or merit. But the amount of interest that World Cup cricket has generated across the globe has been undeniable, particularly with two different formats becoming entrenched. Changes in cricket and in society have resulted in countless alterations to limited overs cricket and the World Cup in general, yet the concept has arguably reached greater and greater heights.

The generally accepted form of cricket involved two innings per side (unless of course a team won by a margin of an innings), until limited overs cricket became a regular part of the English county season following the start of the Gillette Cup in 1963. While the limited overs concept gradually caught on in other countries, rainy weather in Melbourne at a crucial time proved a pivotal moment. A washed out Australia versus England Ashes Test in season 1970–71 resulted in the Test being replaced with the first ever limited overs international, which drew a crowd of 46,006. The game went from strength to strength so rapidly in the next few years, and the first ever World Cup cricket tournament was set in stone for 1975. While Test cricket had not necessarily been devalued, a lot of drawn results in the 1960s meant the international game had arguably gone into something of a lull. In retrospect, perhaps limited overs cricket gave the sport a new lease of life.

In more ways than one, the inauguration of World Cup cricket was a huge risk. Having cricket on the world stage in a format that was still relatively new and evidently not embraced by purists and traditionalists was risky enough. Additionally, it was easy to overlook the fact that a World Cup-type of concept had been tried in Test cricket all the way back in 1912. Marred by rain, the triangular series involving Australia, England and South Africa proved a failure. More than 60 years passed before any initiatives were taken to instigate another cricket tournament that brought numerous playing nations together.

The first three World Cups contained 60 overs per side, before 50 overs became the norm. The chief difference in limited overs cricket – compared with first-class cricket – was the need to score runs more rapidly which inevitably meant the batsmen ('batters' having since become the more common term) had to take more risks in an effort to push the run rate along. Captains also had to learn to rotate their bowlers – regardless of form or fatigue – simply for the reason that each bowler could deliver no more than a fifth of the total number of allotted overs per team.

Incidentally, the first four World Cups had something of a first-class look as they involved the red ball and white clothing, before the white ball and coloured clothing became the norm. Playing some games under floodlights at night became another significant feature, starting in the fifth instalment of World Cup cricket. Other changes such as the third umpire, and the right for players to seek to overturn an on-field umpire's decision, have also placed numerous incidents under increasingly intense scrutiny.

England's James Anderson celebrates a wicket.

Rule changes including fielding restrictions and 'powerplays' have invariably meant changes to batting and bowling plans, while the range of strokeplay has expanded in the meantime. Traditional strokes such as drives, cuts, pulls and hooks have been complemented with more adventurous inventions including ramp shots and switch-hits, as well as other daring and high-risk strokes. With the desire to score rapidly, perhaps it is inevitable that run rates have increased over time. Indeed, an inspection of numerous limited overs scoreboards suggests a competitive total in a 60-over contest now appears small in 50 overs! Additionally, for a number of years it was not unusual for the team batting second to effectively shut up shop when chasing a stiff target, and to simply bat out the overs. When referring to one such contest from 1987 in his book *World Cup Cricket: 1975–1999*, author Mark Browning wrote that in these situations it might be beneficial if a forfeit rule was available in order to avoid having to play many overs of pointless cricket. But with the progression and development of the game – and perhaps the hunger to win with increased amounts of money in the sport – it has become as scarce as hen's teeth for any team to simply 'give up' during a run chase. Likewise, it has also become rare to bowl economically and restrict the opposing team's run rate. Conceding 50 runs in 10 overs has gone from being expensive to being tidy, while the only realistic way to stymy an opposing team's progress has been to take wickets instead of containment.

The advent of 20 overs per side cricket simply added another component to the sport, with an even greater need to score runs as rapidly as possible. With virtually no incentive for bowlers, this shortened format has had mass commercial appeal while attracting a vastly different demographic from Test cricket, and to some extent a different market from the 50 overs per side format. It was little surprise to see the Twenty20 (T20) format become another component of World Cup cricket. This began in 2007 – the only time the two Cricket World Cup tournaments took place in the same year – after the first ever T20 international had taken place in 2005.

While the T20 World Cup has not necessarily overshadowed the limited overs World Cup, it has been abundantly clear that the demand for T20 cricket has led to a downturn in the number of 50 overs per side competitions. Although the limited overs World Cup has generally been played every four years, the T20 World Cup has not had such a consistent pattern. Trying to juggle numerous international and domestic cricket competitions and formats has inevitably become a very trying task for cricket administrators worldwide.

Only time will tell if any more World Cup cricket formats arise, or if any fall by the wayside.

ENGLAND

ODI WORLD CUP (60 AND 50 OVERS PER SIDE)

1975

Windies defy gallant Aussies in first World Cup decider

- The inaugural World Cup cricket competition begins in June 1975, with the fixtures comprising 60 overs per side
- The first game involves a fine century from England's Dennis Amiss, and a 'puzzling innings' from India's Sunil Gavaskar who scores at a snail-like pace as England wins by a huge margin
- An unbroken last-wicket stand of 64 gives West Indies an unbelievable one-wicket victory against Pakistan
- Australia's Gary Gilmour excels with ball and bat in a tense low-scoring semi-final against England at Headingley
- West Indies lift the crown following a Clive Lloyd century, a series of Aussie run-outs and a fighting last-wicket stand from Dennis Lillee and Jeff Thomson

The inaugural Cricket World Cup featured the six countries with Test status (Australia, England, India, New Zealand, Pakistan and West Indies) and two leading 'Associate' nations (East Africa and Sri Lanka). With the teams split into two groups, the top-two teams from each group progressed to the semi-finals. It was by no means surprising that England and New Zealand made the finals from Group A while India and East Africa finished third and fourth respectively. It was also not surprising that West Indies and Australia were the two Group B teams to reach the semi-finals while Pakistan and Sri Lanka missed out. However, Pakistan could just as easily have made the finals instead of West Indies or Australia had Pakistan not squandered what appeared a certain victory against the team from the Caribbean. Interestingly, this was the only tight match in either Group A or B, as nearly all of the group matches were won and lost comprehensively.

One of the semi-finals was a thriller, and the final was also a grand occasion, with West Indies ultimately the maiden titleholder after working hard to overcome a plucky Australian outfit. While the West Indians were worthy winners after being undefeated throughout the tournament, it was easy to overlook the fact that one different result (in this case the West Indies versus Pakistan match) could easily have changed the entire tournament. This sort of thing – a result that could just as easily have gone the other way and changed the course of the tournament – was to become a common theme in World Cup cricket.

A HAT-TRICK OF CLASSICS: Three great contests

Australia v Pakistan at Headingley (Leeds), 7 June

The 73-run margin was highly misleading, after Australia and Pakistan produced a well-fought battle. It was interesting to note Australia had been 5-184 and 6-195 and then tallied 7-278 in its 60 overs, before Pakistan lost its fifth and sixth wickets at 181 and 189 and then fell away.

Australia's openers were on debut in the One Day International (ODI) format, with Alan Turner scoring a brisk 46 in their partnership of 63 while Rick McCosker remained slow. Captain Ian Chappell was in brilliant form before falling for 28, and then the Australians stumbled to 4-124. Greg Chappell played many fine shots in his 45, but it was Ross Edwards who made the biggest difference. Max Walker hung around as 48 runs were added for the seventh wicket, before Jeff Thomson hit a four and a six in the final over on his way to a quickfire 20 not out. Edwards, who reached his half-century with a six, finished on 80.

Pakistan opener Majid Khan scored 44 of his 65 runs in boundaries before he was caught behind down the legside attempting a sweep shot, leaving the team

England's Dennis Amiss hammers the ball during his century in the first World Cup cricket match.

vulnerable at 4-104. Pakistani skipper Asif Iqbal batted solidly while Wasim Raja played his part in a 77-run stand, before the batting team lost its last six wickets for just 24 runs as Dennis Lillee did most of the damage. Australia's other opening bowler, Thomson, had tidy figures of 8-2-25-1 although nearly half of those runs came from illegal deliveries, with his first over containing 11 balls.

Australia 7-278 (Ross Edwards 80 not out; Naseer Malik 2-37) beat Pakistan 205 (Majid Khan 65, Asif Iqbal 53; Dennis Lillee 5-34, Max Walker 2-32) by 73 runs.

West Indian Keith Boyce in action, watched by Australian wicketkeeper Rod Marsh during the World Cup decider.

Pakistan v West Indies at Edgbaston (Birmingham), 11 June

This nail-biting match was a genuine classic. It was definitely a case of one team snatching victory from the jaws of defeat while the other snatched defeat from the jaws of victory.

Pakistan missed captain Asif Iqbal due to illness, while all-rounder and future captain Imran Khan was unavailable due to exams at Oxford University. In the end, the Pakistanis compensated for these absentees and were poised for a comfortable win, but they couldn't land the knockout blow.

Stand-in captain Majid Khan led from the front after winning the toss, scoring a fine 60 at the top of the order. His departure left the team 3-140, before quality half-centuries to Mushtaq Mohammad and Wasim Raja set up a challenging total. Wasim's 58 came from just 57 balls, and ODI debutant Javed Miandad chipped in with 24 on the day before his 18th birthday. There was some ragged fielding from the West Indians, although Pakistan's batting tapered off a little after Wasim's dismissal with the total at 249.

Needing 267 runs, the West Indians were 3-36 after Sarfraz Nawaz dismissed the first three batters, with two of them caught behind and the other one lbw. The score could have been worse had Majid not dropped Rohan Kanhai at mid-wicket, but the West Indians were still in trouble when Kanhai played the ball onto his stumps. The score was 5-99 when Viv Richards hooked a catch to deep backward square leg, leaving captain Clive Lloyd with a huge task on his hands. He passed 50 but then was controversially given out caught behind off Miandad, leaving West Indies 7-151. Another 15 runs were added before Keith Boyce chopped a pull shot onto the stumps, and then Vanburn Holder unleashed some good shots. Deryck Murray edged a streaky boundary, before Holder lashed a catch to cover-point. With the West Indians on 9-203 in the 46th over, the result appeared a formality.

Andy Roberts clouted the economical Miandad through the covers for four, before an all-run four to Murray was followed by a cracking cover drive for another boundary. Parvez Mir bowled a maiden, but the Pakistanis were running out of specialist bowling options while the last-wicket pair chiselled away at the seemingly impossible requirement. Roberts clubbed a four in the second-last over, and just five more runs were needed with one over to spare amid great tension. Wasim Raja was called on to bowl for the first time all day, and he delivered a short ball down legside which Roberts tried to pull. Wicketkeeper Wasim Bari threw erratically to the bowler's end as a run-out option turned into two runs thanks to an extra run from an overthrow. Roberts then nudged the ball into a gap on the legside and managed two runs to tie the scores, before tapping the fourth ball to mid-wicket and scampering through for the winning run. In hindsight, this result had a huge bearing on the tournament as a win to Pakistan may have been enough to knock West Indies out of the finals series.

West Indies 9-267 (Deryck Murray 61 not out, Clive Lloyd 53; Sarfraz Nawaz 4-44, Naseer Malik 2-42) beat Pakistan 7-266 (Majid Khan 60, Wasim Raja 58, Mushtaq Mohammad 55) by one wicket.

New Zealand v India at Old Trafford (Manchester), 14 June

This was by far the most competitive match in Group A, with the winner to progress to the finals series while the loser would be eliminated. There were standout performances from Kiwi captain Glenn Turner and Indian all-rounder Syed Abid Ali, and useful contributions from numerous other players.

After India won the toss, Sunil Gavaskar succumbed to the Hadlee brothers as Richard held a catch off Dayle with the total at 17. Thirty-one runs were added for the next wicket before Richard Hadlee, Brian McKechnie and Hedley Howarth made breakthroughs to leave India struggling at 6-101. At number seven, Abid Ali rescued the situation with a fine 70 while Madan Lal and captain Srinivas Venkataraghavan also made valuable contributions. Fifty-five runs were added for the seventh wicket, and 60 were added for the ninth wicket before a 13-run last-wicket stand ended with a run-out from the final delivery of the 60th over.

The Kiwis lost their first wicket at 45 before stumbling to 3-70 in pursuit of 231. The second victim, Geoff Howarth, was unluckily run out when a straight drive from Turner was deflected by the bowler into the stumps at the non-striker's end. Unfazed, New Zealand's captain held the innings together as partnerships of 65, 50 and 39 unfolded, before the winning runs were scored with only seven balls remaining. Turner finished unconquered on 114 from 177 balls, with 13 fours.

New Zealand 6-233 (Glenn Turner 114 not out, Brian Hastings 34; Syed Abid Ali 2-35) beat India 230 (Syed Abid Ali 70, Anshuman Gaekwad 37; Brian McKechnie 3-49, Dayle Hadlee 2-32) by four wickets.

SIX OF THE BEST: Individual performances

(excluding the finals)

Dennis Amiss 137 off 147 balls: England v India at Lord's (London), 7 June

While Indian opener Sunil Gavaskar's snail-like scoring earned plenty of attention in the England versus India contest, Dennis Amiss's fine century did not deserve to be overlooked. England's opener stroked 18 attractive boundaries as he compiled 137 in the total of 4-334.

Amiss reached his half-century as he gently nudged off-spinner Srinivas Venkataraghavan through point for four, before hitting three successive fours off Mohinder Amarnath's medium-pace. A cracking square drive was followed by a back foot drive slightly in front of point, and then a back foot cover drive. Amiss again turned his attention to Venkataraghavan, as the opener used his feet and lifted a four over mid-on before a cover drive produced his 14th four and took his score to 82. Amiss was just two runs shy of his ton when the score stood at 1-150 during lunch. Soon afterwards, he glided an Abid Ali delivery off his legs to go from 99 to 101. In Eknath Solkar's only over, Amiss advanced the left-arm spinner and hammered the ball wide of long-on where two fielders couldn't prevent another boundary.

England stumbled from 1-230 to 4-245, with Amiss the fourth batter dismissed as he swung at a Madan Lal delivery in the 51st over. Chris Old

The West Indies v Pakistan match was definitely a case of one team snatching victory from the jaws of defeat while the other snatched defeat from the jaws of victory.

promptly came out and blazed an unbeaten 51 from just 30 balls, to ensure a strong total which India never looked like chasing.

Glenn Turner 171 not out off 201 balls: New Zealand v East Africa at Edgbaston (Birmingham), 7 June

While Amiss compiled a stylish century at Lord's on day one of the tournament, New Zealand opener Glenn Turner made an even bigger score against East Africa at Edgbaston. After winning the toss and choosing to bat, Turner batted throughout New Zealand's innings and set up the strong total of 5-309. Turner faced 201 balls for his unbeaten 171 and registered 16 fours and two sixes. The Kiwi skipper played many glorious drives as well as plenty of cross-batted shots, and his innings contained at least one blemish. Turner would have been out for 16 had economical left-arm spinner Parbhu Nana held a sharp caught-and-bowled chance, and the prolific scorer was also reprieved on 27 when a slow-moving fielder could not grasp a chance at mid-off. New Zealand went on to win by 181 runs.

Dennis Lillee 12-2-34-5: Australia v Pakistan at Headingley (Leeds), 7 June

Dennis Lillee's best ODI bowling figures were in the 1975 World Cup, after Australia set Pakistan a target of 279. Lillee claimed the first wicket in the run chase when a brilliant yorker rattled left-hander Sadiq Mohammad's stumps, before the Western Australian sparked a late collapse after Pakistan was soundly placed at 4-181. Lillee crucially dismissed Asif Iqbal for 53, as Pakistan's skipper drove at a ball that swung in and uprooted the off-stump. Lillee's third victim was Sarfraz Nawaz who fiddled outside off-stump and edged behind, and the final two wickets of the match also fell to Lillee. Asif Masood skied a slog and was caught by a running Walker who collided with teammate Ashley Mallett, before Wasim Bari was caught by a diving wicketkeeper.

Keith Fletcher 131 off 147 balls: England v New Zealand at Trent Bridge (Nottingham), 11 June

Keith Fletcher's contribution far outweighed that of anyone else, as he scored nearly half of England's total of 6-266 while his score was 94 runs better than England's second top-scorer. Batting at number three, Fletcher came to the crease with the score at 1-27 before John Jameson departed just one run later.

Fletcher's first boundary was a superbly timed cover drive off the back foot, before he went from 12 to 16 as he flicked a half-volley in front of square leg. Fletcher's half-century yielded seven fours, before the remainder of his innings featured a lot more running between the wickets. A cut shot for three runs raised his century, and his innings included 13 fours before he was run out from the final ball of the innings as he chanced a risky second run.

John Morrison was the only New Zealander to score more than 27 in the run chase, as he made 55 in a disappointing total of 186.

Zaheer Abbas 97 off 89 balls: Pakistan v Sri Lanka at Trent Bridge (Nottingham), 14 June

Pakistan was in control at 1-159 when Zaheer Abbas came to the crease, before his attractive innings of 97 helped build a total of 6-330. Sadiq Mohammad was first out for 74, and captain Majid Khan followed soon after for 84. Zaheer stroked the ball elegantly on both sides of the wicket, as he registered 10 fours and a six while facing just 89 balls. With a century in sight, he played a Tony Opatha delivery onto the stumps.

John Snow 12-6-11-4: England v East Africa at Edgbaston (Birmingham), 14 June

East Africa had no answer to the pace bowling of John Snow, who captured four wickets and conceded just 11 runs in his 12 overs after the host nation set a target of 291. England's opening bowler captured the first four wickets as the Africans fell to 4-21. His victims were Frasat Ali, Yunus Badat, Jawahir Shah and Samuel Walusimbi. Ali made a duck from 17 balls when a Snow delivery flattened his off-stump, before Badat made a third-ball duck as he inside-edged the ball onto his leg-stump. Snow's final two victims were lbw, with the bowler not raising either arm as he appealed which made it look like there was a more enthusiastic appeal from behind the stumps.

England's Keith Fletcher raises his bat after reaching triple figures against New Zealand, while umpire Bill Alley looks on.

HEADLINE MOMENT

Sunil Gavaskar's scoring rate against England

Needing 335 runs to beat England at Lord's on day one of the inaugural Cricket World Cup, India lost only three wickets while batting out its 60 overs but finished 203 runs shy of the target. This justifiably earned a place in Andrew Ward's book *Cricket's Strangest Matches*, with this match headlined 'A Puzzling Innings'.

The puzzling innings came from Indian opener Sunil Gavaskar. He batted throughout the entire innings and faced 174 balls yet scored only 36 runs. His motives and the reasons for his staggeringly slow scoring rate will always remain a matter of conjecture. Given that the Indians were dismissed for a miserable 42 in their previous outing at Lord's, John Woodcock suggested in *The Times*: 'If they could not win on Saturday, as they decided they could not after England's innings, then every effort had to be concentrated on averting another collapse.'

According to a *Cricinfo* article by Martin Williamson, India's manager GS Ramchand said: 'It was the most disgraceful and selfish performance I have ever seen . . . his excuse [to me] was, the wicket was too slow to play shots but that was a stupid thing to say after England had scored 334. The entire party is upset about it. Our national pride is too important to be thrown away like this.' Williamson also reported one rumour was that Gavaskar was unhappy with team selections, while another rumour was that Gavaskar was annoyed with the appointment of Venkataraghavan as captain. Years later, Gavaskar said he couldn't really explain it. He said he had faintly edged the second ball of the innings to the wicketkeeper, but nobody appealed. Had the batter walked or been given out, it would have saved a lot of ensuing trouble – let alone boring cricket. A number of Indian supporters entered the playing arena and urged Gavaskar to show more urgency. Another spectator was arrested for punching a policeman.

Bandula Warnapura strikes the ball through the off side during Sri Lanka's gallant but unsuccessful run chase against Australia.

FIRST SEMI-FINAL

England v Australia at Headingley (Leeds), 18 June

The England versus Australia semi-final had all the makings of a brilliant Ashes contest, except that it featured only one innings per team instead of two. It would have been fascinating to see how the match panned out if it had featured two innings per team.

The game was well known for Gary Gilmour's brilliance. The left-arm bowler captured the first six wickets before finishing his 12 overs with 6-14, and later he made the highest individual score of the match. Only 187 runs were scored in the contest, with England's innings lasting 36.2 overs before the run chase lasted 28.4 overs.

Amiss was lbw with just two runs on the board, and Barry Wood was bowled off his pad before Tony Greig was superbly caught one-handed by a diving Rod Marsh in front of first slip. England crashed from 3-33 to 6-36 as three lbw appeals were upheld, with the first of those victims being Frank Hayes who offered no shot. When Walker had Chris Old caught at second slip, the score was 7-37. The eighth wicket fell at 52, before vital partnerships of 21 and 20 unfolded. England captain Mike Denness fought hard for his 27 before he was ninth out when he edged an inswinger onto the stumps. Geoff Arnold registered a couple of streaky boundaries, including a French cut, before the final wicket was the fifth lbw of the innings.

Although the 94-run target was perhaps 20 or 30 runs higher than it could have been, Australia seemingly had little to worry about. Victory was only 77 runs away when Arnold trapped Alan Turner lbw, before Ian Chappell was lbw to Snow with the total at 24. Greg Chappell's only scoring shot was a four before he too was lbw to Snow, and then Old claimed three wickets in eight balls to have the Australians in dire trouble. Greg Chappell, McCosker and Edwards were dismissed with the total at 32, with McCosker bowled through the gate before Edwards inside-edged a ball that dislodged his middle-stump. When Marsh chanced his arm and lost his off-bail, Gilmour came to the crease with the score a worrying 6-39.

Doug Walters always seemed to struggle in England, but he made a precious contribution on this occasion. He pushed a Snow delivery just wide of second slip, before a cracking off drive from Gilmour raised Australia's 50. A misfield at mid-wicket enabled Walters to turn a single into a three, before a turning point came as Gilmour edged Snow through the slips at catchable height and obtained four runs. Gilmour twice drove Old past cover for four before edging a Peter Lever delivery to second slip, only for another crucial chance to go begging. Walters drove Arnold for four before cutting the same bowler for another boundary, and soon the Australians were home as the batting duo scampered a short single.

Australia 6-94 (Gary Gilmour 28 not out, Doug Walters 20 not out; Chris Old 3-29, John Snow 2-30) beat England 93 (Mike Denness 27; Gary Gilmour 6-14, Max Walker 3-22) by four wickets.

SECOND SEMI-FINAL

New Zealand v West Indies at The Oval (London), 18 June

It was hardly surprising that West Indies won comfortably, but for a little while it appeared that New Zealand could mount a decent challenge. Ultimately, the Kiwis did not score nearly enough runs, before having to defend the sub-standard total without Richard Hadlee.

Sent in, New Zealand began uncertainly as John Morrison scratched around for five runs before being trapped lbw. Geoff Howarth and captain Glenn Turner consolidated the innings and steered the Kiwis into a sound position at lunch: 1-92 from 29 overs. The complexion changed sharply in the first over after the break as Kanhai held a splendid diving slips catch to account for Turner. John Parker fell cheaply and then Howarth, having just passed 50, edged a low catch to the wicketkeeper to leave the Kiwis wobbling at 4-106.

A 19-run stand ensued but then the collapse resumed as Ken Wadsworth attempted a big hit and was easily caught at mid-on. Bernard Julien and Roberts did the main damage with the ball while Lloyd claimed one vital wicket in his tidy spell, before Holder cleaned up the tail. After taking a catch, Holder bowled the final three batters. Lance Cairns perished to a wild swing before Hedley Howarth was out first ball, and then Richard Collinge hung around briefly until a Holder delivery penetrated his defence. The Kiwis tallied only 158 runs and failed by 46 balls to bat out their overs.

New Zealand's hopes were raised as Roy Fredericks hooked a catch to backward square leg. Coincidentally, both teams lost their first wicket with eight runs on the board. As it turned out, a second-wicket stand of 125 virtually guaranteed a West Indian victory. Gordon Greenidge scored the bulk of his runs in boundaries despite a modest strike rate, while Alvin Kallicharran produced a player-of-the-match innings. Collinge held a return catch before winning two appeals for lbw as West Indies slipped from 1-133 to 4-142, but the mini collapse was too late for the Kiwis. Lloyd fell with the total at 151, before Julien whipped a four off his legs. When Kanhai drove a full-toss through cover for an all-run four as spectators entered the arena, the West Indians had won with nearly 20 overs to spare.

West Indies 5-159 (Alvin Kallicharran 72, Gordon Greenidge 55; Richard Collinge 3-28) beat New Zealand 158 (Geoff Howarth 51; Bernard Julien 4-27, Vanburn Holder 3-30) by five wickets.

Gavaskar's motives and the reasons for his staggeringly slow scoring rate will always remain a matter of conjecture.

FINAL

West Indies v Australia at Lord's (London), 21 June

The first World Cup final was a grand occasion in more ways than one, as Lord's was a hive of activity despite the absence of the English team. A high quality contest unfolded, with fielding ultimately making all the difference.

Sent in, West Indies had bad luck early on when Fredericks hooked a bumper over the fence and was out hit wicket as he lost his balance and hit the stumps with his foot. Kallicharran began well but then departed for 12 after lasting 26 minutes, and Greenidge scored just 13 in 80 minutes before his exit left West Indies 3-50.

The pendulum swung as Lloyd struck two sixes and 12 sumptuous fours in his outstanding knock of 102 from 85 balls. Before reaching 50, the West Indian skipper was crucially reprieved as Edwards spilled a catch at mid-wicket. Kanhai, who was bogged down for a lengthy period, was also dropped by Edwards before Lillee gave Kanhai another reprieve. The total was 199 when Lloyd was ruled caught behind down the legside off Gilmour, who soon bowled Kanhai and Richards to reduce the West Indians to 6-209 in the 46th over. Boyce, Julien and Murray made crucial runs before Holder scored a two off the final ball when a run-out chance was butchered. Despite Gilmour's five-wicket haul, Australia faced a stiff target of 292.

Australian opener Alan Turner made his limited overs international debut during the inaugural Cricket World Cup.

Australia was 1-25 when McCosker edged Boyce to second slip, before a string of useful partnerships followed. Several decent starts were wasted as Richards produced three run-outs while Ian Chappell was batting. Alan Turner and Greg Chappell succumbed to direct hits, with the former seeking a short single before the latter chanced a run from a misfield. Ian Chappell, who was earlier reprieved when Boyce spilled a return catch, became another run-out victim when he steered the ball to mid-wicket where Richards threw to the bowler who broke the wicket. When an in-form Walters played all around a delivery from Lloyd, Australia was in trouble at 5-170.

The next two wickets fell at 195 and 221, with Marsh bowled before Gilmour hooked a catch to Kanhai who was mobbed by spectators. Edwards lobbed an easy catch to cover, before Walker turned the ball to square leg and was run out by a direct hit from Holder as Walker momentarily left his crease. Australia's last pair required 59 runs from 43 balls, but it was not a lost cause as Thomson struck Roberts down the ground for four before flicking the same bowler through square leg for another boundary. Lillee hit Holder for four over mid-on, before Thomson scored a two as another run-out chance arose. When Thomson dived to complete another two as the bails were dislodged, a crowd invasion occurred. Shortly after play resumed, Thomson clipped a simple catch to Fredericks at cover off a no-ball, and the fielder threw unsuccessfully to the bowler's end as ignorant spectators again dashed onto the arena. Thomson and Lillee ran three but then stopped amid the chaos, and Lloyd was unaware of the no-ball call until he sought clarification from umpire Tom Spencer.

Finally, with Holder bowling to Thomson as Australia needed 18 runs from nine balls, a desperate swing failed to connect. Thomson left his crease as he thought of a run, and then he dived in vain as Murray underarmed the ball into the stumps to produce the fifth run-out of the innings. Security staff had their hands full as another invasion occurred, before Lloyd held aloft the main prize. He was also an obvious player of the match for his masterful batting, while it was easy to overlook that he was the most economical bowler in the match with his figures of 12-1-38-1.

West Indies

West Indies		R	B
Roy Fredericks	hit wicket b Lillee	7	13
Gordon Greenidge	c Marsh b Thomson	13	61
Alvin Kallicharran	c Marsh b Gilmour	12	18
Rohan Kanhai	b Gilmour	55	105
Clive Lloyd (c)	c Marsh b Gilmour	102	85
Viv Richards	b Gilmour	5	11
Keith Boyce	c Greg Chappell b Thomson	34	37
Bernard Julien	not out	26	37
Deryck Murray (+)	c & b Gilmour	14	10
Vanburn Holder	not out	6	2
Sundries	(lb 6, nb 11)	17	
TOTAL	**(60 overs) 8-291**		

DID NOT BAT: Andy Roberts

FALL: 12, 27, 50, 199, 206, 209, 261, 285

Lillee 12-1-55-1, Gilmour 12-2-48-5, Thomson 12-1-44-2, Walker 12-1-71-0, Greg Chappell 7-0-33-0, Walters 5-0-23-0

Australia

Australia		R	B
Alan Turner	run out (Richards)	40	54
Rick McCosker	c Kallicharran b Boyce	7	24
Ian Chappell (c)	run out (Richards/Lloyd)	62	93
Greg Chappell	run out (Richards)	15	23
Doug Walters	b Lloyd	35	51
Rod Marsh (+)	b Boyce	11	24
Ross Edwards	c Fredericks b Boyce	28	37
Gary Gilmour	c Kanhai b Boyce	14	11
Max Walker	run out (Holder)	7	9
Jeff Thomson	run out (Murray)	21	21
Dennis Lillee	not out	16	19
Sundries	(b 2, lb 9, nb 7)	18	
TOTAL	**(58.4 overs) 274**		

FALL: 25, 81, 115, 162, 170, 195, 221, 231, 233, 274

Julien 12-0-58-0, Roberts 11-1-45-0, Boyce 12-0-50-4, Holder 11.4-1-65-0, Lloyd 12-1-38-1

UMPIRES: Dickie Bird, Tom Spencer

TOSS: Australia

PLAYER OF THE MATCH: Clive Lloyd

WEST INDIES WON BY 17 RUNS

1979

King for one day; Richards on fire as Windies go back-to-back

- Australia fields understrength teams as authorities reward players who didn't play 'rebel' cricket under Kerry Packer
- An associate ICC member defeats a full ICC member, as Sri Lanka accounts for India
- Geoff Boycott bags two wickets before being dismissed for a single run when England contests Australia
- England and West Indies win hard-fought semi-finals
- West Indies reign supreme again as a sluggish 129-run opening partnership involving Mike Brearley and Geoff Boycott hurts England's run chase in the decider

Cricket had changed enormously since the 1975 World Cup due to the emergence of World Series Cricket in 1977, spearheaded by Australian media magnate Kerry Packer. The cricket world was essentially split into two, with players signed by the 'rebel' organisation earning a lot more money than those who remained with the traditional format. For the sake of the World Cup in particular, it was fortunate that a truce took place in May 1979; just a couple of weeks before the start of the tournament. With every team, it was a matter of conjecture as to how harmonious things were behind the scenes after World Series Cricket had created countless factions. The situation for Australia appeared unsettled as the team which toured England was well below full strength. The Australian authorities repaid the loyalty shown by the players who remained with the establishment from 1977 to 1979, which meant no Ian Chappell, Greg Chappell, Dennis Lillee, Jeff Thomson and Rod Marsh in the 1979 World Cup. Lillee was in England to do some newspaper reporting for the tournament, and he dropped into the Australian dressing room to wish the players good luck for their opening encounter with England. Rightly or wrongly, fairly or unfairly, many of the players showed no warmth towards him.

As was the case four years earlier, the 1979 World Cup was staged in England with eight teams split into two groups. All bar one of eight countries backed up from the 1975 tournament, with the exception being East Africa which was excluded in favour of Canada. With the six Test nations guaranteed a place in the World Cup, Sri Lanka and Canada joined them after defeating Denmark and Bermuda respectively in the qualifying fixtures.

The groups were different from 1975, as England was the only team in Group A on both occasions. In 1979, the host nation was grouped with Australia, Canada and Pakistan, while India, New Zealand, Sri Lanka and West Indies were in Group B. It was perhaps fitting that England and West Indies contested the final after they went through the round-robin and semi-final matches unbeaten, although West Indies had a washed out game against Sri Lanka. Pakistan and New Zealand earned second place in their respective groups before coming off second best in the semi-finals, while Sri Lanka and Australia enjoyed victory only once each. The Canadians and Indians were unable to register a win, with Canada outplayed in its three matches while India was competitive in one.

In the end, the West Indian line-up was again just too strong.

Joel Garner savours World Cup glory after capturing five wickets against England in the final.

Glenroy Sealy is caught at second slip by Ian Botham off the bowling of Mike Hendrick, during Canada's miserable total of 45 in an eight-wicket loss to England.

A HAT-TRICK OF CLASSICS: Three great contests

England v Pakistan at Headingley (Leeds), 16 June

The struggle for supremacy was evident as bowlers held sway while the scoring was very slow. Lower order partnerships played a huge part, particularly in the first innings.

After losing the toss and being sent in to bat, England captain Mike Brearley snicked the second ball of the match to diving wicketkeeper Wasim Bari. England soon plunged to 2-4 as Derek Randall was also caught behind. A slow 47-run third-wicket stand unfolded, and then a television commentator said 'a good recovery going on here' as Majid Khan was about to start the 22nd over. This very delivery trapped Geoff Boycott plumb lbw, ensuring Pakistan remained on top. Graham Gooch top-scored with 33 until he was well caught at backward point, and David Gower looked confident until a Majid yorker removed his off-stump. Ian Botham played some attacking shots before he slashed at Majid and lost his leg-stump, and the score tumbled to 8-118 when Chris Old offered Asif Iqbal an easy return catch. The ninth-wicket partnership produced 43 precious runs, with Bob Willis riding his luck at times in his crucial knock of 24. Nonetheless, Pakistan's target of 166 seemed very achievable.

Sadiq Mohammad made a positive start before Pakistan inexplicably crashed from 0-27 to 6-34 in five overs, with Mike Hendrick capturing four wickets and Botham nabbing two. Pakistan's hopes were revived as 52 runs were added for the seventh wicket, before Old had Wasim Raja lbw. Asif raised the only individual half-century of the game with his fifth boundary, but then he gloved the next ball to first slip to leave his team 8-115; only a slightly worse position than England had been in.

Imran was gritty but very slow, while Bari showed a little more urgency as a 30-run stand set up a very tense finish. Boycott broke through as Bari was streakily caught behind from an edge onto the pad. The last pair added six runs in 23 minutes, and so another 15 runs were required from 25 balls when a delivery from Boycott landed in the slot. Sikander Bakht tried to loft it over the infield but Hendrick was up for it, as he leapt to take a fine catch at mid-off to win the game. Ironically, Sikander had earlier reprieved Willis when he failed to hold an overhead catch in the same fielding position.

England 9-165 (Graham Gooch 33; Majid Khan 3-27, Sikander Bakht 3-32) beat Pakistan 151 (Asif Iqbal 51; Mike Hendrick 4-15, Geoff Boycott 2-14) by 14 runs.

Sri Lanka v India at Old Trafford (Manchester), 16-18 June

Sri Lanka's 47-run victory over India was notable, as an associate ICC member defeated a full ICC member. The start was delayed due to rain, and Sri Lanka missed its captain Anura Tennekoon due to a hamstring injury.

Stand-in captain Bandula Warnapura was the first wicket to fall before Sunil Wettimuny and Roy Dias produced some attractive strokes during a 96-run second-wicket stand. They posted solid half-centuries before Duleep Mendis boosted the scoring as his 64 from 57 balls included one four and three sixes. Sudath Pasqual made a quick 23 not out to help set India a worthy but not daunting target of 239 on day two, which took place two days after the opening day.

India's top-six made double figures but none could go on with the job as the top-six tallied 143 runs. The team was soundly placed at 0-60 and 2-119, before the run-out of Gundappa Viswanath was a huge turning point. Wickets began to tumble regularly, with Somachandra de Silva's leg-spin causing a lot of damage before Tony Opatha captured the final three wickets to seal a comfortable victory for the Sri Lankans.

Sri Lanka 5-238 (Sunil Wettimuny 67, Duleep Mendis 64, Roy Dias 50; Mohinder Amarnath 3-40) beat India 191 (Dilip Vengsarkar 36, Anshuman Gaekwad 33; Somachandra de Silva 3-29, Tony Opatha 3-31) by 47 runs.

West Indies v New Zealand at Trent Bridge (Nottingham), 16 June

The contest featuring West Indies and New Zealand on a flat deck turned out to be the second-closest contest in the round-robin series. With the Kiwis missing captain Geoff Howarth for the second straight match due to a hamstring injury, stand-in skipper Mark Burgess opted to chase a target. Although Desmond Haynes and Viv Richards failed, with Richards scoring an uncharacteristic nine off 30 balls, Gordon Greenidge and Alvin Kallicharran set the platform for a decent total. Following Greenidge's departure for 65, captain Clive Lloyd assumed responsibility and went on to make the top score. There were a couple of hiccups as the West Indians stuttered to 7-204, before Joel Garner made an unbeaten nine during an unbroken eighth wicket stand of 40.

New Zealand's openers departed before the total reached 40, and then Jeremy Coney and Glenn Turner hinted at a revival until they fell in quick succession as the Kiwis went from 2-90 to 4-91. Richard Hadlee scored a lively 42 at number eight, but all five West Indian bowlers conceded fewer than 3.8 runs per over as the Kiwis never looked like reaching the target.

West Indies 7-244 (Clive Lloyd 73 not out, Gordon Greenidge 65, Alvin Kallicharran 39; Jeremy Coney 2-40, Lance Cairns 2-48) beat New Zealand 9-212 (Richard Hadlee 42, Jeremy Coney 36; Andy Roberts 3-43, Joel Garner 2-45) by 32 runs.

SIX OF THE BEST: Individual performances

(excluding the finals)

Gordon Greenidge 106 not out off 173 balls: West Indies v India at Edgbaston (Birmingham), 9 June

On the first day of the tournament, India's total of 190 never looked sufficient when West Indian openers Gordon Greenidge and Desmond Haynes began the run chase. Greenidge made the first century of the tournament to set up a nine-wicket victory with 8.3 overs to spare. Greenidge hit nine fours and a six in his undefeated 106, with the six coming as he swung a Mohinder Amarnath delivery over square leg.

Greenidge was on 81 when Haynes was dismissed for 47, with West Indies just 53 runs shy of the target. As soon as Greenidge turned a delivery behind square to go from 99 to 101, play was held up due to a crowd invasion. Greenidge appeared the worse for wear from the buffeting, as the damage was done despite the intervention of security guards. Greenidge hit the winning boundary soon afterwards, then promptly grabbed two stumps and sprinted off the field to avoid being swamped as the crowd again swarmed the arena.

Chris Old 10-5-8-4: England v Canada at Old Trafford (Manchester), 13-14 June

It was highly unusual for Chris Old to be England's fourth change bowler, particularly after Boycott delivered one tidy over as the third change bowler. Old nonetheless conceded just eight runs in his 10 overs while taking four wickets in damp conditions in this contest with Canada.

The Canadians had their highest partnership of the innings, 12, when Old won an lbw appeal against Tariq Javed to make the score 3-25. Old's other three victims were bowled as Canada tumbled to 7-41, before succumbing for a miserable 45. For the record, England went on to win by eight wickets.

Bob Willis 10.3-3-11-4: England v Canada at Old Trafford (Manchester), 13-14 June

While Chris Old won player of the match honours for his 4-8 against Canada, opening bowler Bob Willis's figures were almost as good as Old's. Like Old, Willis did not require any support from a teammate for his wickets. Willis's first victim was Canada's captain and wicketkeeper Bryan Mauricette, who was bowled to leave Canada 6-38. Willis's second victim was Franklyn Dennis, who scored a defiant 21 in nearly two hours at number three before losing his balance and falling on his wicket as he encountered a short ball. This made the score 8-41, and soon the Canadians were all out for 45 in 40.3 overs after Robert Callender and Jitendra Patel were bowled by Willis.

Majid Khan 61 off 100 balls and 12-0-53- 3: Pakistan v Australia at Trent Bridge (Nottingham), 13-14 June

With Pakistan trouncing Australia by 89 runs, Pakistani captain Asif Iqbal was named player of the match after scoring 61 off 57 balls at number six and then returning tidy figures of 12-0-36-0 as an opening bowler. Majid Khan could have considered himself unlucky not to receive the individual prize, having made the same score off 100 balls as an opener before returning figures of 12-0-53-3 as the other opening bowler. Asif and Majid hit seven fours each, while Majid also hit a six.

Majid was into stride with a pull for four off Graeme Porter, before a copybook cut shot off Geoff Dymock also found the boundary. Majid played the late cut to good effect against change bowlers Gary Cosier and Allan Border, before swatting a full-toss from Border to the mid-wicket boundary. When Majid lofted Border over the long-on boundary to reach his half-century, a small crowd invasion took place. Majid and his opening partner Sadiq were dismissed with the total on 99, before Asif's innings helped set up the total of 7-286.

Australia progressed from 3-46 to 3-117 before Majid bowled the left-handed Graham Yallop to ensure Pakistan maintained the upper hand. When Majid held a catch off his own bowling to dismiss Cosier for a first-ball duck, the score was 6-137. Majid's final wicket came when his opening batting partner held a catch to account for Porter, making the score 8-175.

Mike Hendrick 12-6-15-4: England v Pakistan at Headingley (Leeds), 16 June

With England needing to bowl well to have any chance of defending a seemingly sub-standard total of 9-165 against Pakistan, Mike Hendrick produced one of the best spells of the tournament. In addition to snaring four wickets, he delivered six maidens in his dozen overs.

It appeared that luck might not be on Hendrick's side as wicketkeeper Bob Taylor dropped a regulation catch off his bowling to reprieve Majid. Incidentally, it didn't take long to compensate, as Hendrick captured 4-3 in eight deliveries to break the back of the innings. Majid was caught at second slip, and then Mudassar Nazar was lbw before the left-handed Sadiq played the ball onto his stumps. Haroon Rasheed was Hendrick's final victim when he snicked a catch to first slip, and Pakistan had sunk to 6-34 after Botham also chipped in with a couple of wickets. Hendrick also featured in the final wicket as he held a fine catch to secure a nervous 14-run triumph.

Graham Gooch earned player-of-the-match honours in England's victories against Australia and New Zealand.

Alan Hurst 10-3-21-5: Australia v Canada at Edgbaston (Birmingham), 16 June

Canada's innings against Australia began spectacularly as two dot balls were followed by four successive boundaries to 39-year-old Glenroy Sealy in the first over. The bowler, Rodney Hogg, was soon replaced after his two overs cost 26 runs. The other opening bowler, Alan Hurst, was a different matter as he delivered five times as many overs, took five more wickets and conceded five fewer runs.

Hurst had two lbw appeals upheld before he bowled Charles Baksh as the score went from 1-50 to 4-51. As the Canadians later slumped from 5-97 to 105 all out, Callender was caught behind off Hurst who then claimed his fifth wicket when Cornelius Henry was caught by Australian captain Kim Hughes. Nobody reached 30 with the bat in this match while every bowler conceded fewer than 30 runs, with Australia winning by seven wickets.

HEADLINE MOMENT

More wickets than runs for Geoff Boycott against Australia

Known as a stonewalling opening batter who could be very difficult to dislodge, Geoff Boycott seldom bowled but there were occasions that his right-arm medium-pacers came in handy. One such occasion was on the first day of the 1979 World Cup. He came on as the fourth change bowler and returned excellent figures of 6-0-15-2. Of England's six bowlers, he was the only one to capture more than one wicket!

Australia was solidly placed at 1-97 until Boycott broke through as Andrew Hilditch dragged the ball onto his wicket. Boycott also claimed the next wicket as Australian skipper Kim Hughes was superbly caught by Hendrick at mid-wicket. Four run-outs subsequently cruelled the innings, and Australia finished with a disappointing 9-159 from its 60 overs. The run chase began disastrously as Boycott was lbw for a single, before Randall also departed for one run. England eventually won by the comfortable margin of six wickets, with numerous scribes noting the oddity of Boycott accumulating more wickets than runs.

FIRST SEMI-FINAL

England v New Zealand at Old Trafford (Manchester), 20 June

The England versus New Zealand semi-final was a contender for game of the tournament, with only nine runs separating the two teams. Sent in, England struggled to 2-38 but Brearley played a captain's knock at the top of the order, while Gooch showed more urgency. Gooch slammed a straight six off Brian McKechnie, and then played a fine back foot drive for four. England reached 2-96 before falling to 4-98 with the dismissals of Brearley and Gower, who was run out as he sought a risky second run. Gooch passed 50 with successive boundaries, and shared a useful 47-run stand with Botham before the latter departed. Gooch reached 71 before perishing to a yorker which he tried to crunch through the off side, and then the second-ball dismissal of Old made the score a shaky 7-178. Randall found form at a crucial time following a string of failures, and he hammered a six during a vital 41-run stand which helped set a target of 222.

Four lbw verdicts and two run-outs hindered New Zealand's progress after the openers put on 47 runs. The score was 3-104 when Jeremy Coney became the third lbw victim, before another huge turning point came just eight runs later. On 69 and seeking a second run, John Wright was run out after Turner sent him back.

The Kiwis had a stroke of good fortune as Gooch spilled a catch, but the respite was short-lived as Burgess was foolishly run out while pursuing a single that was never on. Willis suffered a critical knee injury, but in his final over he had Turner lbw to make the score 6-162. The twists and turns continued as Warren Lees was caught by Boycott at long-on, only for the fielder to step over the boundary and concede six runs. The pendulum swung back England's way as Richard Hadlee was bowled with the total on 180. Lance Cairns hammered a six but then belted a catch to mid-wicket, and another 13 runs were added before Lees succumbed to a yorker. The last pair of McKechnie and Gary Troup could scrape together only four runs from the final over when 14 were needed, with Botham bowling.

England 8-221 (Graham Gooch 71, Mike Brearley 53; Brian McKechnie 2-46) beat New Zealand 9-212 (John Wright 69; Mike Hendrick 3-55) by nine runs.

SECOND SEMI-FINAL

West Indies v Pakistan at The Oval (London), 20 June

Although not as close as the other semi-final, the West Indies versus Pakistan semi-final was another magnificent contest. Greenidge and Haynes set the tone for a game featuring nearly 550 runs as they put on 132 for the first wicket. Haynes had a crucial reprieve with his score on 32 when Imran dropped what television commentator Richie Benaud described as 'as close to a sitter as you can have'. Greenidge's innings included a vicious hook for six off Sarfraz Nawaz, before being smartly caught behind off Asif Iqbal. The second wicket fell at 165 as Asif held a low return catch to account for Haynes, and later he dismissed Lloyd and Richards in one over as they tried to force the pace when well set. From 4-236, West Indies progressed towards 300 thanks largely to Collis King's 34 from 25 balls. Despite not taking a wicket, Majid had fine figures as his 12 overs cost just 26 runs.

Pakistan lost an early wicket before Zaheer Abbas combined with Majid for a 166-run second-wicket stand. There were some superb strokes but the partnership was by no means unblemished, with Majid dropped in the slips early on before a few edged shots went to the boundary. Zaheer was seven runs shy of a ton when he succumbed softly, as he glanced a catch down the legside. Soon the score changed from 2-187 to 4-187 with successive balls, with Majid hitting an easy catch to cover before Javed Miandad was lbw for a golden duck. A catch was badly missed at deep mid-on to reprieve Asif, but another chance was taken in the same position soon afterwards. Haroon was sent packing as he chanced a risky second run, and then Mudassar clipped a legside catch. Imran hit a four but then he was superbly caught-and-bowled by Richards, and Pakistan was all but gone at 8-228. Sarfraz and Bari resisted temporarily before succumbing to Andy Roberts, with the last wicket falling with 22 balls remaining as the batting team was 44 runs shy of the target.

West Indies 6-293 (Gordon Greenidge 73, Desmond Haynes 65; Asif Iqbal 4-56) beat Pakistan 250 (Zaheer Abbas 93, Majid Khan 81; Colin Croft 3-29, Viv Richards 3-52) by 43 runs.

FINAL

West Indies v England at Lord's (London), 23 June

England was counting the cost before a ball was even bowled as Willis withdrew due to the knee injury he sustained in the semi-final. Interestingly, England's selectors replaced the right-arm fast bowler with left-arm orthodox spinner Phil Edmonds. West Indies fielded the same team as in the semi-final and had Lloyd, Greenidge, Kallicharran, Richards, Murray and Roberts backing up from the 1975 decider.

After Brearley invited the West Indians to bat, Greenidge struggled before he was run out by a direct hit from Randall. The score was 3-55 following the departures of Haynes and Kallicharran but a turning point came when Richards, on 22, survived a confident lbw appeal against Hendrick. Having begun a little scratchily, Richards became ominous as he pulled a short ball from Boycott for six and then clipped a full-toss for four.

West Indies was 4-99 as Old took a fine return catch to dismiss Lloyd, but then a bit of luck eluded England in the lead-up to lunch. Richards passed 50 as an edge flew just wide of first slip, and King top-edged a hook shot which soared over the cordon for four. The score was 4-125 at the 34-over mark when lunch was taken, before King outscored Richards during an onslaught as the former recorded his only ODI half-century. England paid dearly for playing only four specialist bowlers as part-timers Boycott, Gooch and Wayne Larkins were expensive while filling the void. King creamed two half-trackers into the crowd during a Larkins over which cost 16 runs, before a Boycott over cost 15 runs. When King holed

Surrounded by teammates, West Indian captain Clive Lloyd holds aloft the World Cup trophy on the Lord's balcony at the conclusion of the final.

'In a parallel universe, Hendrick dismissed Richards for 22 and is the hero of England's first World Cup victory.'

– 2019 Wisden Cricketers' Almanack

out to deep square leg in the 51st over to leave West Indies 5-238, he had blasted 10 fours and three sixes in his 86 from 66 balls. Richards raised his ton in the next over as he glided a full-toss to the mid-wicket boundary, and then took charge as wickets fell around him.

Following the departure of Deryck Murray for five, the next three batters were dismissed without scoring. An unfazed Richards slammed 14 runs off Hendrick in the final over, including a four from a bullet-like straight drive which luckily eluded the bowler and umpire. The highlight was the last ball as Richards stepped to the off side and flicked a low full-toss over square leg in a highly unorthodox fashion for his third six. Having also hit 11 powerful fours, Richards finished on 138 from 157 balls as West Indies tallied 9-286. Curiously, England's bowlers did not deliver a single wide or no-ball.

England's openers made a steady but slow start, with Brearley surviving a couple of chances as he and Boycott put on 79 runs in 25 overs before the tea break. The West Indians had been 3-84 at the same stage before reaching 100 in the 30th over for the loss of four wickets, whereas England reached triple figures in the 32nd over with the openers still batting. Lloyd dropped his second catch, with Boycott the beneficiary this time, but there was no indication it would prove costly. Although England's openers tallied 10 fours between them, they could not boost the run rate to sufficient proportions. The partnership ended at 129 when Brearley hooked a catch to deep square leg in the 38th over, and Boycott departed in the 40th over when he spooned an easy catch to mid-wicket.

With 151 runs needed in the final 20 overs, England virtually needed a partnership to match that of Richards and King. Gooch unleashed a flurry of strokes while Randall supported him during a lively 48-run stand, which left England needing 104 runs from 80 balls. Incredibly, the match was over just 26 balls later as the hosts lost 8-11, with Croft starting and finishing the rout while Garner took 5-4 in 11 balls. Randall was bowled as he swished at Croft before Garner bowled Gooch, Gower and Larkins in quick succession, with Gower out for a fourth-ball duck before Larkins was out first ball. Gooch and Larkins were no match for Garner's lethal yorker, whereas the left-handed Gower tried to crack the ball through the off side.

Botham tried to belt Croft for six and was superbly caught by Richards in the deep, and Garner was again on a hat-trick as he bowled Old and then had Bob Taylor edging behind. Hendrick was the sixth England player to hear the 'death rattle' and, astonishingly, five England batters including the last three had failed to score, after the last four West Indian batters also scored nothing. The 92-run margin was highly misleading, given how hard fought the game was until England's batting collapse. Intriguingly, the century partnership in the West Indian innings was ultimately match-winning while England's century partnership virtually enhanced West Indies' chances due to how many overs it used up. England also rued Willis's absence, and the non-selection of a designated fifth bowler. As usual, a bit of luck also played a part. This was especially the case for Hendrick, who held a catch and had figures of 12-2-50-2 before souveniring a stump when he was last out. In the *2019 Wisden Cricketers' Almanack*, Rob Smyth reported: 'In a parallel universe, Hendrick dismissed Richards for 22 and is the hero of England's first World Cup victory.' Had that been the case, Richards' astonishing last-ball six would have been one of many things not to occur.

In the end, Richards and King reigned supreme with the bat before Roberts, Holding, Croft and Garner played their part with the ball. Richards and King also bowled tidily, with Richards having figures of 10-0-35-0 while King had 3-0-13-0. They also held a catch each.

West Indies

West Indies		R	B
Gordon Greenidge	run out (Randall)	9	31
Desmond Haynes	c Hendrick b Old	20	27
Viv Richards	not out	138	157
Alvin Kallicharran	b Hendrick	4	17
Clive Lloyd (c)	c & b Old	13	33
Collis King	c Randall b Edmonds	86	66
Deryck Murray (+)	c Gower b Edmonds	5	9
Andy Roberts	c Brearley b Hendrick	0	7
Joel Garner	c Taylor b Botham	0	5
Michael Holding	b Botham	0	6
Colin Croft	not out	0	2
Sundries	(b 1, lb 10)	11	
TOTAL	**(60 overs) 9-286**		

FALL: 22, 36, 55, 99, 238, 252, 258, 260, 272

Botham 12-2-44-2, Hendrick 12-2-50-2, Old 12-0-55-2, Boycott 6-0-38-0, Edmonds 12-2-40-2, Gooch 4-0-27-0, Larkins 2-0-21-0

England

England		R	B
Mike Brearley (c)	c King b Holding	64	130
Geoff Boycott	c Kallicharran b Holding	57	105
Derek Randall	b Croft	15	22
Graham Gooch	b Garner	32	28
David Gower	b Garner	0	4
Ian Botham	c Richards b Croft	4	3
Wayne Larkins	b Garner	0	1
Phil Edmonds	not out	5	8
Chris Old	b Garner	0	2
Bob Taylor (+)	c Murray b Garner	0	1
Mike Hendrick	b Croft	0	5
Sundries	(lb 12, nb 3, w 2)	17	
TOTAL	**(51 overs) 194**		

FALL: 129, 135, 183, 183, 186, 186, 188, 192, 192, 194

Roberts 9-2-33-0, Holding 8-1-16-2, Croft 10-1-42-3, Garner 11-0-38-5, Richards 10-0-35-0, King 3-0-13-0

UMPIRES: Dickie Bird, Barrie Meyer

TOSS: England

PLAYER OF THE MATCH: Viv Richards

WEST INDIES WON BY 92 RUNS

1983

Indians stun Windies

- Zimbabwe upsets Australia in African nation's World Cup debut
- Kapil Dev's heroics prevent Zimbabwe from recording two shock wins
- Headlines of 'The Davis Cup' arise after West Indian quick Winston Davis nabs seven wickets in an innings
- Despite a loss to India in the round-robin series, West Indies romps to a third straight final appearance
- With a hat-trick of titles in sight, West Indians crumble in low-scoring finale after a match-turning catch from Kapil Dev sends Viv Richards on his way

While English venues again hosted World Cup matches, a difference in 1983 was that Wales did as well. Another change was the inclusion of Zimbabwe for the first time, while Canada was omitted.

Although there were again two groups of four, there were twice as many group matches as previously due to each team contesting each other team twice in the group stage. It was a sign of expansion, while it was useful for each team to have a second chance against each other team in its group. England was the pacesetter in Group A while Pakistan and New Zealand finished equal-second on points, and the Kiwis unfortunately missed the finals as their run rate was 3.927 compared to Pakistan's 4.014. New Zealand's 11-run loss to Pakistan in the last of the Group A matches was one of many decisive factors.

West Indies lost one match in Group B but topped the ladder while India was second. With Greg Chappell missing the tournament because of a neck injury while Dennis Lillee played despite battling a knee injury, Australia had a disappointing time. After a shock loss to Zimbabwe on day one, Australia was on the back foot. A huge win against India revived Australia's chances, before India turned the tables a week later and ensured Australia would not make the play-offs. The unpredictable nature of the tournament showed as India upset West Indies four days prior to being thrashed by Australia, before West Indies later beat the Indians who ultimately upstaged the team from the Caribbean in the game that mattered the most.

A HAT-TRICK OF CLASSICS: Three great contests

England v New Zealand at Edgbaston (Birmingham), 15 June

Six days after England thrashed New Zealand by 106 runs, a very different match unfolded between the two countries. Remarkably, it was the first time the Kiwis beat the Poms in an international cricket fixture on England soil.

When England lost its first wicket at 63, Ian Botham came in at number three for a change. He struck a four and a six, only to depart from the ninth ball he faced as John Bracewell took a sharp return catch. Opener Graeme Fowler went on to score a composed 69, and fellow left-hander David Gower batted superbly but was badly let down by his teammates below him. England's last seven batters tallied just 28 runs, and the hosts went from 7-233 to 234 all out. Gower hit six fours and four sixes in his unbeaten 92 from just 96 balls, but England had wasted the chance to score at least another 25 runs after losing its final wicket with 28 balls remaining in the allotted overs.

The Kiwis were reeling at 2-3 after Bob Willis dismissed the openers, although the lbw verdict was a little suspect before there was doubt that the catch behind the

Malcolm Marshall (bowler) and Jeff Dujon (wicketkeeper) celebrate the dismissal of Wasim Raja in the West Indies versus Pakistan semi-final at The Oval.

wicket was a clean one. After the fourth wicket fell at 75, Geoff Howarth and Jeremy Coney nearly doubled the total before Howarth was run out as he chanced Graham Dilley's arm. The cheap dismissal of Ian Smith left New Zealand 6-151, but Coney pushed on while Richard Hadlee showed his batting ability. Only 14 runs were needed when Willis bowled Hadlee, before the England captain accounted for Lance Cairns as well. Needing four runs from the last over with Paul Allott bowling, the Kiwis earned two byes from the second ball. With the scores level, John Bracewell settled the issue as he struck the penultimate delivery to the boundary. Coney's 66 not out came from 97 balls, after he earlier took 1-27 from 12 overs.

New Zealand 8-238 (Jeremy Coney 66 not out, Geoff Howarth 60; Bob Willis 4-42) beat England 234 (David Gower 92 not out, Graeme Fowler 69; Richard Hadlee 3-32, Lance Cairns 3-44) by two wickets.

Pakistan v Sri Lanka at Headingley (Leeds), 16 June

When Pakistan and Sri Lanka first met in the 1983 World Cup, Pakistan won by 50 runs after tallying 5-338. In the rematch seven days later, the margin was much closer while there were considerably fewer runs. There were four standout displays, with Sri Lankan medium-fast bowler Ashantha de Mel and Pakistani leg-spinner Abdul Qadir bagging five wickets each while Pakistani skipper Imran Khan and teammate Shahid Mahboob starred with the bat.

Sri Lankan skipper Duleep Mendis's decision to bowl first appeared vindicated as de Mel captured the first three wickets, before Rumesh Ratnayake won two lbw appeals from successive balls as Pakistan slumped to 5-43. A match-turning sixth-wicket partnership produced 144 runs before Mahboob fell for a solid 77. Imran farmed the strike in the closing overs as he worked his way to a century to set up a total of 7-235.

Sri Lanka lost its first wicket at 22 before partnerships of 79 and 61 put the team in the box seat, but none of its batters could go on with the job. The Sri Lankans lost 5-9 as they crashed to 7-171, with a wicket to Rashid Khan followed by three to Qadir before Somachandra de Silva was run out. After Qadir held a catch off Mahboob, Sri Lanka's last pair needed to score 37 runs in six overs. De Mel and number 11 Vinothen John reduced the requirement to 12 from 10 balls before de Mel drove a Sarfraz Nawaz delivery to long-off where Imran took the catch. Ultimately, Sri Lanka rued its middle-order collapse and its inability to capitalise after having Pakistan on the ropes. It was incredible to think the winning team had been 5-43 before the losing team was 2-162 in reply.

Pakistan 7-235 (Imran Khan 102 not out, Shahid Mahboob 77; Ashantha de Mel 5-39, Rumesh Ratnayake 2-42) beat Sri Lanka 224 (Sidath Wettimuny 50, Roy Dias 47; Abdul Qadir 5-44, Rashid Khan 2-31) by 11 runs.

India v Zimbabwe at Nevill Ground (Royal Tunbridge Wells), 18 June

It would be fair to say Zimbabwe really lost this match to India's skipper Kapil Dev, rather than to the Indian team. Rarely has one batter dominated a team's innings as much as Kapil did this time. It was impossible to imagine what India's total and the match outcome would have been without his contribution.

India's openers failed to score, before the loss of another three quick wickets left the team 5-17. Sixty runs were added for the sixth wicket, and then the departures of Roger Binny and Ravi Shastri left India 7-78. The ensuing partnership produced 62 runs, but India was still in dire straits when the eighth wicket fell. It was a sign for Kapil to throw caution to the wind, while Syed Kirmani held firm and made the second top score of the innings. An unbroken ninth-wicket stand of 126 unfolded, with Kirmani grafting his way to an unbeaten 24 from 56 balls. Kapil finished with 175 not out, with 100 of his runs coming in boundaries.

Zimbabwe began soundly in reply before crumbling to 6-113, and the result seemed a foregone conclusion although India had been in a worse position. Kevin Curran did his best to keep the match alive as he dominated a seventh wicket stand of 55, before the eighth wicket fell at 189. With Curran able to keep most of the strike during the ninth-wicket stand, Zimbabwe had an outside chance of winning until he was caught for 73. The last pair had little hope of scoring the 37 runs required for victory, and Kapil fittingly ended the match with a caught-and-bowled to seal a 31-run triumph with three overs remaining.

India 8-266 (Kapil Dev 175 not out; Peter Rawson 3-47) beat Zimbabwe 235 (Kevin Curran 73; Madan Lal 3-42) by 31 runs.

Pakistan's Javed Miandad departs the scene after being dismissed against England.

SIX OF THE BEST: Individual performances

(excluding the finals)

Duncan Fletcher 69 not out off 84 balls and 11-1-42-4: Zimbabwe v Australia at Trent Bridge (Nottingham), 9 June

The saying 'catches win matches' was never more evident than in Zimbabwe's opening World Cup match, particularly for Duncan Fletcher. The left-handed batter arrived at the crease with the score at 4-86, and soon the Australians reduced the African nation to a worrying 5-94. But Fletcher produced a captain's knock and found the required support at the other end. Fletcher registered five fours and hit some powerful shots as he made 69 not out, having crucially been reprieved twice.

With his team defending a total of 239, Fletcher achieved the best bowling figures with his right-arm medium-fast bowling. He captured the first four wickets – all to catches including a couple of classics. He was the second change bowler, with Vince Hogg having returned tidy figures of 0-15 from six overs before a back injury prevented him bowling any more on the day.

Fletcher played only six ODIs but his debut was memorable as plenty of good fortune went his way. Twenty-two years later, there was also some luck and good fortune that went his way as he coached England to its first Ashes series win in 18-and-a-half years.

David Gower 130 off 120 balls: England v Sri Lanka at County Ground (Taunton), 11 June

David Gower's international record did not necessarily reflect his talent, but most of his centuries were a sight to behold. One case in point was on 11 June 1983, as England hosted Sri Lanka at Taunton. Gower's elegant and delightful innings of 130 included 12 fours and five sixes. After coming to the wicket at 1-49, Gower departed at 7-298. England slid from 3-193 to 5-194 as Mike Gatting and Ian Botham were run out, but Gower overcame these setbacks as his superb knock set up a total of 9-333.

Gower opened his account as he flicked a legside full-toss to the fine leg boundary. His first six was a flick over mid-wicket, and later an edge flew away streakily to take him from 93 to 97. Gower reached triple figures with an authoritative clout over the mid-wicket boundary before he replicated the stroke a couple more times with the same result. Gower's final six was struck over extra cover, before he was bowled as he chanced his arm once too often. Sri Lanka batted gallantly in reply before falling 48 runs shy of victory. England off-spinner Vic Marks took 5-39 from 12 overs, while Dilley also had a brilliant match with 29 runs off 16 balls and bowling figures of 11-0-45-4.

Winston Davis 10.3-0-51-7: West Indies v Australia at Headingley (Leeds), 11-12 June

A headline reading 'The Davis Cup' would relate to tennis, except for one occasion when it pertained to World Cup cricket. The play on words (and names)

was too good for at least one newspaper writer to resist, after West Indian fast bowler Winston Davis captured seven wickets against Australia in a World Cup fixture. Interestingly, Davis and teammate Wayne Daniel were only included due to the absence of Joel Garner and Malcolm Marshall to injury.

The match was played over two days, after rain delayed the start. After being 3-32 with Gordon Greenidge, Desmond Haynes and Viv Richards dismissed, West Indies reached 5-160 after 42 overs on day one before finishing on 9-252 following 18 overs the next day. After Andy Roberts claimed a wicket, Australia was effectively 2-18 when Graeme Wood retired hurt after a Michael Holding delivery took off and struck him on the side of the head.

Davis claimed his first scalp with the total at 55 when Hughes edged a cut shot and was caught at first slip by opposing skipper Clive Lloyd. A speedy 59-run stand followed, and Davis had unflattering figures of 5-0-37-1 until he ripped through the Australian line-up. His second, third and sixth victims were left-handers. Yallop tried to whip a delivery through the legside but the ball flew high between the wicketkeeper and third man, and was well caught by a running Holding. David Hookes edged a low catch to the wicketkeeper, before Ken MacLeay's hook shot lobbed to square leg. Following a wicket to Holding, Davis snared his fifth when an airy drive from Lawson produced an edge behind. Border skied a slog to mid-wicket where Lloyd lost sight of the ball in the sun before reaching forward to hold the catch while his body moved backwards. Lillee was last to depart when a yorker rattled his leg-stump.

Incidentally, Davis took only one wicket in the next four matches and lost his place for the finals series.

Richard Hadlee 10.1-4-25-5: New Zealand v Sri Lanka at County Ground (Bristol), 13 June

Richard Hadlee's figures of 5-25 were all the more impressive for the fact that none of his teammates were involved in any of his wickets. Sri Lanka was 1-16 when Hadlee had Sidath Wettimuny lbw, before Hadlee held a catch off Ewen Chatfield with the total at 56. The batting team was soundly placed at 3-144 before stuttering to 5-144 in the space of four balls, as Hadlee bowled Mendis and then trapped Arjuna Ranatunga in front of the stumps. Hadlee later polished off the innings as he held a catch off his own bowling to dismiss de Mel, and then bowled Rumesh Ratnayake. Chatfield was even more economical than Hadlee as the former finished with 2-24 from 12 overs, and neither of them were required to bat as the Kiwis passed the target of 207 for the loss of five wickets in less than 40 overs.

England skipper Bob Willis appeals for the run out of Pakistan's Javed Miandad.

A headline reading 'The Davis Cup' would relate to tennis, except for one occasion when it pertained to World Cup cricket.

Ken MacLeay 11.5-3-39-6: Australia v India at Trent Bridge (Nottingham), 13 June

Trevor Chappell was named player of the match in Australia's 162-run thumping of India, having hit 11 fours in his 110 from 131 balls in a total of 9-320. Kapil Dev shone for India with figures of 12-2-43-5, before Ken MacLeay claimed outstanding figures of 11.5-3-39-6. MacLeay was the standout bowler in this game as veterans Lillee and Thomson were excluded. Astonishingly, MacLeay needed assistance from a teammate for only one of his six dismissals.

Dilip Vengsarkar was MacLeay's first victim as India's number four batter was adjudged lbw, and then Sandeep Patil was bowled by the Western Australian medium-fast bowler before another run was added. MacLeay used his height to take a return catch and send Yashpal Sharma packing, leaving India 5-64. Following a seventh wicket partnership of 58, MacLeay had Madan Lal caught by the bowler's state and international teammate Tom Hogan. Roger Binny became MacLeay's fifth victim when another lbw appeal was upheld, before MacLeay wrapped up the match when he bowled Kirmani.

Australian captain Kim Hughes sweeps against West Indies. Hughes didn't have a happy tournament as Australia failed to reach the finals while he encountered some problems within the team.

Zimbabwe's first ODI appearance would be a contender for the biggest upset in World Cup cricket history.

Kapil Dev 175 not out off 138 balls: India v Zimbabwe at Nevill Ground (Royal Tunbridge Wells), 18 June

Kapil Dev finished his 225-game ODI career with just one century and a modest batting average of 23.79. His lone ton was memorable nonetheless, as he skippered his country in the 1983 World Cup. Were it not for his amazing 175 not out, India would surely have lost to Zimbabwe on 18 June, and the outcome of the tournament could have been entirely different.

India's captain came to the crease with the score at 4-9, and soon it became 5-17. Further wickets fell at 77, 78 and 140, before India finished with an unlikely 8-266 to set up a 31-run victory. Kapil hit the ball powerfully without being reckless, as his innings yielded 16 fours and six sixes. At one stage he struck three fours and three sixes in the space of 18 balls. A few miscued airy strokes fell safely, and a difficult catch went to ground when Kapil was in the 90s. His score was the highest by an individual in a World Cup match at the time, before it was surpassed a little over four years later.

For the record, Kapil was also the most economical bowler in the India versus Zimbabwe clash on 18 June as he returned figures of 11-1-32-1. He finished the match with a catch off his own bowling, after he had earlier held a catch in the field.

HEADLINE MOMENT

Zimbabwe knocks over Australia

Zimbabwe's first ODI appearance would be a contender for biggest upset in World Cup cricket history. Another 31 years passed before the African nation beat Australia again in international cricket.

The difference in fielding probably determined the outcome, as the Australians spilled several catches before the Zimbabweans held some excellent catches. With an entire team of ODI debutants, Zimbabwe enjoyed an opening stand of 55 before Lillee, as first change bowler, dismissed the openers with consecutive balls. A 31-run third-wicket stand was again followed by two wickets from successive deliveries, with Graham Yallop's part-time left-arm medium-pace doing the trick. Jack Heron and David Houghton were caught behind, although there was doubt over the legitimacy of the latter catch. The next wicket left Zimbabwe 5-94, but slipshod fielding from the Australians enabled the so-called novices to boost their total substantially. Curran and skipper Duncan Fletcher produced a 70-run partnership, before Iain Butchart combined with Fletcher for an undefeated 75-run stand.

Needing to score at exactly four runs per over, Australia slipped from 0-61 to 2-63 as Fletcher produced a double breakthrough. The only right-hander in the top-seven was captain Kim Hughes, who made a duck. The other top-six batters were tied down against an honest and consistent bowling line-up. Fletcher claimed another two wickets before another turning point arose as a direct hit from Heron ran out top-scorer Kepler Wessels. A brilliant catch by Andy Pycroft in the deep sent Allan Border packing, before Geoff Lawson's dismissal left Australia 7-176. Despite some pugnacious batting from Rod Marsh and some brisk runs from Rodney Hogg, the requirement was beyond Australia's reach. Not even a towering six to Marsh in the final over could rescue Australia, as the African nation recorded a shock 13-run victory. It remained one of Houghton's favourite days of cricket despite scoring a golden duck, while it was also a memorable time for Egyptian-born off-spinner John Traicos despite being wicketless. Traicos conceded just 27 runs in his 12 overs and had the unique honour of being in this momentous occasion for Zimbabwe after playing in South Africa's final Test series – in 1969–70 when the Springboks trounced Australia – before the nation's exile from international cricket. Another quirk was the surnames of the opening bowlers, with Rodney Hogg and Geoff Lawson sharing the new ball for Australia before Vince Hogg and Peter Rawson opened for Zimbabwe.

Zimbabwe 6-239 (Duncan Fletcher 69 not out, Iain Butchart 34 not out; Graham Yallop 2-28, Dennis Lillee 2-47) beat Australia 7-226 (Kepler Wessels 76, Rod Marsh 50 not out; Duncan Fletcher 4-42) by 13 runs.

FIRST SEMI-FINAL

England v India at Old Trafford (Manchester), 22 June

Following five convincing victories and just one defeat before the finals, England came crashing down as one sub-standard performance ended the host nation's campaign. Frustratingly for the hosts, their top-five batters made starts before being dismissed for scores between 17 and 33 after Willis chose to set a target. After being 0-69, England could not produce another lengthy partnership as the score stumbled to 8-177. The run-outs of Allan Lamb and Ian Gould did not help, and the ball failed to reach the boundary for more than an hour at one point. Dilley made a useful if streaky 20 not out, and some wayward bowling and fielding enabled 36 runs to be added for the final two wickets. The final wicket fell from the last allotted delivery in the 60 overs.

India went from 0-46 to 2-50 with the departures of openers Sunil Gavaskar and Kris Srikkanth. Ninety-two runs were added for the next wicket but an Indian win was far from a certainty as the run rate was sedate, while a couple of appeals were turned down. Mohinder Amarnath also had a narrow escape when he was nearly caught at square leg. When he was run out, England was right back in the game.

The momentum quickly changed as the incoming batter, Patil, unleashed a flurry of strokes. Sixty-three runs were added at around seven per over before Yashpal was well caught for a sensible 61. Patil finished with 51 not out from just 32 balls, and the outcome was somewhat misleading as India won with 5.2 overs to spare and with six wickets in hand.

India 4-217 (Yashpal Sharma 61, Sandeep Patil 51 not out) beat England 213 (Graeme Fowler 33, Chris Tavaré 32; Kapil Dev 3-35, Mohinder Amarnath 2-27) by six wickets.

SECOND SEMI-FINAL

West Indies v Pakistan at The Oval (London), 22 June

The second semi-final was more anti-climactic than the first one, which was played on the same day. There was little point wondering what might have been if Javed Miandad had played for Pakistan, rather than being sidelined with influenza.

After the Pakistanis were sent in to bat, opener Mohsin Khan played an anchoring role as he produced a Test match type of innings. Pakistan wobbled at 2-34 before a 54-run stand hinted at a revival, only for Zaheer Abbas to depart in the last over before lunch. The addition of 51 runs for the next wicket again suggested a competitive total could eventuate, until Marshall struck twice without the addition of a run. Pakistan was unable to gain any momentum, with the entire innings yielding only two boundaries including one to Mohsin. When the opener departed with three overs left, he had scored just 70 off 176 balls. Pakistan still had two wickets in hand at the expiration of the 60 overs, yet had scored at just 3.067 runs per over.

The West Indian openers were not at their best, before their dismissals left the defending titleholders uncertainly placed at 2-56. There was no further joy for the Pakistanis as Richards powered to 80 not out from 96 balls, including 11 fours and a six. Richards had had a narrow escape early in his innings when he was nearly caught at short leg off Abdul Qadir, who caused some problems in his first few overs and claimed the second wicket when Haynes succumbed to a googly. But it was not Pakistan's day. While Richards was in commanding form, Larry Gomes made a composed 50 not out from 100 balls to help set up the landslide victory with 11.2 overs left.

West Indies 2-188 (Viv Richards 80 not out, Larry Gomes 50 not out) beat Pakistan 8-184 (Mohsin Khan 70; Malcolm Marshall 3-28, Andy Roberts 2-25) by eight wickets.

FINAL

India v West Indies at Lord's (London), 25 June

Although India had beaten West Indies in one encounter during the round-robin part of the tournament, the powerful West Indian line-up was an overwhelming favourite to win another World Cup title. Lloyd, Greenidge, Richards and Roberts remained from the 1975 and 1979 finals while Haynes, Holding and Garner backed up from the 1979 decider. Lloyd sustained a groin injury during the semi-final but passed fit for the decider, although he was fortunate to be allowed a runner when he batted.

After Lloyd won the toss and sent India in, Gavaskar scored the first two runs before he edged a catch behind in the fifth over. Srikkanth unleashed some cracking shots including a hook for six, and a square drive which rocketed to the boundary. Srikkanth had hit 34 of his 38 runs in boundaries when he was trapped lbw, leaving India 2-59. Amarnath crawled to 26 from 80 balls despite finding the rope three times, before his dismissal was soon followed by Yashpal's exit as India went from 2-90 to 4-92. Kapil slammed three fours before he holed out from the eighth ball he faced, and then another wicket made the score 6-111. Forty-two precious runs were added for the next two wickets, before the ninth fell at 161. The tail continued to wag as another 22 runs were scored before the final wicket fell with 32 balls left in the allotted 60 overs.

Chasing only 184, West Indies had an early setback as Greenidge offered no stroke to a ball that seamed in and hit the off-stump. Richards, however, began even more ominously than he had in the 1979 decider. He struck a series of boundaries while Haynes played a supporting role, until Haynes drove a catch to cover just after the total reached 50. Seven more runs were added before Richards mistimed a pull and was well caught by a running Kapil at deep mid-wicket. This monumental breakthrough was undoubtedly the turning point in the game, and it reinforced the saying 'catches win matches'.

Lloyd, Gomes and Faoud Bacchus failed as West Indies crumbled to 6-76. Jeff Dujon and Marshall staged a recovery as they slowly added 43 runs, before Dujon edged an Amarnath delivery onto his wicket as he seemed unsure whether or not to play at the ball. Amarnath struck again when he had Marshall caught at slip, before Kapil won an lbw appeal against Roberts. Needing a last-wicket partnership of 58 for a West Indian victory, Garner and Holding added 14 runs in 28 minutes before Amarnath delivered the knockout blow. Holding played across the line and was trapped lbw, and the West Indians were all out with eight overs to spare. Amarnath was named player of the match, as the scoreboard suggested most of the Indians had made a handy contribution. It was a remarkable victory for India against all odds, while the West Indians were a dejected lot. Little did anyone know how long it would take for West Indies to reach another World Cup cricket decider.

India

India		R	B
Sunil Gavaskar	c Dujon b Roberts	2	12
Kris Srikkanth	lbw b Marshall	38	57
Mohinder Amarnath	b Holding	26	80
Yashpal Sharma	c sub (Logie) b Gomes	11	32
Sandeep Patil	c Gomes b Garner	27	29
Kapil Dev (c)	c Holding b Gomes	15	8
Kirti Azad	c Garner b Roberts	0	3
Roger Binny	c Garner b Roberts	2	8
Madan Lal	b Marshall	17	27
Syed Kirmani (+)	b Holding	14	43
Balwinder Sandhu	not out	11	30
Sundries	(b 5, lb 5, nb 1, w 9)	20	
TOTAL	**(54.4 overs) 183**		

FALL: 2, 59, 90, 92, 110, 111, 130, 153, 161, 183

Roberts 10-3-32-3, Garner 12-4-24-1, Marshall 11-1-24-2, Holding 9.4-2-26-2, Gomes 11-1-49-2, Richards 1-0-8-0

West Indies

West Indies		R	B
Gordon Greenidge	b Sandhu	1	12
Desmond Haynes	c Binny b Madan Lal	13	33
Viv Richards	c Kapil Dev b Madan Lal	33	28
Clive Lloyd (c)	c Kapil Dev b Binny	8	17
Larry Gomes	c Gavaskar b Madan Lal	5	16
Faoud Bacchus	c Kirmani b Sandhu	8	25
Jeff Dujon (+)	b Amarnath	25	73
Malcolm Marshall	c Gavaskar b Amarnath	18	51
Andy Roberts	lbw b Kapil Dev	4	14
Joel Garner	not out	5	19
Michael Holding	lbw b Amarnath	6	24
Sundries	(lb 4, w 10)	14	
TOTAL	**(52 overs) 140**		

FALL: 5, 50, 57, 66, 66, 76, 119, 124, 126, 140

Kapil Dev 11-4-21-1, Sandhu 9-1-32-2, Madan Lal 12-2-31-3, Binny 10-1-23-1, Amarnath 7-0-12-3, Azad 3-0-7-0

UMPIRES: Dickie Bird, Barrie Meyer

TOSS: West Indies

PLAYER OF THE MATCH: Mohinder Amarnath

INDIA WON BY 43 RUNS

1987

The Aussie revolution

- 50 overs per side contests become the norm
- Several tight matches are decided in the final over
- West Indies snatch defeat from jaws of victory on two occasions when Courtney Walsh delivers the final over
- Chetan Sharma captures the first hat-trick in World Cup cricket
- Australia and England contest the decider on Indian soil, in the first World Cup decider held outside England

The 1987 Cricket World Cup was the first to be held outside of England, as India and Pakistan won the right to host. The matches were reduced from 60 to 50 overs per side, with 50 becoming the standard figure in the ODI format although the figure was 55 in England until the mid-1990s.

The competition format for the 1987 tournament was the same as in 1983, while there were changes to each of the two groups as usual. India and Australia were far and away the pacesetters in Group A as New Zealand struggled without Richard Hadlee, while Zimbabwe was unable to record a win. Pakistan and England made the semi-finals from Group B while West Indies and the winless Sri Lanka missed out, although the outcome could have been completely different had West Indies not squandered two very winnable games. Pakistan beat England twice but the Pakistanis ultimately lost to Australia in a semi-final, while India went down to England in the other semi-final. It was commendable for England to reach the final as Ian Botham and David Gower were conspicuously absent for the tournament, while the Australian side had changed immensely after Allan Border assumed the captaincy since the 1983 World Cup. Australia had had some lean times since 1983, but the glory of 1987 was a revelation of sorts as Australia was destined to become a regular powerhouse of world cricket.

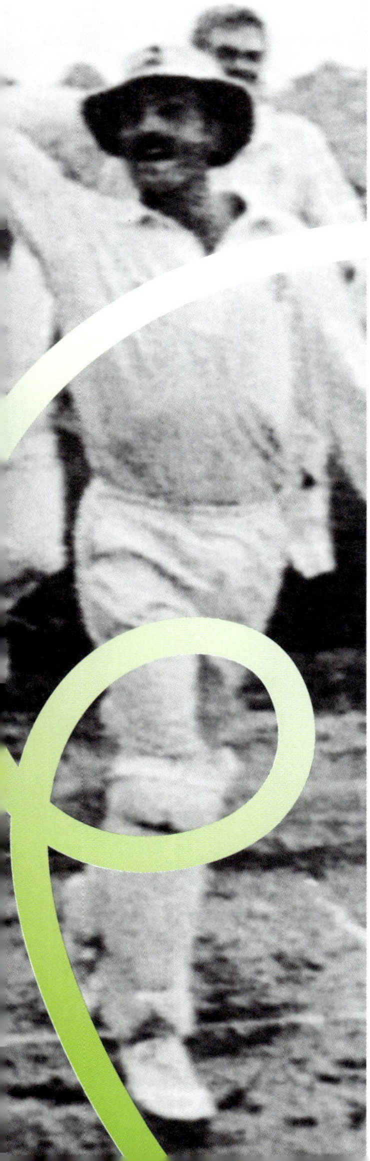

A HAT-TRICK OF CLASSICS: Three great contests

India v Australia at M.A. Chidambaram Stadium (Chennai), 9 October

Writing about this contest, experienced commentator Henry Blofeld remarked: 'It had been a wonderful spicy day which had almost smelt of hot curry.'

Australia had a 110-run opening stand before David Boon was unhappy at being ruled lbw. Dean Jones struck a quick 39, and then Geoff Marsh combined with Border to take the total past 200 in the 40th over. Marsh posted a century but wickets fell regularly after the total reached 228, and Simon O'Donnell was run out from the final ball. The final total of 6-270 was perhaps 15 runs shy of what it could have been. Significantly, one of Jones's boundaries was signalled as a four before being changed to a six during the innings break. In hindsight, this could have been the difference between winning and losing.

Sunil Gavaskar gave India a great start with six fours and a six before he holed out to long-off with the total on 69. Kris Srikkanth and debutant Navjot

Australian skipper Allan Border leads his team on a victory lap at Eden Gardens after winning the World Cup final against England.

Sidhu put India in the box seat as partnerships of 62 and 76 occurred. Sidhu struck four fours and five sixes, and the result appeared a formality as only 64 runs were needed from the last 13 overs with eight wickets standing. A yorker from Craig McDermott ended Sidhu's entertaining innings, before India stumbled from 3-229 to 5-232 as Mohammad Azharuddin and Dilip Vengsarkar succumbed to poor strokes. Ravi Shastri became McDermott's fourth victim, but India was still soundly placed until Kapil Dev was caught and Roger Binny run out with the total on 256. Another nine runs were added before Manoj Prabhakar was another run-out victim, and six runs were needed from the final over with Steve Waugh bowling.

Number 11 Maninder Singh turned the first ball to fine leg before steering the third ball to third man, and managed two runs each time. Just two more runs were needed as he swished wildly at the fifth ball and lost his off-stump. To be fair to Maninder, he should not have been required to bat considering his teammates should have carried the hosts to victory.

Australia 6-270 (Geoff Marsh 110, David Boon 49; Manoj Prabhakar 2-47) beat India 269 (Navjot Sidhu 73, Kris Srikkanth 70; Craig McDermott 4-56) by one run.

New Zealand v Zimbabwe at Lal Bahadur Shastri Stadium (Hyderabad), 10 October

The Kiwis sprang a surprise as Martin Snedden opened the batting, although it was not surprising that he later opened the bowling. He outscored regular opener John Wright, who contributed just 18 to the opening stand of 59. Snedden went on to score a solid 64, while Martin Crowe top-scored with 72 at first drop. The Kiwis stumbled from 1-143 to 5-169, before captain Jeff Crowe and wicketkeeper Ian Smith made useful runs. Forty-year-old Zimbabwean off-spinner John Traicos was the standout bowler as his 10 overs cost just 28 runs.

Chasing 243, the African nation was 2-10 before wicketkeeper David Houghton boosted the scoring. Andy Pycroft made just 12 in a partnership of 51 before his run-out dismissal sparked a collapse, with the Zimbabweans plummeting to 7-104 in the 23rd over. A hefty defeat appeared inevitable, but Houghton and all-rounder Iain Butchart had other ideas. Houghton's innings included 13 fours and six sixes while Butchart stuck with him and also kept the runs ticking over in the steamy conditions. Houghton smacked 14 runs from the first four balls of the 47th over so that Zimbabwe needed just 22 more runs, but the next ball potentially changed the game as Martin Crowe held a spectacular catch at deep mid-on. Eddo Brandes was run out without facing a ball, meaning 22 runs were still needed with only one wicket remaining. Butchart and Traicos whittled away at the deficit, and Butchart passed 50 as he pulled a six in the 49th over. Six runs were needed from the last over, with left-arm spinner Steve Boock bowling. Two singles were followed by a dot ball, and then Butchart swung at the fourth ball but failed to put it away. Traicos hared down the pitch but Butchart did not want the single, and he was run out to seal a thrilling three-run win to the Kiwis.

New Zealand 7-242 (Martin Crowe 72, Martin Snedden 64; Ali Shah 2-42) beat Zimbabwe 239 (David Houghton 142, Iain Butchart 54; Willie Watson 2-36) by three runs.

Pakistan v West Indies at Gaddafi Stadium (Lahore), 16 October

West Indies reached 0-91 but then lost 4-30, before Viv Richards and Carl Hooper resurrected the innings. After reaching 4-169, however, the West Indians faltered again as they succumbed for 216 in 49.3 overs, with Imran Khan, Saleem Jaffar and Tauseef Ahmed restricting the scoring.

The run chase also had plenty of stops and starts, with the hosts going from 0-23 to 2-28 and then reaching 2-92, before falling to 5-110. Saleem Yousuf had extraordinary luck as he struck three successive balls into the air and survived each one, with either a catch dropped or the ball landing near a fielder. The reprieves appeared costly as the sixth-wicket stand produced 73 runs, before Imran flicked a catch to deep mid-wicket. The hosts were back on course as the 200 was reached with four wickets still remaining, but there were more twists and turns to come. Yousuf swept an easy catch to square leg in the 48th over before the 49th yielded 2-2, with Wasim Akram caught off a skied shot before Tauseef was run out. Saleem Jaffar survived Patrick Patterson's final two deliveries, leaving Abdul Qadir on strike as Courtney Walsh began the final over with Pakistan needing 14 runs. The tail-enders managed only a single each, followed by a two to Qadir thanks to erratic fielding which resulted in a bonus run. There was no way of knowing what would have ensued had Jaffer been on strike, as Qadir clubbed the fourth ball for six and then sliced successive full-tosses through the off side for two runs each to steal a famous one-wicket victory. Just as memorable was Walsh declining to run out Jaffer in the 'Mankad' fashion, which would have sealed a one-run win for West Indies.

Pakistan 9-217 (Saleem Yousuf 56, Ramiz Raja 42; Courtney Walsh 4-40) beat West Indies 216 (Viv Richards 51, Phil Simmons 50; Imran Khan 4-37, Saleem Jaffar 3-30) by one wicket.

SIX OF THE BEST: Individual performances

(excluding the finals)

David Houghton 142 off 137 balls: Zimbabwe v New Zealand at Lal Bahadur Shastri Stadium (Hyderabad), 10 October

David Houghton lost weight as he scored a wonderful 142 in very hot and humid conditions, but unfortunately for him it was not enough to prevent an agonising three-run defeat against New Zealand. Several years later, he said he probably would have felt better to score a golden duck and be on the winning side, as he had been against Australia in 1983.

With the Zimbabweans chasing 243, Houghton came to the crease at 1-8 and lost partners regularly until Butchart stayed with him. As three of New Zealand's six bowlers were spinners, Houghton played the reverse sweep a number of times. He also cleared the boundary with straight drives and pull shots, before a sweep to the boundary brought up his century.

As the heat began to take a hefty toll, Houghton suffered dehydration and found it increasingly difficult to run. He resorted to slogging in the 47th over, and he hammered 14 runs in four balls before another slog went a little too high and not quite long enough, and resulted in a brilliant running and diving catch from Martin Crowe. For the record, Houghton was the first player to score a World Cup century and be on the losing side.

Viv Richards 181 off 125 balls: West Indies v Sri Lanka at National Stadium (Karachi), 13 October

In his final World Cup campaign, Viv Richards repeatedly made starts without going on to a big score. 13 October was an exception, as he was simply unstoppable. He survived a hat-trick ball from Ravi Ratnayake with the score at 2-45, and then made another sound start before he really turned up the heat. His first 50 runs took 62 balls and featured just three fours, before another four fours and a six helped him to a century from 97 balls.

Richards needed only 15 balls to go from 100 to 150 as he hammered the ball around the park, including sixes over long-off and down the ground. Richards took 20 runs off Ratnayake's seventh over and 22 runs off his eighth over, after Gus Logie scored a single from the first ball each time. The

Australia's World Cup-winning squad.

‘It had been a wonderful spicy day which had almost smelt of hot curry.’

– Henry Blofeld after Australia beat India by 1 run.

first double-century in ODIs beckoned until one hand came off Richards's bat as he sought another boundary and resulted in a high catch being skewed behind point. The 'Master Blaster' had clubbed 16 fours and seven sixes, while his 181 was his second highest ODI score. Ashantha de Mel's 10 overs cost 97 runs although he could claim that he captured Richards's wicket. Meanwhile, Desmond Haynes made a fine but overlooked 105 off 124 balls and combined with Richards for a 182-run third-wicket stand. Interestingly, Don Anurasiri had tidy figures of 10-0-39-0 while the West Indian total of 4-360 was a record for ODIs at the time, regardless of 50 or 60 overs.

The Sri Lankans were 0-24 after just eight balls before losing momentum, and they opted for survival as they made their way to 4-169 in their 50 overs.

Mohammad Azharuddin 54 not out off 45 balls and 3.5-0-19-3: India v Australia at Feroz Shah Kotla (Delhi), 22 October

Mohammad Azharuddin had a splendid all-round match as he made an undefeated half-century and followed up with three wickets. He came to the crease at 4-178 and shared a 65-run stand with Vengsarkar before scoring the bulk of India's runs after Vengsarkar's dismissal.

Azharuddin hit one streaky boundary wide of the wicketkeeper before producing some cracking shots through the off side. He struck a Waugh delivery between the bowler and mid-on for six, before turning his attention to left-armer Bruce Reid in the final over. A clip to the mid-wicket boundary was followed by a drive behind point for another four which took him past 50.

Azharuddin was India's fourth change bowler, with Australia falling away after being 0-88 in pursuit of 290. The score was 6-182 when O'Donnell charged at an Azharuddin delivery which turned into a yorker and knocked out the leg-stump. McDermott was Azharuddin's second victim, as the bowler impressively held a return catch when a bullet-like hit flew at his head. Australia succumbed for 233 with an over to spare as Azharuddin accounted for Reid, who somewhat belied his batting bunny reputation as he lofted a catch to long-on. Interestingly, Reid was similarly dismissed in the opening match of the following tournament when Australia needed 38 runs from the final two overs.

Geoff Marsh 126 not out off 149 balls: Australia v New Zealand at Sector 16 Stadium (Chandigarh), 27 October

In the 27 October clash involving the Trans-Tasman teams, Australia finished with 8-251 as Geoff Marsh faced nearly half of the 50 overs and scored fractionally more than half of the total. He registered 12 fours and three sixes.

Marsh played a role in the run-out of Boon with the total at 25, before adding 126 with Dean Jones. Marsh swept Boock for six before cover-driving, cutting, sweeping and flicking New Zealand's spinners to the boundary. An on-drive for four off medium-fast bowler Willie Watson was followed by an off drive for four off the same bowler, before the middle order collapsed. After reaching three figures, Marsh twice drove Ewen Chatfield behind square for four. Then with Chatfield straying down the legside in the 50th over, Marsh hoicked two consecutive sixes. The final over, which cost 19 runs, made a huge difference as Australia ultimately won by 17 runs.

Chetan Sharma hat-trick: India v New Zealand at Vidarbha Cricket Association Stadium Ground (Nagpur), 31 October

Chetan Sharma captured the first hat-trick in World Cup cricket history. For good measure, all three of his victims were bowled. The moment came in the last round-robin match of the 1987 tournament.

New Zealand sank to 8-182 after Sharma's three-from-three feat in the 42nd over. Ken Rutherford was the first victim, as he swung across the line and had his middle-stump bent back. Next, Ian Smith played neither forward nor back as the ball went through the gate and knocked back the off-stump. The crowd roared as Sharma raced in for the ensuing delivery, with Chatfield stepping towards the line of off-stump and attempting to leg glance a full-pitched delivery which dislodged the leg-stump, sparking plenty of jubilation. Sharma finished with 10-2-51-3 in India's nine-wicket victory.

Chetan Sharma captured the first hat-trick in World Cup cricket history. For good measure, all three of his victims were bowled.

Sunil Gavaskar 103 not out off 88 balls: India v New Zealand at Vidarbha Cricket Association Stadium (Nagpur), 31 October

While Sunil Gavaskar was temporarily the leading run-scorer in Test cricket, his style did not always translate effectively to limited overs cricket. His scoring rate was generally quite good in the 1987 tournament, and was far removed from his snail-paced 36 not out on day one of the 1975 tournament; however, he attracted the ire of captain Kapil Dev once in the 1987 World Cup for scoring 50 off 114 balls in a seven-wicket win over Zimbabwe.

Just five days after his tardy efforts against Zimbabwe, Gavaskar made his sole century in limited overs internationals. It was his 107th ODI appearance, and he was fated to play just one more. Gavaskar's ODI milestone came against New Zealand in the final round-robin match of the 1987 World Cup, as India passed its target of 222 in 32.1 overs for the loss of just one wicket. The hosts had the incentive of reaching the target in 42.2 overs or less, to finish atop Group A. Srikkanth made 75 in the opening stand of 136, before Azharuddin made 41 not out in the unbroken second-wicket stand of 88. Gavaskar and Srikkanth set the tone with 18 runs in the first two overs before Gavaskar took 21 runs off a Chatfield over, with successive sixes followed by successive fours and a single. Gavaskar struck 10 fours and three sixes as he needed just 85 balls to reach triple figures.

The England contingent of Graham Gooch, John Emburey, Chris Broad, Paul Downton and Mike Gatting (front).

HEADLINE MOMENT

Courtney Walsh in the last over as West Indies contest England and Pakistan

Courtney Walsh was the first to take 500 Test wickets, but the 1987 World Cup was not among his career highlights. His bowling at the death proved detrimental to West Indies' fortunes in the tournament, as England and Pakistan stole victories which appeared in West Indies' grasp. Yet the results could have been much different had a fielder been stationed at third man, or if an outfield throw had not been wayward, or if Walsh had not been so generous when a number 11 committed an indiscretion.

Chasing 244, England was in trouble at 8-210 with three overs remaining. Having struck 18 runs from five balls in the last over to steal an unlikely victory in a one-dayer on Australian soil early in the year, Lamb sought a repeat. He took 15 runs off the 48th over, bowled by Walsh. England required 13 runs from the last over, with Walsh continuing as the other four bowlers had bowled out their 10 overs.

Lamb struck the first ball of the final over to deep mid-wicket for two, before he backed away and slammed a full-toss to the unattended third man boundary. The next ball proved fatal for West Indies as Walsh, anticipating Lamb's movement, sprayed it too far down the legside and gave away four runs in wides. Suddenly England needed just three runs from four balls, and then Walsh bowled a no-ball which Lamb clipped for a single. Neil Foster then advanced the erratic bowler and opened the face of the bat to run the ball down to the still-unattended third man region for the winning boundary. Walsh had conceded 29 runs from his final nine legitimate deliveries.

A week later, the Pakistanis faced a 217-run target. They were 6-200 before the loss of 3-3 left them on the brink of defeat, and the last-wicket pair needed 14 runs from the final over. The first two balls yielded only a single each, with Qadir driving to long-on before a booming drive from Jaffar rolled into the covers. Qadir again struck the ball to long-on for what appeared another single, but Walsh fumbled a wayward throw which resulted in an extra run, with Jaffar nearly run out at the bowler's end. With

the equation now 10 runs from three deliveries, Qadir backed away and smacked a six over long-off. He also backed away from the second-last ball, and skewed a full-toss to deep cover for two which meant two runs were needed from the last ball for victory. A single would be enough to give Pakistan victory on the 'fewer wickets lost' rule, in the event of a tied result.

Walsh stopped in his delivery stride while Jaffar started running and, rather than run out the non-striker in the 'Mankad' fashion to secure a one-run victory for West Indies, Walsh merely folded his arms and watched Jaffar scurry back to the crease. Walsh belatedly delivered the final ball – another full-toss – which Qadir dispatched to third man for a comfortable two to seal a dramatic one-wicket win for the hosts. Qadir received £20,000 courtesy of two Pakistani businesses, while Walsh received a hand-woven carpet for his sporting gesture.

FIRST SEMI-FINAL

Pakistan v Australia at Gaddafi Stadium (Lahore), 4 November

Pakistan was set back as all-rounder Mudassar Nazar withdrew on the morning of the game, and the second ball of the match was another sign that luck was not on Pakistan's side as Marsh edged it just short of second slip. Australia's openers added 73 runs before Marsh was run out, and the Pakistanis had another setback when a delivery deflected off Dean Jones's pad and struck wicketkeeper Saleem Yousuf in the mouth. Yousuf left the field, and Javed Miandad took over as wicketkeeper.

Jones and Boon added 82 before both were dismissed with the total on 155. Border and Mike Veletta added 60 runs before Australia's skipper became another run-out victim, and another 21 runs were added before the visiting team lost 4-13. Three of the victims were bowled by Imran and the other – O'Donnell – was the third run-out victim. Australia was 8-249 with one over left, to be bowled by Jaffar. The 50th over was another turning point as Steve Waugh smashed 18 runs; the difference between the two teams in the final washup. A six and a four were followed by two twos and a dot ball, before a misfield from the final ball resulted in another boundary. Jaffar and fellow left-arm paceman Wasim Akram had been disappointing while Imran, Tauseef and Qadir conceded fewer than four runs per over.

The hosts had a horror start to the run chase as their leading scorer in the tournament – Ramiz Raja – was disastrously run out in the first over. Mudassar's replacement Mansoor Akhtar also failed, and the score was a worrying 3-38 when Saleem Malik was caught off a leading edge.

Javed and Imran produced a century partnership, but never took charge nor scored too rapidly. The asking rate was above seven-and-a-half runs per over when Imran edged a catch off Border's part-time left-arm spin. Akram creamed two sixes but soon fell for a quickfire 20, and the score was 6-192 when Ijaz Ahmed departed. Another 20 runs were added, and then Pakistan's hopes were almost dead as Javed took a swing and was bowled by Reid. Despite gallant efforts from Yousuf and Qadir, the Pakistanis were all out with an over to spare after McDermott claimed the last three wickets to catches behind the stumps. Imran wrote in his book *All Round View*: 'It was a match in which everything went wrong, and the day was a complete nightmare . . . I felt particularly annoyed at losing in that, although we played our worst cricket in all three aspects of the game – batting, bowling and fielding – and although the Australians

Australian coach Bob Simpson (back row far left) with his World Cup title-winning team after the 1987 final.

excelled themselves, there was a difference of only eighteen runs at the end, and we undoubtedly had the better team. On the day we let ourselves down.'

Little did anyone know how Imran's and Pakistan's destiny would unfold in the next World Cup!

Australia 8-267 (David Boon 65, Mike Veletta 48; Imran Khan 3-36) beat Pakistan 249 (Javed Miandad 70, Imran Khan 58; Craig McDermott 5-44) by 18 runs.

SECOND SEMI-FINAL

India v England at Wankhede Stadium (Mumbai), 5 November

While a promoter's dream of an India versus Pakistan final was dashed, India's chances of back-to-back titles were on the line. On a pitch that was low and slow with the ball turning sharply at any random time, India won the toss and chose to bowl. India missed Vengsarkar due to illness, meaning Chandra Pandit and Kiran More both played.

England's openers started cautiously with 20 runs in the first 10 overs. Commentator Henry Blofeld later criticised Kapil's decision to introduce Maninder Singh's left-arm spin for the 11th over, which cost eight runs. Yet Maninder's first delivery turned a long way and kept very low, for no result, before his second over featured the wicket of Tim Robinson to a stumping. Bill Athey contributed only four runs to a second-wicket partnership of 39, before captain Mike Gatting joined Graham Gooch. They played the sweep shot regularly as they added 117 runs in 19 overs. Gooch raised a century, and Gatting passed 50 before the sweep shot brought about his downfall. Another seven runs were added before Gooch's hard-fought innings ended, and then Lamb made a vital 32 not out to help the total beyond 250.

India began dreadfully as Gavaskar produced just one scoring stroke before a Phil DeFreitas delivery clipped his pad and uprooted the off-stump. It was a sad farewell to international cricket for Gavaskar. Srikkanth rode his luck during a second-wicket stand of 51 before he fell to Neil Foster, who also struck next with the wicket of Sidhu to leave India 3-73. Eddie Hemmings bowled three expensive overs and was taken off, before Foster trapped Pandit lbw. Kapil then combined with Azharuddin for a potentially winning partnership, as 47 runs were quickly added. Gatting riskily brought back Hemmings and, after Kapil clubbed him to the mid-wicket boundary, England's captain stationed himself at deep mid-wicket. India's captain promptly hit a catch straight to his counterpart, and suddenly the hosts were back under the pump. Azharuddin kept going, however, and a tight finish loomed as India needed 56 runs from 10 overs with five wickets in hand. Incredibly, the match was over just 33 balls later.

After Azharuddin was out lbw trying to sweep, several indiscreet strokes caused a flood of wickets when giving Shastri the strike might have been a better option. The last three wickets fell for just one run,

Australian captain Allan Border with the World Cup trophy after Australia defeated England in the final.

The powers-that-be had to settle for a decider featuring cricket's oldest rivals, rather than the sub-continental rivals.

with Shastri the last to go when a wild shot produced a skied catch. The powers-that-be had to settle for a decider featuring cricket's oldest rivals, rather than the sub-continental rivals.

England 6-254 (Graham Gooch 115, Mike Gatting 56; Maninder Singh 3-54, Kapil Dev 2-38) beat India 219 (Mohammad Azharuddin 64; Eddie Hemmings 4-52, Neil Foster 3-47) by 35 runs.

FINAL

Australia v England at Eden Gardens (Calcutta), 8 November

It was unusual for Australia and England to have a major cricketing showdown in India with World Cup glory up for grabs, rather than to contest an Ashes Test on either Australian or English turf. Gooch was the only player from either side to have previously played in a World Cup final.

Wayward bowling from DeFreitas and Gladstone Small enabled Australia to reach 0-48 after nine overs. Foster then applied the brakes and accounted for Marsh when the total was 75. Boon and Jones had to work hard for their runs, and the score was 2-151 when Jones departed in the 35th over. As a pinch-hitter, McDermott made 14 off eight balls before Boon's innings of 75 ended soon afterwards, leaving Australia 4-168 in the 39th over. A brilliant 45 not out off 31 balls from Veletta, as well as a run-a-ball 31 from Border, turned the tide. Waugh helped Veletta add 11 runs in the final over, leaving England a target of 254.

McDermott trapped Robinson for a golden duck in the first over, before O'Donnell won an lbw shout against Gooch in the 18th over to render England 2-66. Athey batted steadily but slowly while Gatting showed more urgency. It appeared that luck might be on Gatting's side as he recorded a six when caught at long-on, with the fielder stepping on the boundary. On another occasion, England gained four runs from overthrows. But England's skipper paid dearly for trying to reverse sweep Border's first ball, which strayed down the legside and produced an easy catch for wicketkeeper Greg Dyer. When Athey was run out as he sought a risky third run, England was in a similar position to what Australia had been in the 39th over.

Despite a couple of dropped catches, England could not capitalise. Paul Downton's impact was brief, and then Lamb and Emburey added 30 before England slid from 5-218 to 7-220, with Lamb bowled before Emburey was run out. DeFreitas cracked 14 runs from three balls in the 48th over to keep alive the possibility of a miracle for England. Waugh again showed nerves of steel as he bowled a tidy over which yielded the wicket of DeFreitas, who was caught as he sought another boundary. England needed 17 runs from the last over, and never looked like getting them as Foster and Small could only manage singles and twos. The last two balls cost two runs each when Foster was faced with the task of hitting back-to-back sixes. While Gatting's dismissal gained instant notoriety, there had been many key moments and turning points.

Australia		R	B
David Boon	c Downton b Hemmings	75	125
Geoff Marsh	b Foster	24	49
Dean Jones	c Athey b Hemmings	33	57
Craig McDermott	b Gooch	14	8
Allan Border (c)	run out (Robinson/Downton)	31	31
Mike Veletta	not out	45	31
Steve Waugh	not out	5	4
Sundries	(b 1, lb 13, nb 7, w 5)	26	
TOTAL	**(50 overs) 5-253**		

DID NOT BAT: Simon O'Donnell, Greg Dyer (+), Tim May, Bruce Reid

FALL: 75, 151, 166, 168, 241

DeFreitas 6-1-34-0, Small 6-0-33-0, Foster 10-0-38-1, Hemmings 10-1-48-2, Emburey 10-0-44-0, Gooch 8-1-42-1

England		R	B
Graham Gooch	lbw b O'Donnell	35	57
Tim Robinson	lbw b McDermott	0	1
Bill Athey	run out (Waugh/Reid)	58	103
Mike Gatting (c)	c Dyer b Border	41	45
Allan Lamb	b Waugh	45	55
Paul Downton (+)	c O'Donnell b Border	9	8
John Emburey	run out (Boon/McDermott)	10	16
Phil DeFreitas	c Reid b Waugh	17	10
Neil Foster	not out	7	6
Gladstone Small	not out	3	3
Sundries	(b 1, lb 14, nb 4, w 2)	21	
TOTAL	**(50 overs) 8-246**		

DID NOT BAT: Eddie Hemmings

FALL: 1, 66, 135, 170, 188, 218, 220, 235

McDermott 10-1-51-1, Reid 10-0-43-0, Waugh 9-0-37-2, O'Donnell 10-1-35-1, May 4-0-27-0, Border 7-0-38-2

UMPIRES: Ram Gupta, Mahboob Shah

TOSS: Australia

PLAYER OF THE MATCH: David Boon

AUSTRALIA WON BY SEVEN RUNS

1992

Cornered Tigers come from out of the blue

- Coloured uniforms are worn for the first time in World Cup cricket
- South Africa appears in World Cup cricket for the first time, following the country's exile from international sport
- Inspired by inaugural player of the tournament award winner Martin Crowe, competition co-host New Zealand wins seven from seven before missing the final following back-to-back losses against Pakistan
- Rain interruption at an untimely stage of the second semi-final cruels South Africa's hopes against England
- Brilliant spell of bowling from Wasim Akram swings the final Pakistan's way, after Pakistan had won only one of its first five matches

The 1992 tournament had several new aspects. It was the first time that the competition featured coloured uniforms and the white ball, and the first time that a 'player of the tournament' was named. With Australia and New Zealand as co-hosts, this was also the first Cricket World Cup played in the southern hemisphere. Another significant development was the addition of South Africa, which had been banned from international sport for more than 20 years due to apartheid. Rather than have the nine teams divided into groups, the countries opposed each other once in a round-robin format before the top-four contested the semi-finals.

New Zealand was the surprise packet, as the co-hosts won their first seven matches to secure top spot before losing to the fourth-placed Pakistan in the first semi-final. England was second on the ladder, although its player depth was tested as there were numerous injuries as the tournament unfolded. Finishing third was a remarkable effort for South Africa after being starved of international cricket for so long. With former Australian World Cup campaigner Kepler Wessels as captain, South Africa shocked the cricket world in its first match with a nine-wicket trouncing of Australia, before two successive defeats were followed by three consecutive victories. Were it not for a rain disruption at a crucial stage in the second semi-final, South Africa may have reached the decider.

Pakistan ultimately came from nowhere to win the tournament after being in danger of missing the top-four. The Pakistanis were already set back as fast bowler Waqar Younis was absent with a back injury. They won only one of their first five matches, and were lucky to gain a point when rain robbed England of a certain victory after the second-placed team skittled the Pakistanis for 74. In the long run, that single competition point made a huge difference to Pakistan's fortunes. The Pakistanis won their final three round-robin matches – against Australia, Sri Lanka and New Zealand – but were not assured of a finals spot until Australia beat West Indies just hours after Pakistan upstaged New Zealand. With Pakistani captain Imran Khan wanting his team to play like 'cornered tigers', the Pakistanis also had some luck go their way in the semi-final and final before lifting the coveted trophy.

Reigning titleholder Australia had a disappointing campaign on home soil, and it was not easy to understand where it all went wrong. Australia's batting was particularly underwhelming in its four losses, although the co-hosts would have made the finals had Pakistan lost either of its round-robin matches against England or New Zealand. West Indies, like Australia, had four wins and four losses, and also would have made the finals at Pakistan's (and Australia's) expense had one or two results been different. India and Sri Lanka each had two wins, five losses and one no-result, with India left to wonder what might have been. The India versus Sri Lanka match was washed out with just two balls bowled, and India also had agonisingly narrow losses to Australia and England. Sri Lanka lost only one of its first four matches, before losing its final four. Zimbabwe, having failed to defend a large total against Sri Lanka, rarely threatened the other teams until the African nation finished on a high with a shock victory over England.

Oddly, the 1992 World Cup was the first to be held in an even-numbered year, as the tournament took place following the completion of the Australian-based international cricket season.

The jubilant Pakistanis celebrate winning the World Cup.

South Africa shocked the cricket world in its first match with a nine-wicket trouncing of Australia.

A HAT-TRICK OF CLASSICS: Three great contests

England v India at WACA (Perth), 22 February

Individual performances from Robin Smith and Ian Botham were vital in England's winning start to the tournament. Botham's impact as an opening batter was minimal, before his bowling and fielding stood out.

England skipper Graham Gooch combined with Smith for a second-wicket stand of 110. England was well placed at 3-197 before losing 6-27, with Smith falling nine runs short of a century when he was brilliantly caught by Indian captain Mohammad Azharuddin behind point. An unbroken last-wicket stand of 12 ultimately proved decisive, and Azharuddin also rued his bowlers conceding 13 runs in wides. England's total of 9-236 was competitive but far from daunting in any case.

India's openers put on 63 runs in as many minutes, with Kris Srikkanth hitting seven boundaries before two wickets fell without the addition of a run. Wicketkeeper Alec Stewart took a fine catch off Dermot Reeve to dismiss Azharuddin first ball, before gifted teen Sachin Tendulkar made a stylish 35. India was 2-126 with 20 overs left, before Botham turned the game with a great delivery which squared Tendulkar up and had him snicking behind. Vinod Kambli was Botham's second scalp, and Ravi Shastri passed 50 before being run out off a dropped catch. Pravin Amre and Kapil Dev boosted the scoring until the loss of 4-14 left the last-wicket pair needing 36 runs. Subroto Banerjee and Javagal Srinath hung in there, and a miracle was possible when a six from Banerjee reduced the requirement to 11 runs from the last over. From the second ball, a mix-up between the wickets resulted in Botham running out Srinath to seal England's nine-run triumph.

England 9-236 (Robin Smith 91, Graham Gooch 51; Manoj Prabhakar 2-34, Kapil Dev 2-38) beat India 227 (Ravi Shastri 57, Kris Srikkanth 39; Dermot Reeve 3-38, Ian Botham 2-27) by nine runs.

Sri Lanka v Zimbabwe at Pukekura Park (New Plymouth), 23 February

With neither Sri Lanka nor Zimbabwe expected to be a title contender, it was somewhat surprising to see the two teams engage in a rare run glut. The totals and outcome may not seem unusual according to one-day cricket since 2000, but in 1992 the result was extraordinary.

There was no sign of anything special when Zimbabwe lost its third wicket with the score at 82. Kevin Arnott's 52 off 56 balls provided some spark, and then the carnage unfolded following his dismissal as the final 13 overs featured an unbroken 145-run stand. Andy Waller creamed nine fours and three sixes in his undefeated 83 from just 45 balls, while opener Andy Flower worked his way to 115 not out from 152 balls in his ODI debut.

Sri Lankan openers Roshan Mahanama and Athula Samarasekera came out with all guns blazing, putting on 128 at almost a run per ball. The Sri Lankans stumbled, and like their opponents they lost their fourth wicket at 167. Sanath Jayasuriya then hit a quick 32 before Arjuna Ranatunga took control and had useful support as partnerships of 61 and 36 unfolded. A key moment occurred in the 48th over when Ranatunga was caught off a no-ball, before the Sri Lankans won with four balls to spare. Intriguingly, the oldest player in the World Cup, 44-year-old John Traicos, returned tight figures of 10-1-33-1 for the vanquished team.

Sri Lanka 7-313 (Arjuna Ranatunga 88 not out, Athula Samarasekera 75, Roshan Mahanama 59; Eddo Brandes 3-70) beat Zimbabwe 4-312 (Andy Flower 115 not out, Andy Waller 83 not out, Kevin Arnott 52; Pramodya Wickramasinghe 2-50) by three wickets.

Australia v India at The Gabba (Brisbane), 1 March

Amazingly, Australia beat India by a single run in a World Cup match for the second time. Eight Australians and six Indians played in both matches. One of those Australians, David Boon, kept wickets on the latter occasion in the absence of an injured Ian Healy.

After Kapil dismissed the openers to leave Australia 2-31, Dean Jones produced a superb knock. He was just two hits short of a century when a skier was caught by the bowler, Manoj Prabhakar. Boon, Steve Waugh and Tom Moody also made handy middle-order contributions, but too many wickets were thrown away in the latter part of the innings. India initially needed 238 runs in 50 overs, before a shower of rain resulted in a revised target of 236 runs in 47 overs. Having been 1-45 after 16.2 overs when play was halted, India relied heavily on Azharuddin whose innings was of similar quality to Jones's. Shastri took 70 balls to score 25, and Tendulkar and Kapil departed before they could make much impact. Sanjay Manjrekar lifted the tempo, but another turning point came when Allan Border ran out Azharuddin for 93 with a direct hit. Manjrekar was also run out at a crucial time, having unwisely chanced a second run on Craig McDermott's arm.

Needing 13 runs from the final over, India was on track as Kiran More tucked away consecutive legside full-tosses for four. Moody's third delivery shattered the middle-stump, before a single from the fourth ball as followed by another run-out from the fifth ball and a premature crowd invasion. Needing a last-ball four for victory, Srinath lofted a regulation catch to long-on but Waugh dropped it. The fielder promptly picked up the ball and hurled it a little wide of the wicketkeeper, but Boon gathered it and scurried to break the stumps as Venkatapathy Raju was a metre short of tying the match.

Australia 9-237 (Dean Jones 90, David Boon 43; Kapil Dev and Manoj Prabhakar 3-41) beat India 234 (Mohammad Azharuddin 93, Sanjay Manjrekar 47; Tom Moody 3-56) by one run.

The nine teams in the 1992 World Cup line up on the deck of the HMAS Canberra on Sydney Harbour.

SIX OF THE BEST: Individual performances

(excluding player of the tournament, and the finals)

Mark Greatbatch 68 off 60 balls: New Zealand v South Africa at Eden Park (Auckland), 29 February

An innings of 68 from 60 balls does not sound extraordinary since T20 cricket began, but in 1992 it was virtually unheard of, especially for an opener. In reply to South Africa's modest total of 190, Mark Greatbatch took a short time to get his eye in before hammering the ball with vicious power as he registered nine fours and three sixes. When he departed, New Zealand's total was 114 in the 18th over.

Greatbatch adopted a similar approach in the remaining matches, with a top score of 73 from 76 balls. At least another four years passed before this type of strike rate became a regular feature for openers in ODIs.

Meyrick Pringle 8-4-11-4: South Africa v West Indies at Lancaster Park (Christchurch), 5 March

South Africa's finals prospects looked shaky, until second opening bowler Meyrick Pringle produced the best bowling figures of the tournament. After South Africa made 200, Pringle produced a spell of 4-0 in 11 balls on a seaming wicket to leave the West Indians reeling at 4-19. Brian Lara cut a catch to point, and then skipper Richie Richardson was trapped lbw before Carl Hooper and Keith Arthurton edged catches to first slip. There were only four scoring shots in Pringle's eight overs as West Indies succumbed for 136.

Ian Botham 10-1-31-4 and 53 off 77 balls: England v Australia at Sydney Cricket Ground (Sydney), 5 March

When the 1992 World Cup came around, Ian Botham's heroics in the 1981 Ashes were a distant memory. He had had very poor figures with bat and ball in the 1989 Ashes, and since then his newly adopted role as an opening batter in limited overs cricket did not pay off although his bowling was tidy. He was among the leading wicket-takers in the 1992 World Cup, with his crowning moment coming against arch-rival Australia.

The hosts were 4-145, before Botham took 4-0 in seven balls to rip the heart out of the Australians. He bowled Allan Border through the gate, before the following dismissals were caught at mid-wicket, lbw, and caught at mid-on as Australia tumbled to 171 all out.

In the run chase, Botham easily passed his previous highest World Cup score of 22. He struck six boundaries as he played his natural attacking game, and the result was all but decided when his departure for 53 left England 1-107.

Andrew Jones 9-0-42-2 and 78 off 113 balls: New Zealand v England at Basin Reserve (Wellington), 15 March

Andrew Jones's rarely used off-breaks claimed two wickets, with Robin Smith and Derek Pringle hitting catches into the deep in the final 10 overs. Jones then came to the crease at 1-5, as the hosts chased a target of 201. He added 59 with Mark Greatbatch and 108 with Crowe, who finished with 73 not out. Jones scored 52 of his 78 runs in boundaries, before being run out.

Eddo Brandes 10-4-21-4: Zimbabwe v England at Lavington Sports Oval (Albury), 18 March

After the bottom-placed Zimbabwe tallied a paltry 134 against the second-placed England, Eddo Brandes was chiefly responsible for Zimbabwe's shock victory. He trapped Gooch lbw with the first ball of the run chase, and later took a spell of 3-2 to leave England 5-43. Allan Lamb miscued a pull to mid-on, before Robin Smith and expatriate Zimbabwean Graeme Hick had their stumps wrecked.

Ramiz Raja 119 not out off 155 balls: Pakistan v New Zealand at Lancaster Park (Christchurch), 18 March

Pakistani opener Ramiz Raja made the highest score of the 1992 World Cup, when he compiled an undefeated century against New Zealand on the last day of the round-robin fixtures. His score, which included 16 fours, stood out as Pakistan won by

Martin Crowe captained the Kiwis to seven consecutive wins, but an injury during the first semi-final had a detrimental effect on New Zealand's fortunes.

Martin Crowe (New Zealand)

Matches	Innings	Not outs	Runs	Highest score	Average	50s	100s	Catches
9	9	5	456	100*	114	4	1	3

Overs	Maidens	Runs	Wickets	Average
1	-	6	-	-

seven wickets after dismissing New Zealand for 166. Pakistan's second top score was 30, after the Kiwi total included 42 sundries while New Zealand's top-scorer also made 42.

Interestingly, Ramiz did not earn the player of the match award, which went to Mushtaq Ahmed for his 2-18 from 10 overs. Just as interestingly, Ramiz also did not earn player of the match honours on the two other occasions that he scored a World Cup ton. The first occasion was in 1987 when his 113 helped Pakistan to a seven-wicket victory against England, which had tallied 9-244. His second World Cup ton was on the second day of the 1992 tournament when he made 102 not out in a total of 2-220 against the West Indians, who went on to win by 10 wickets.

HEADLINE MOMENT

Upset win for Zimbabwe as England fails to reach small target

There appeared to be little interest in this fixture at the Lavington Sports Ground, with England guaranteed to finish second on the ladder while Zimbabwe had not won a game. Zimbabwe's batters struggled as usual, with no partnerships of substance while England's medium-fast bowlers and spinners were economical. Thirty-one runs were added for the eighth wicket before the loss of 3-7 ended Zimbabwe's innings at 134 with 23 balls remaining.

Brandes dismissed Gooch first ball and made further breakthroughs as England fell to 5-43. Neil Fairbrother and Stewart took 24 overs to compile a 52-run partnership, but the required run rate was well within reach until another collapse left England 8-108. Following a run-out, England's last pair needed to score 10 runs in the final over. Gladstone Small chipped the first ball to mid-wicket, and the Zimbabweans were beside themselves while schoolchildren swarmed the arena. The result was arguably as much of a surprise as Zimbabwe's only previous World Cup win, against Australia nearly nine years earlier.

Zimbabwe 134 (David Houghton 29, Iain Butchart 24; Ian Botham 3-23, Richard Illingworth 3-33) beat England 125 (Alec Stewart 29, Neil Fairbrother 20; Eddo Brandes 4-21, Ali Shah 2-17) by nine runs.

PLAYER OF THE TOURNAMENT

Martin Crowe won the inaugural award for his prolific run scoring, while also earning player of the match honours against Australia, Zimbabwe and West Indies. Crowe also captained the Kiwis to seven consecutive wins, but an injury during the first semi-final had a detrimental effect on New Zealand's fortunes.

Crowe began the tournament with a fine 100 not out, as the Kiwis made 6-248 and then defeated reigning titleholder and competition co-host Australia by 37 runs. Crowe's innovative captaincy included 15 bowling changes in the first 40 overs of Australia's innings, and opening the bowling with off-spinner Dipak Patel.

The Kiwis followed up with a six-wicket win over Sri Lanka and a seven-wicket win over South Africa, with Crowe making just five against Sri Lanka before his unbeaten three against the Africans included the winning runs.

New Zealand's clash with Zimbabwe was marred by rain, with Crowe blasting eight fours and two sixes in his unconquered 74 from 44 balls in a total of 3-162 from 20.5 overs. Crowe again used his bowlers cleverly in the 48-run triumph, with Patel not used due to the conditions. In New Zealand's next game, Patel reverted to opening the bowling and had wonderful figures of 1-19 from 10 overs. In pursuit of the 204-run target against West Indies, Crowe scored

England all-rounder Ian Botham celebrates one of his four wickets against Australia at the Sydney Cricket Ground.

A classic finish appeared imminent (in the second semi-final), but a 12-minute rain interruption proved fatal for the team chasing the target.

a majestic 81 not out from as many balls, including 12 fours in the five-wicket triumph.

Crowe was freakishly run out for 26 during a successful run chase against India, before he scored 73 not out in a winning run chase against England. Although the Kiwis had won seven from seven, their subsequent loss to Pakistan on the last day of round-robin fixtures had a decisive impact on the remainder of the tournament. Pakistan's shock victory not only eliminated Australia but also set up a Pakistan versus New Zealand semi-final showdown. In the first encounter with Pakistan, Crowe departed for three as his team succumbed for 166. Despite umpteen bowling changes as nine of Crowe's teammates rolled the arm over, only three wickets fell in the run chase.

Crowe won the toss in the semi-final and wanted to bat second, but he chose otherwise due to concerns about rain which didn't eventuate. His masterful 91 included seven fours and three sixes, although he injured a hamstring when running between the wickets during Ken Rutherford's dismissal. Crowe soon called for a runner, and was helpless when he was run out. With New Zealand defending a strong total of 262, Crowe opted to watch from the sidelines and rest his injury. The Kiwis had their counterparts 4-140 in the 35th over, but the match slipped away. Stand-in skipper John Wright was seemingly not familiar with Crowe's tactics, and there was little point wondering what might have happened if Crowe had taken the field.

FIRST SEMI-FINAL

New Zealand v Pakistan at Eden Park (Auckland), 21 March

The first semi-final was among the best games of the 1992 World Cup, as there were many twists and turns.

Greatbatch struck two sixes but made only 17 before he was bizarrely bowled by Aaqib Javed's slower ball. Having been named player of the tournament, Crowe continued his sparkling form but he lacked sufficient support for a while. Rutherford would have been lbw for a duck had Wasim Akram not bowled a no-ball, and he took 20 balls to open his account before racing from 10 to 50 in 21 balls during a potentially match-turning 107-run fourth wicket partnership.

New Zealand stumbled again, as Rutherford spooned a catch to the wicketkeeper while Crowe injured a hamstring and soon called for a runner. Chris Harris scored a quick 13, and Crowe was run out for 91 after his runner – Greatbatch – got in a mix-up with Ian Smith. Smith, Patel and Gavin Larsen hit out to good effect as New Zealand reached 7-262, following 161 runs in the final 20 overs and 91 in the last 10. The Kiwis were set back as Crowe was sidelined with his injury, which led to Wright deputising as skipper.

Pakistan lost its first wicket at 30 when Aamer Sohail miscued a sweep shot in the seventh over. With his score on 17, Ramiz flicked a simple catch to square leg but Andrew Jones spilled it after he had caught the other opener. A couple of expensive overs followed, before the run rate slowed. Ramiz skied a catch to deep mid-on, and then Javed Miandad survived a run-out which would have resulted in his dismissal had technology been available to assist the umpires.

Ramiz's 44 came from 55 balls while Imran made the same score off 93 balls, before Saleem Malik was out second ball to leave Pakistan 4-140 in the 35th over. Inzamam-ul-Haq changed the game as he blazed 60 runs off just 37 balls, while Miandad methodically worked towards a half-century. The Kiwis narrowly failed to capitalise on a couple of run-out opportunities before Harris produced a direct hit to dismiss Inzamam. Only 36 runs were needed from the final 32 balls.

Akram was bowled by Willie Watson with the second ball of the 47th over as Pakistan still needed 25 runs, but the bowler faltered with his final delivery as Moin Khan clipped a legside full-toss for four. A subsequent misfield enabled Miandad to turn a single into a two and reduce the requirement to 17 runs from as many balls. With nine needed off eight balls, Moin sliced a half-volley over the long-off boundary and then pulled a four to seal the result with an over to spare.

Pakistan 6-264 (Inzamam-ul-Haq 60, Javed Miandad 57 not out; Willie Watson 2-39) beat New Zealand 7-262 (Martin Crowe 91, Ken Rutherford 50; Wasim Akram and Mushtaq Ahmed 2-40) by four wickets.

Dean Jones plays an attacking shot during Australia's defeat against Pakistan in Perth. The wicketkeeper is Moin Khan.

SECOND SEMI-FINAL

England v South Africa at Sydney Cricket Ground (Sydney), 22 March

A classic finish appeared imminent, but a 12-minute rain interruption proved fatal for the team chasing the target and resulted in England progressing to the final in farcical circumstances.

Rain delayed the start by 10 minutes, with Wessels electing to bowl. A number of illegal deliveries were sent down early on, before Gooch was dubiously adjudged caught behind in the third over. England was 2-39 in the eighth over when Botham departed, before the next two deliveries were critical in the long run. Hick survived a confident appeal for lbw, and then edged a catch to Wessels at slip off a no-ball. Stewart and Fairbrother gave Hick solid support as partnerships of 71 and 73 unfolded, and then England was 5-187 when Hick exited for a well-made 83. Lamb and Chris Lewis boosted the scoring, before the 45th over was the last of the innings due to South Africa's slow over rate. Reeve clouted 17 runs off Allan Donald's bowling as the over yielded 18 runs and took the total to 6-252.

Eight South Africans were required to bat, and they all registered double figures without reaching a half-century. Opener Andrew Hudson top-scored before his departure made the score 3-90. Adrian Kuiper looked dangerous until he was bowled for 36 as he swung wildly, and Hansie Cronje was tied down before Jonty Rhodes scored a brisk 43. A boundary from Dave Richardson left South Africa needing 27 runs from 16 balls, but the rain soon arrived. A two to Brian McMillan reduced the task to 22 from 13, and then the players were forced from the field although the batters wanted to play on. The rules for rain-reduced games hampered the team batting second, as the most economical overs in the first innings were used in favour of the team that batted first. England's innings yielded two maidens, with one featuring a leg bye. South Africa's requirement became 22 runs off seven balls as one over was lost, before the loss of another over changed the target to an impossible 21 runs off one ball (although the scoreboard erroneously revealed 22 runs were needed off the final ball). McMillan prodded a slow yorker to mid-wicket for a single and looked furious while the England players appeared a little sheepish. Both captains showed good sportsmanship, with Gooch saying his heart went out to the South Africans while Wessels said he too would have accepted the offer to leave the field had he been in Gooch's position.

England 6-252 (Graeme Hick 83, Alec Stewart 33; Meyrick Pringle 2-36) beat South Africa 6-232 (Andrew Hudson 46, Jonty Rhodes 43; Richard Illingworth 2-46) by 19 runs.

FINAL

England v Pakistan at Melbourne Cricket Ground (Melbourne), 25 March

A few dubious umpiring decisions may well have affected the outcome, but there was no doubt that both teams had their chances to win after Imran chose to bat.

Back from an injury layoff, Derek Pringle had Aamer caught behind before trapping Ramiz lbw to have Pakistan 2-24. The 39-year-old Imran and 34-year-old Miandad embarked on a rescue mission, but were painfully slow for a while and were fortuitously reprieved. With his score on 2 while Pakistan was 2-31 in the 15th over, Miandad luckily survived two lbw appeals off successive Pringle deliveries. Another turning point came in the 21st over as Gooch spilled a running catch which could have dismissed Imran for nine and left Pakistan 3-56.

Imran lofted Richard Illingworth for six in the 28th over, but the scoring remained slow as Pakistan was only 2-113 with 16 overs remaining. A boundary to each batter in the 35th over sparked an increase in urgency, and soon the duo posted half-centuries. Miandad sought a runner due to a back injury, but the runner wasn't needed for long as a reverse sweep from Miandad found Botham at point in the 40th over with the total at 163. Inzamam hit 28 runs from his first 14 deliveries as the total raced towards 200, before Imran smacked a catch to long-on in the 44th over. Akram then hammered 33 off just 18 balls, and Inzamam finished with 42 off 35. The final over yielded just two runs, with Inzamam bowled as he swung at the penultimate delivery before Akram was run out by the wicketkeeper from the final ball.

Needing 250, England controversially lost Botham for a duck in the third over as he was ruled caught behind after the ball appeared to flick his sleeve. Stewart luckily survived an appeal for caught behind, but he departed in a similar manner soon afterwards to leave England 2-21. It would have been 3-27 had the wicketkeeper not spilled a tough chance which Gooch offered. Mushtaq Ahmed's leg-spin troubled Hick who ultimately succumbed to a superb googly, before a miscued sweep from Gooch was well caught by a diving Aaqib.

England recovered from 4-69 as Fairbrother and Lamb added 72 runs, before the return of Akram changed the game irrevocably. Coming around the wicket in the 35th over, Akram produced a cracking delivery which straightened and then hit Lamb's off-stump. From the next delivery, Lewis lurched forward and edged the ball onto the middle-stump.

Fairbrother passed 50 and soon called for a runner due to a leg strain. Reeve was tied down, before the duo departed to skied shots in quick succession to leave England down and out at 8-183 with six overs remaining. The tail-enders merely added respectability to the total as partnerships of 25 and 19 unfolded. With 27 runs needed from the final over, Illingworth flicked the first ball for four and then mistimed a slower ball from Imran and was caught by a running Ramiz at mid-off. The situation was sombre for England, having been the runner-up in three World Cup deciders. Gooch was in all three, while Lamb and DeFreitas were in the latter two. Rather than focus on his team, Imran somewhat unusually said he hoped his country's triumph would help his mission to build a hospital to help cancer patients.

Pakistan

Pakistan		R	B
Aamer Sohail	c Stewart b Pringle	4	19
Ramiz Raja	lbw b Pringle	8	26
Imran Khan (c)	c Illingworth b Botham	72	110
Javed Miandad	c Botham b Illingworth	58	98
Inzamam-ul-Haq	b Pringle	42	35
Wasim Akram	run out (Stewart)	33	18
Saleem Malik	not out	0	1
Sundries	(lb 19, nb 7, w 6)	32	
TOTAL	**(50 overs) 6-249**		

DID NOT BAT: Ijaz Ahmed, Moin Khan (+), Mushtaq Ahmed, Aaqib Javed

FALL: 20, 24, 163, 197, 249, 249

Pringle 10-2-22-3, Lewis 10-2-52-0, Botham 7-0-42-1, DeFreitas 10-1-42-0, Illingworth 10-0-50-1, Reeve 3-0-22-0

England

England		R	B
Graham Gooch (c)	c Aaqib b Mushtaq	29	66
Ian Botham	c Moin b Akram	0	6
Alec Stewart (+)	c Moin b Aaqib	7	16
Graeme Hick	lbw b Mushtaq	17	36
Neil Fairbrother	c Moin b Aaqib	62	70
Allan Lamb	b Akram	31	41
Chris Lewis	b Akram	0	1
Dermot Reeve	c Ramiz b Mushtaq	15	32
Derek Pringle	not out	18	16
Phil DeFreitas	run out (Malik/Moin)	10	8
Richard Illingworth	c Ramiz b Imran	14	10
Sundries	(lb 5, nb 6, w 13)	24	
TOTAL	**(49.2 overs) 227**		

FALL: 6, 21, 59, 69, 141, 141, 180, 183, 208, 227

Wasim Akram 10-0-49-3, Aaqib Javed 10-2-27-2, Mushtaq Ahmed 10-1-41-3, Ijaz Ahmed 3-0-13-0, Imran Khan 6.2-0-43-1, Aamer Sohail 10-0-49-0

UMPIRES: Brian Aldridge, Steve Bucknor

TOSS: Pakistan

PLAYER OF THE MATCH: Wasim Akram

PAKISTAN WON BY 22 RUNS

1996

Green and Gold no match for de Silva

- Sri Lanka wins two matches on forfeit due to security concerns from Australia and West Indies
- Kenya records a shock 73-run victory against West Indies
- Pakistan's Javed Miandad competes in the first six World Cup cricket tournaments
- Sri Lanka versus India semi-final ends prematurely, farcically and on a sad note due to spectator unrest
- Sri Lanka wins the crown after never previously reaching the World Cup semi-finals

The number of teams increased from nine to 12 due to the addition of Kenya, United Arab Emirates and the Netherlands. This resulted in the competition being split into two groups of six, meaning each country would only oppose someone from another group from the quarter-finals stage. While it was a big thing for the non-Test-playing nations to play on the global stage, there were many lopsided results.

While 1996 was the second time that the Cricket World Cup was played in the sub-continent, a key difference from 1987 was that Sri Lanka joined India and Pakistan as co-hosts. India hosted 17 contests at 17 different venues, while Pakistan hosted 16 matches but used only six venues. Sri Lanka was scheduled to use three venues and host four matches, but this turned into a highly contentious matter.

Sri Lanka was slated to host Australia and West Indies, but these two teams chose not to play these fixtures due to safety concerns after a terrorist bomb in Colombo. Despite an increase in security, the two touring sides still refused to play on Sri Lankan soil. The co-hosts were subsequently awarded two wins on forfeit, enabling them to reach the quarter-finals before the first ball was even bowled. Sri Lanka also won its other three round-robin matches, and ultimately had an undefeated tournament. Two of its wins were at home, as struggling teams Zimbabwe and Kenya chose to play on Sri Lankan soil. In the Sri Lanka versus Zimbabwe fixture, there was strong security in the form of police and bomb-sniffing dogs. As a cricketing nation, Sri Lanka had evidently come on in leaps and bounds. Captain Arjuna Ranatunga was in his fourth World Cup while Aravinda de Silva, Asanka Gurusinha and Roshan Mahanama were in their third. Batting was the team's strong point, as the Sri Lankans were starting to master a changed approach to the game. Rather than try to score at three to four runs per over in the first 15 overs, Sri Lanka's openers went on the attack during this period before the middle order sought to capitalise on the platform. Against Kenya, the Sri Lankans amassed a gigantic total of 398 for the loss of five wickets.

Australia and India each won three games and lost two during the round-robin format, with India falling one game shy of the decider while Australia reached the decider but was beaten by a better team on the day (and night). The West Indians, having finished fourth in Group A, were left to ponder what might have been after snatching defeat from the jaws of victory in the second semi-final. Who's to know what would have happened had the West Indians rather than the Australians contested Sri Lanka in the decider?

It was little surprise that Zimbabwe and Kenya were the bottom two teams in Group A, although the Kenyans sprang the biggest shock when they knocked off the team from the Caribbean.

In Group B, South Africa went through the round-robin competition unbeaten before faltering in the quarter-finals. Pakistan lost only once before the finals, and then lost to arch-rival India in a quarter-final. New Zealand and England made the quarter-finals but could go no further, although the Kiwis made a big total of 286 which ultimately proved unsuccessful against Australia. With largely different looking line-ups from the previous World Cup, New Zealand and England were not the same force as in 1992.

In the battle of the cellar dwellers, United Arab Emirates came away with one win: against the Netherlands.

Sri Lankan skipper Arjuna Ranatunga accepts the World Cup trophy after victory against Australia in the final.

Richie Richardson played in his third World Cup tournament for West Indies, and was the not-out batter as his team choked in the first semi-final when victory was in sight.

One significant change from previous World Cups was the introduction of the third umpire to adjudicate on dismissals – mainly run-outs and stumpings – if the on-field umpire was undecided.

A HAT-TRICK OF CLASSICS: Three great contests

India v Australia at Wankhede Stadium (Mumbai), 27 February

Australia didn't beat India by a single run this time, but another great World Cup contest involving the two nations still unfolded. Mark Waugh produced a superb 126 at the top of the Australian order, while his captain and opening partner Mark Taylor made 59. Australia was 3-231 with five overs left before the last four wickets fell without the addition of a run in the final over. The innings yielded five run-outs, including when Venkatapathy Raju deflected a straight drive from Mark Waugh into the stumps at the bowler's end to run out the batter's twin brother Steve. Raju had earlier claimed the first two wickets, with Taylor caught by Javagal Srinath before Sanjay Manjrekar held a great catch at backward point to send Ricky Ponting on his way.

The Indians were 2-7 following a double strike from Damien Fleming, who struck again with the total at 70. A wonderful innings of 90 from Sachin Tendulkar kept India well on track, until he was stumped off a wide from Mark Waugh to leave India 4-143. A run-out soon afterwards was another setback, but India progressed to 5-201 before another two quick wickets swung the momentum Australia's way. India's tail had too much to do, and Fleming finished with five scalps when he captured the final wicket with two overs left as India was 17 runs shy of the target.

Australia 258 (Mark Waugh 126, Mark Taylor 59; Venkatapathy Raju 2-48, Venkatesh Prasad 2-49) beat India 242 (Sachin Tendulkar 90, Sanjay Manjrekar 62; Damien Fleming 5-36, Steve Waugh 2-22) by 16 runs.

India v Pakistan at M. Chinnaswamy Stadium (Bengaluru), 9 March

A clash involving India and Pakistan was a promoter's dream, although the occasion was a quarter-final rather than a semi-final or decider. One conspicuous absentee was Wasim Akram, who was unavailable due to a side strain. At day's end, there was little point wondering if he would have changed the result had he played.

Stand-in Pakistani captain Aamer Sohail lost the toss and was made to field first. Waqar Younis troubled India's openers in his first few overs, but they survived the early pressure. Tendulkar was slower than usual, contributing just 31 to the 90-run opening stand before falling to Akram's replacement Ata-ur-Rehman, who finished as Pakistan's most economical bowler with 1-40 from 10 overs.

Navjot Sidhu's 93 and Mohammad Azharuddin's quick 27 helped India to 200 in the 42nd over, before Ajay Jadeja produced a match-turning cameo. He whacked 45 off 26 balls, and Anil Kumble and Javagal Srinath chipped in with a combined 22 runs from just 10 balls. With 51 runs added in the final three overs – Waqar conceding 40 from two of them – a likely target of 250 or 260 had swollen to 288. To make matters worse for the Pakistanis, they had to do it in 49 overs after being penalised one over for slow over rates.

Sohail and Saeed Anwar hammered 84 runs in 10 overs before Anwar's attacking approach led to his downfall. The Pakistanis reached 1-113 before three dismissals to Venkatesh Prasad reduced them to 4-132. A 52-run stand revived their hopes somewhat, as did a subsequent 47-run stand which featured two sixes from Rashid Latif and a brave effort from veteran Javed Miandad. But with the required run rate getting steep, Pakistan lost 4-8 and any hope of a miracle. The last pair added just nine runs as they batted out the last few overs. It was a disappointing farewell for Miandad, who was the only player to compete in the first six cricket World Cups: an incredible achievement.

India 8-287 (Navjot Sidhu 93, Ajay Jadeja 45; Mushtaq Ahmed 2-56) beat Pakistan 9-248 (Aamer Sohail 55, Saeed Anwar 48; Venkatesh Prasad 3-45, Anil Kumble 3-48) by 39 runs.

South Africa v West Indies at National Stadium (Karachi), 11 March

South Africa's five-match winning streak and World Cup campaign ended as the Proteas faltered at vital moments in their quarter-final. South Africa's best bowler in the tournament, Allan Donald, was mysteriously omitted in favour of unorthodox spinner Paul Adams. In hindsight, it was easy to think Donald's exclusion was a dreadful mistake from the selectors. His absence was arguably just as decisive as Wasim Akram's in the Pakistan versus India quarter-final.

Courtney Browne gave West Indies a bright start before Brian Lara overcame a scratchy start to produce one of his scintillating knocks which made him a nightmare to bowl to. Fellow left-hander Shivnarine Chanderpaul played a supportive role before the second wicket fell with the total at 180. A total in the vicinity of 300 was still possible as another 30 runs were added, but then West Indies lost 5-20, including the wicket of Lara for 111. Were it not for Ian Bishop's 17, the West Indians might have had to settle for even less than their eventual 8-264.

The Proteas were set back when Gary Kirsten trod on his wicket for just 3, before half-centuries from Andrew Hudson and Daryll Cullinan provided the necessary platform for victory. They wasted the hance to post big scores as they were caught in the deep off part-time left-arm orthodox spinner Jimmy Adams, but captain Hansie Cronje kept the scoring rate moving until he too played a fatal attacking shot against Jimmy Adams. South Africa suddenly crumbled as Roger Harper grabbed three quick wickets, including a superb return catch, as the score slid to 7-198. Pat Symcox smacked a quick 24, but then Shaun Pollock became Harper's fourth victim to leave the Proteas needing 38 from five overs with only two wickets left. With Symcox departing just moments later, the West Indians were all but home. A last-wicket stand of 18 was of little concern, as 20 runs were still needed when the final wicket fell with three balls to spare.

West Indies 8-264 (Brian Lara 111, Shivnarine Chanderpaul 56; Brian McMillan 2-37) beat South Africa 245 (Daryll Cullinan 69, Andrew Hudson 54; Roger Harper 4-47, Jimmy Adams 3-53) by 19 runs.

Members of the Australian cricket team line up prior to the final of the 1996 Cricket World Cup.

SIX OF THE BEST: Individual performances

(excluding player of the tournament, and the finals)

Gary Kirsten 188 not out off 159 balls: South Africa v United Arab Emirates at Rawalpindi Cricket Stadium (Rawalpindi), 16 February

Gary Kirsten's unbeaten 188 was the highest individual score in a World Cup match until another left-handed opener – Chris Gayle – surpassed it 19 years later.

Kirsten's then record score came in the second match of the 1996 tournament. The fixture was postponed 24 hours following heavy rain, and it was the first time Kirsten and his opponents – United Arab Emirates – appeared in a Cricket World Cup. After the Proteas were sent in to bat, Kirsten struck 13 fours and four sixes and fell just one run short of Viv Richards' then record for highest individual score in a one-day international. Having been dropped on 118, Kirsten needed a four from the last ball of the innings to reach 190, but managed only two. In any case, Kirsten set up a huge total of 2-321 which was always going to be impossible for the World Cup rookies to overcome.

Paul Strang 9.4-1-21-5: Zimbabwe v Kenya at Moin-ul-Haq Stadium (Patna), 27 February

Zimbabwe and United Arab Emirates won just once each in the 1996 tournament, yet the two bowlers with the best individual figures of the tournament came from these two nations. Admittedly, both opponents were wooden-spooners in their respective groups.

Emirates off-spinner Shaukat Dukanwala claimed 5-29 against the Netherlands, after Zimbabwean leg-spinner Paul Strang captured 5-21 against Kenya three days earlier. Interestingly, the Kenyans were five wickets down before Strang claimed his first victim. The leg-spinner was not brought on until the 32nd over, and his first six overs were unremarkable before he captured three wickets in four balls during his seventh over. A fine catch at point was followed by a catch at cover before the third victim was lbw. The final two wickets fell in the 50th over, with catches to deep point and deep mid-wicket as Kenya succumbed for 134 on its way to a five-wicket defeat.

Maurice Odumbe 10-3-15-3: Kenya v West Indies at Nehru Stadium (Pune), 29 February

Maurice Odumbe bowled magnificently as his team achieved a stunning victory against the West Indians, who fell well short of their small target of 167.

The West Indians were struggling at 4-55 before three successive wickets to Odumbe left them on the brink of defeat at 7-78. Odumbe bowled his 10 overs in one spell and conceded only 15 runs. His first victim was Chanderpaul, who cut a loose delivery to backward point. Next, Jimmy Adams was caught at silly point via bat and pad before Harper glanced a catch to the wicketkeeper down the legside. Coincidentally, Harper had earlier returned 3-15 from his 10 overs.

Sachin Tendulkar 137 off 137 balls: India v Sri Lanka at Feroz Shah Kotla Ground (New Delhi), 2 March

Sachin Tendulkar produced several sparkling knocks in the 1996 World Cup, with his 137 from as many balls against Sri Lanka perhaps the pick of them.

Tendulkar reached his half-century from 72 balls, having hit five fours and a six. It took him just 50 more deliveries to reach triple figures, with just one four and one six in this period. He then hit the accelerator, as he finished his innings with eight fours and five sixes. Two fours and two sixes came in the 49th over, bowled by Ravi Pushpakumara, before Tendulkar was denied the satisfaction of being not out when he was run out in the final over.

Tendulkar then returned tidy figures of 0-41 from 10 overs while Kumble had 2-39, but Sri Lanka won by six wickets and with eight balls to spare as the target was 272.

Brian Lara 111 off 94 balls: West Indies v South Africa at National Stadium (Karachi), 11 March

Brian Lara produced one of his masterclasses in the third quarter-final, as West Indies ended South Africa's campaign. After coming to the crease at 1-42, Lara began uncertainly as he played and missed repeatedly early on. But as soon as he got his eye in, he was simply unstoppable.

Lara hit five fours in an over from off-spinner Symcox, and reached his half-century from 45 balls before registering his ton from 83 balls. Lara struck 16 of the 94 balls he faced to the boundary, before succumbing to a sweep shot to leave the team 4-214. Ultimately, West Indies won by 19 runs after making 8-264.

One significant change from previous World Cups was the introduction of the third umpire.

Mark Waugh 110 off 112 balls: Australia v New Zealand at M.A. Chidambaram Stadium (Chennai), 11 March

Mark Waugh made three brilliant centuries in the tournament, with the third one making this list due to the pressure he was under. Waugh's centuries against Kenya and India came when Australia batted first, before his third came in a quarter-final when Australia chased a target of 287 against New Zealand. Waugh also took 1-43 from eight overs in this match. It was a pity for Kiwi all-rounder Chris Harris that his own brilliance was not enough for New Zealand. He made a splendid 130 and then escaped the onslaught as his 10 overs conceded a respectable 41 runs.

Waugh paced himself perfectly, taking 67 balls to reach his 50 before needing just 34 more deliveries to crack triple figures. His departure for 110 left the

Coca-Cola
Coca-Cola
Coca-Cola
WILLS
LANKA
WILLS
LANKA

Sanath Jayasuriya (Sri Lanka)

Matches	Innings	Not outs	Runs	Highest score	Average	50s	100s	Catches
6	6	-	221	82	36.83	2	-	5

Overs	Maidens	Runs	Wickets	Average	Best figures
51	1	231	7	33	3-12

team needing 74 from 70 balls, before Steve Waugh and Stuart Law sealed a six-wicket victory with 13 balls to spare. The century-maker's innings included six fours and two sixes.

HEADLINE MOMENT

Kenya upstages West Indies

West Indian captain Richie Richardson was almost lost for words after his team suffered a defeat that defied belief. In his 1996 Australian cricket annual, Allan Miller described it as the biggest upset in the history of international limited overs cricket. Three other rare aspects were the date (29 February), one of the dismissals (hit wicket), and a part-time wicketkeeper (Jimmy Adams) completing five dismissals with the gloves.

Nothing seemed unusual as Kenya fell to 6-81, before a seventh wicket stand of 44 and a ninth-wicket stand of 29 took place. Kenya's 166-run total, which occupied 49.3 overs, included 35 extras while none of the batters reached 30. The West Indian pacemen gave away 27 runs in illegal deliveries while off-spinner Harper was the best bowler, and there were signs of unrest and frustration from the West Indians during Kenya's lower order revival. A West Indian win seemed a formality in any case, and the openers put on 18 before an extraordinary collapse unfolded. A turning point came when Lara edged a catch behind to make the score 3-33, and resistance was minimal as only two West Indians reached double figures while none reached 20. The last wicket fell from the second ball of the 36th over as the West Indians were 74 runs shy of the target. Kenyan skipper Maurice Odumbe, who suffered the misfortune of being out hit wicket for 6, later claimed 3-15 from 10 overs. Rajab Ali's role could also not be underestimated, as he claimed the prized scalps of Richardson and Lara before capturing the final wicket.

Kenya 166 (Steve Tikolo 29, Hitesh Modi 28; Roger Harper 3-15, Courtney Walsh 3-46) beat West Indies 93 (Shivnarine Chanderpaul 19; Maurice Odumbe 3-15, Rajab Ali 3-17) by 73 runs.

PLAYER OF THE TOURNAMENT

The choice for player of the 1996 World Cup was controversial to say the least. Although Sanath Jayasuriya's influence at the top of the Sri Lankan order could not be underestimated – hence his strike rate of 131.55 – his figures paled in comparison to many other players, particularly Sachin Tendulkar and Mark Waugh. While Jayasuriya made just two half-centuries and no centuries, Tendulkar made three half-centuries and two centuries while Waugh made three centuries and one half-century. Although he admittedly had fewer opportunities than many other players due to Sri Lanka winning two matches on forfeit, Jayasuriya was merely the 17th highest run-scorer of the tournament. His left-arm orthodox spinners, while useful, produced exceptional figures just once.

In his first outing, Jayasuriya returned figures of 1-44 from 10 overs and was subsequently bowled for just 6, in a comfortable six-wicket win over Zimbabwe. In his next outing, Jayasuriya took 0-52 from 10 overs and then hammered 79 runs off 76 balls in Sri Lanka's six-wicket triumph against India when chasing 272. Jayasuriya's innings included nine fours and two sixes. In Sri Lanka's mammoth total of 5-398 against Kenya, Jayasuriya set the tone with five fours and three sixes in his 44 from 27 deliveries before he returned 0-34 from seven overs.

Romesh Kaluwitharana and Sanath Jayasuriya played a vital role in Sri Lanka's successful tournament as they were tasked with getting the innings off to a flying start. Jayasuriya was nonetheless a somewhat unusual choice for player of the tournament.

Australia's Mark Taylor and Sri Lanka's Arjuna Ranatunga prepare to lead their respective teams in the World Cup decider.

Jayasuriya's best match was the first quarter-final, which Sri Lanka won by five wickets and with 9.2 overs to spare after England set a target of 236. Jayasuriya nabbed 2-46 from nine overs and then smashed 82 runs from 44 balls. His staggering knock included 13 fours and three sixes, but it was the last time he made any impact with the bat during the tournament. His adventuresome approach cost him dearly in the semi-final as he was caught at third man for one in the opening over. His bowling was vital, however, as he captured 3-12 from seven overs and started India's astonishing collapse with the prized dismissal of Tendulkar to a stumping. He also held two catches in this match and was involved in a run-out. Jayasuriya also held two catches in the final, and took one wicket while conceding 43 runs in eight overs, before being run out for 9.

FIRST SEMI-FINAL

India v Sri Lanka at Eden Gardens (Calcutta, since changed to Kolkata), 13 March

The first semi-final turned into a sad and shameful occasion, as crowd unrest led to the match being called off early with Sri Lanka on course for a convincing victory.

The first four balls of the match were unlike anything ever seen in any game of cricket, and suggested Sri Lanka could be skittled for a miserable total in front of a crowd of about 110,000. The right-handed Romesh Kaluwitharana slashed the second ball of the match to third man for a catch, before the left-handed Jayasuriya did likewise two balls later. Although Aravinda de Silva stroked a majestic 66 from 47 balls, including 14 glorious boundaries, Sri Lanka was still uncomfortably placed at 4-85 when he departed. Mahanama made a vital half-century before succumbing to cramp, and there were also crucial contributions from left-handers Ranatunga, Hashan Tillakaratne and Chaminda Vaas to help the total to 8-251.

India lost Sidhu in the second over, but another classy knock from Tendulkar put the hosts on track. He was on 65 and the team total was 98 when he lapsed and was stumped. With Azharuddin pushing back a return catch and Manjrekar bowled off his thigh, India was suddenly in freefall at 4-101. A run-out occurred next, and Sri Lanka's spinners continued to rip through the batting as a number of cross-batted shots proved fatal on the pitch that suddenly crumbled. With India needing 132 runs from 95 balls and only two wickets remaining, a number of restless and upset spectators vented their spleen by throwing bottles and other objects onto the field. Other spectators lit fires in the stands, and match referee Clive Lloyd had little choice but to remove the players from the field. Attempts to resume the match were unsuccessful as the rioting continued, and Lloyd justifiably awarded victory to Sri Lanka. The agony was too much for the Indian players, with not-out batter Vinod Kambli in tears as the deplorable actions of some of the spectators could not be excused or justified in any era.

Sri Lanka 8-251 (Aravinda de Silva 66, Roshan Mahanama 58 retired hurt; Javagal Srinath 3-34, Sachin Tendulkar 2-34) beat India 8-120 (Sachin Tendulkar 65; Sanath Jayasuriya 3-12) by default.

SECOND SEMI-FINAL

Australia v West Indies at Mohali Stadium (Chandigarh), 14 March

Similarly to the first semi-final, the second semi-final involved a nightmare start for the team batting first, and then a revival, followed by the team batting second being in a very sound position and then losing the plot. The second semi-final, nonetheless, went down to the wire while fortunately there was no crowd disturbance.

It would be fair to say the West Indians lost it more than the Australians won it.

Australia was instantly in strife as the in-form Mark Waugh was trapped lbw with the second ball of the match. Curtly Ambrose and Ian Bishop ripped through the top order to leave Australia 4-15 in the 10th over. A vital 138-run partnership for the next wicket revived Australia's hopes, with Law scoring 72 and Michael Bevan going on to make 69 before departing with the total on 171. A lively 31 from Ian Healy helped Australia reach 207 for the loss of eight wickets, but the total still appeared sub-standard.

The first wicket fell at 25 in the run chase before left-handers Chanderpaul and Lara guided West Indies into a winning position. A brilliant delivery from Steve Waugh rattled Lara's off-stump with the total at 93, before Richardson combined with Chanderpaul for a seemingly match-winning 72-run stand. A needless slog brought about Chanderpaul's downfall and triggered an astonishing collapse as a series of lbws and caught-behinds unfolded. Richardson remained defiant under pressure, and the requirement came down to 10 runs from the last over, which was to be bowled by Fleming. Richardson dispatched the first ball for four but then chanced a risky single, which resulted in Ambrose being run out at the striker's end. Courtney Walsh drove at the third ball but it bowled him, and the Australians were overjoyed as they had reached the World Cup final following a collapse of 8-37. It would be fair to say the West Indians lost it more than the Australians won it.

Australia 8-207 (Stuart Law 72, Michael Bevan 69; Curtly Ambrose 2-26, Ian Bishop 2-35) beat West Indies 202 (Shivnarine Chanderpaul 80, Richie Richardson 49 not out; Shane Warne 4-36, Glenn McGrath 2-30) by five runs.

FINAL

Sri Lanka v Australia at Gaddafi Stadium (Lahore), 17 March

The 1996 World Cup final was a rare occasion when Sri Lanka had the overwhelming support of a crowd at a Pakistani stadium. It also marked the first time in World Cup history that one of the tournament co-hosts lifted the trophy.

Although every previous World Cup decider was won by the team batting first, Sri Lanka's skipper asked Australia to bat first when he won the toss. Overnight rain may have played a part in Ranatunga's decision. Mark Waugh failed for the second successive time, but a 101-run second-wicket stand involving Taylor and Ponting put Australia on course for a big total. The score was 1-134 after 25 overs, but then Sri Lanka's spinners enjoyed a purple patch as Australia fell to 5-170 with 15 overs remaining. Law and Bevan were not as effective as they had been in the semi-final, although Bevan progressed to 36 not out as Australia had to settle for 7-241.

Dewy conditions under lights made it hard for the Australians to grip the ball, but two early breakthroughs temporarily gave them the upper hand. The score was 2-23 as both openers succumbed for single-figure scores, with Jayasuriya run out and Kaluwitharana caught at square leg. The pendulum turned as a chancy 125-run stand unfolded for the third wicket. Shane Warne's first over cost 11 runs, with de Silva gaining a crucial reprieve as the wicketkeeper failed to hold a tough chance. Gurusinha had more luck as he was dropped twice in the outfield. When Gurusinha was bowled for 65, Sri Lanka required 94 runs from a little under 20 overs. Fifty-one were required from the last 10, and then Ranatunga offered Warne a stinging return catch which resulted in a boundary. The next ball was dispatched for six, and Australia's hopes were all but gone. Sri Lanka still had seven wickets in hand when the winning runs were scored with 22 balls to spare. De Silva finished on 107 from 124 balls, including 13 fours, while Ranatunga's 47 came from 37 balls and included four fours and a six. De Silva had an outstanding match, having earlier claimed 3-42 from nine overs with Taylor, Ponting and Healy his victims. He also caught Steve Waugh and Law.

Australia		R	B
Mark Taylor (c)	c Jayasuriya b de Silva	74	83
Mark Waugh	c Jayasuriya b Vaas	12	15
Ricky Ponting	b de Silva	45	73
Steve Waugh	c de Silva b Dharmasena	13	25
Shane Warne	st Kaluwitharana b Muralidaran	2	5
Stuart Law	c de Silva b Jayasuriya	22	30
Michael Bevan	not out	36	49
Ian Healy (+)	b de Silva	2	3
Paul Reiffel	not out	13	18
Sundries	(lb 10, nb 1, w 11)	22	
TOTAL	**(50 overs) 7-241**		

DID NOT BAT: Damien Fleming, Glenn McGrath

FALL: 36, 137, 152, 156, 170, 202, 205

Wickramasinghe 7-0-38-0, Vaas 6-1-30-1, Muralidaran 10-0-31-1, Dharmasena 10-0-47-1, Jayasuriya 8-0-43-1, de Silva 9-0-42-3

Sri Lanka		R	B
Sanath Jayasuriya	run out (McGrath/Healy)	9	7
Romesh Kaluwitharana (+)	c Bevan b Fleming	6	13
Asanka Gurusinha	b Reiffel	65	99
Aravinda de Silva	not out	107	124
Arjuna Ranatunga (c)	not out	47	37
Sundries	(b 1, lb 4, nb 1, w 5)	11	
TOTAL	**(46.2 overs) 3-245**		

DID NOT BAT: Hashan Tillakaratne, Roshan Mahanama, Kumar Dharmasena, Chaminda Vaas, Muttiah Muralidaran, Pramodya Wickramasinghe

FALL: 12, 23, 148

McGrath 8.2-1-28-0, Fleming 6-0-43-1, Warne 10-0-58-0, Reiffel 10-0-49-1, Mark Waugh 6-0-35-0, Steve Waugh 3-0-15-0, Michael Bevan 3-0-12-0

UMPIRES: Steve Bucknor, David Shepherd (TV: Cyril Mitchley)

TOSS: Sri Lanka

PLAYER OF THE MATCH: Aravinda de Silva

SRI LANKA WON BY SEVEN WICKETS

1999

Aussies reign supreme after early setbacks

- Zimbabwe defeats India and South Africa
- Sourav Ganguly and Rahul Dravid produce the first 300-run partnership in a limited overs international
- Following two defeats in its first three games, Australia wins the tournament after being undefeated in its final seven fixtures
- South Africa squanders two chances to knock Australia out of contention, with a comical dropped catch proving costly in one match and a suicidal run-out ending South Africa's title hopes in a tied semi-final
- Pakistan crushes New Zealand in a semi-final before being slaughtered in the final

The return to odd-numbered years for the Cricket World Cup meant only a little over three years had passed between the 1996 World Cup and the next one.

World Cup cricket had a much different look and feel about it when it returned to England in 1999, after the previous time England hosted the limited overs showpiece was 16 years earlier. Another change in 1999 was that the Netherlands, Ireland and Wales staged one match each while there were two fixtures in Scotland. As in 1996, a dozen teams fought out the 1999 title although there were two changes, with Scotland and Bangladesh coming in at the expense of the Netherlands and United Arab Emirates. Once again the competition was split into two groups, although there was a change to the format as there was a 'Super Six' phase before the finals. The top-three teams from each group qualified for the 'Super Six' phase, with points brought forward according to the head-to-head results among these teams.

The two groups had an identical look about them as the top team in each group had four wins and a loss, followed by three teams with three wins and two losses. Both groups also had a team with two wins and three losses, and one team without a win. While South Africa was the standout team in Group A as India, Zimbabwe and England were just one win behind, it appeared Zimbabwe might give the competition a real shake. Although placing third in Group A, Zimbabwe entered the 'Super Six' phase ahead of India and South Africa after beating them in the round-robin phase. However, the Zimbabweans subsequently suffered a fatal hefty loss to the top-placed team in Group B: Pakistan. The Proteas had their chances in their two contests with Australia, only for a victory to slip through their fingers on both occasions including when a spot in the decider was up for grabs. Reigning titleholder Sri Lanka missed the finals series after an underwhelming tournament, while Kenya was unable to win a game.

Pakistan topped Group B and lost only once on its way to reaching the final, although its defeat to Bangladesh was one of the biggest shocks in World Cup history. Pakistan's tournament also finished disastrously when the team was simply annihilated in the final. The Bangladeshis were never likely to make the finals, and the only team below them on the Group B ladder was the winless Scotland. The three Group B teams locked on six points were Australia, New Zealand and West Indies, none of which appeared a genuine contender for a while.

As history has shown, Australia lost two of its first three matches before being undefeated in its remaining seven matches to hold aloft the trophy. Had one or two things gone slightly differently, South Africa or Pakistan or even Zimbabwe could just as easily have been the tournament winner.

Pakistan fast bowler Shoaib Akhtar shows his frustration as he kicks out in the direction of Australia's Mark Waugh. Pakistan narrowly won this fixture at Headingley, before the Australians turned the tables in the decider as they demolished Pakistan.

England's Nasser Hussain is bowled during a loss to India, as England tumbles out of contention for the 1999 title.

A HAT-TRICK OF CLASSICS: Three great contests

India v Zimbabwe at Grace Road (Leicester), 19 May

There were many decisive aspects of this match which went down to the wire. India, which chose to field first, missed Sachin Tendulkar who flew home for his father's funeral. More crucially, the Indians conceded 51 runs in sundries – including 37 from illegal deliveries – and were allowed to face only 46 overs due to their slow over rate. All of these things made India's task much stiffer than it otherwise would have been.

Zimbabwe lost opener Neil Johnson cheaply, before the next three batters rued their inability to capitalise on a decent start. Grant Flower added 57 runs with brother Andy for the fourth wicket, before a 60-run stand took the total beyond 200. Andy Flower held the innings together with a crucial 68 not out, before the run chase featured many twists and turns. India needed to score at 5.5 runs per over, and Zimbabwe's bowlers were also wayward as they conceded 34 runs from illegitimate deliveries. From 3-56 after nine overs, India progressed to 3-155 as a couple of chances were missed, before stumbling to 6-175 and then recovering with a 44-run partnership. The eighth wicket stand put India back on track for victory, with only seven runs needed from the last 11 balls before Henry Olonga captured three quick wickets to seal a three-run triumph with an over to spare. Zimbabwe captain Alistair Campbell took a diving catch at cover to account for Robin Singh before a single was followed by a two, courtesy of overthrows. Olonga kept his cool while the tail-enders lost theirs, with a full-length ball rattling Javagal Srinath's stumps before another accurate ball trapped Venkatesh Prasad lbw.

Zimbabwe 9-252 (Andy Flower 68 not out, Grant Flower 45; Javagal Srinath 2-35, Venkatesh Prasad 2-37) beat India 249 (Sadagoppan Ramesh 55, Ajay Jadeja 43; Henry Olonga 3-22, Heath Streak 3-36) by three runs.

Australia v Pakistan at Headingley (Leeds), 23 May

Australia's decision to bowl first appeared to pay off when Pakistan stumbled to 3-46 in the 13th over. Inzamam-ul-Haq and Abdul Razzaq were subsequently tied down, and a disastrous mix-up in the 27th over resulted in the duo being stranded at the same end. But a run-out was comically avoided after a throw ricocheted from the stumps.

Pakistan was 3-130 with 15 overs remaining, before Inzamam and Razzaq hit the accelerator. Razzaq was caught in the 40th over, and then 13 runs in the next over was a sign of what was to come as 108 runs were added in the final 10 overs. Mohammad Yousuf was run out in the 45th over after slamming 29 off 16 balls, before Inzamam was run out in the 47th over. Despite a further two wickets – including another run-out – Pakistan scored 39 runs in the final three overs. Moin Khan hit the last two balls for a six and a four, and little did anyone know just how priceless those 10 runs would be.

Chasing 276, Australia lost Adam Gilchrist for a third-ball duck before Mark Waugh and Ricky Ponting added 91. The loss of 3-10 put Pakistan back on top, only for Steve Waugh and Michael Bevan to turn the tide with a 113-run stand. Australia required 38 from 31 balls when a brilliant Shoaib Akhtar yorker rattled Steve Waugh's stumps. With 11 runs needed from four balls and two wickets in hand, Damien Martyn was bowled which prompted a crowd invasion from Pakistani fans who thought the game was over. Two balls later, they had their wish as another Wasim Akram delivery crashed into the stumps.

Pakistan 8-275 (Inzamam-ul-Haq 81, Abdul Razzaq 60; Damien Fleming 2-37) beat Australia 265 (Michael Bevan 61, Steve Waugh 49; Wasim Akram 4-40, Saqlain Mushtaq 3-51) by 10 runs.

Australia v South Africa at Headingley (Leeds), 13 June

Australia faced a crunch clash with South Africa, as Australia and Zimbabwe were in contention for one semi-final spot. Ultimately, a tight win to the Australians set up a rematch with the Proteas.

South Africa's openers put on 45 runs before 95 were added for the second wicket. Despite the Proteas stumbling from 1-140 to 3-141 as Shane Warne dismissed Daryll Cullinan and Hansie Cronje in one over, a big total always looked likely as Herschelle Gibbs was in fine form. He worked his way to triple figures, before quick scoring from Jonty Rhodes and Lance Klusener helped the total to 271. Klusener was caught from the penultimate delivery, before Shaun Pollock was bowled from the final ball.

Steve Elworthy struck early with the key wicket of Gilchrist, before the run-out of Mark Waugh left Australia 2-20. Martyn perished to a miscued pull with the total on 48, but hope was restored with the fourth wicket stand. Ricky Ponting was more subdued than usual while Steve Waugh showed more urgency. The total was only 3-97 after 25 overs, before 30 runs were added in the next two overs. Australia was 3-152 in the 31st over when Waugh, on 56, flicked a simple catch to mid-wicket where Gibbs comically muffed the chance as he tried to throw the ball away in celebration. It turned out to be a sliding doors moment in the game and in the tournament.

Australia needed 98 runs from 16 overs when Ponting skied a catch, before Bevan helped move the score along. Waugh reached his century in the 43rd over, before Bevan's departure left Australia needing 25 runs from 26 balls. With eight runs needed from the last over, Tom Moody struck a two and a four from the first two balls, before Steve Waugh edged a single from the fourth ball to seal his team's victory.

Australia 5-272 (Steve Waugh 120 not out, Ricky Ponting 69; Steve Elworthy 2-46) beat South Africa 7-271 (Herschelle Gibbs 101, Daryll Cullinan 50; Damien Fleming 3-57, Shane Warne 2-33) by five wickets.

SIX OF THE BEST: Individual performances

(excluding player of the tournament, and the finals)

Allan Donald 8-1-17-4: South Africa v England at The Oval (London), 22 May

Usually an opening bowler, Allan Donald was used as a first or second change bowler throughout the 1999 World Cup, with plenty of success. His spell against England was simply breathtaking, as England crumbled for 103 in reply to South Africa's 7-225.

Graham Thorpe was Donald's first victim as an lbw appeal was upheld, and Andrew Flintoff was the fast bowler's second victim as the all-rounder presented a catch to backward point. Mark Ealham edged a leg-cutter to first slip, before Neil Fairbrother became the second left-hander to be trapped in front of the stumps.

Had one or two things gone slightly differently, South Africa or Pakistan or even Zimbabwe could just as easily have been the tournament winner (rather than Australia).

Ridley Jacobs five catches and 80 not out off 131 balls: West Indies v New Zealand at County Ground (Southampton), 24 May

Ridley Jacobs had the honour of being the first player in an ODI to achieve the double of five dismissals with the gloves and a half-century with the bat. It was also the first time in a World Cup match that all 10 dismissals in an innings were catches.

Four West Indian bowlers benefited from Jacobs' glovework as New Zealand managed only 156. The left-hander went on to open the batting, as he usually did in the tournament, and he showed plenty of patience and composure as he held the innings together. Jacobs took 88 balls to reach his half-century, before finishing with 80 not out which included eight fours and a six. Wickets fell at 29, 49 and 121 before Stuart Williams hit the winning runs in the 45th over.

Sourav Ganguly 183 off 158 balls: India v Sri Lanka at County Ground (Taunton), 26 May

Sourav Ganguly and Rahul Dravid produced the first ever 300-run partnership in an ODI as they added 318 for the second wicket, after India lost a wicket in the first over. The left-handed Ganguly and right-handed Dravid were simply outstanding as they played an array of brilliant strokes while the Sri Lankan bowlers had no answer.

Dravid hit 17 fours and one six in his 145 from 129 balls before being run out in the 46th over. He outscored Ganguly for the most part, with the left-hander taking 68 balls to reach his half-century before taking another 51 to reach three figures. Ganguly upped the tempo, to put it mildly, as he raced from 100 to 183 in just 39 balls. In the 45th over he hammered three fours and a six from successive balls, with the first of those boundaries coming from a dropped catch. Ganguly finished with 17 fours and seven sixes, and he was caught from the penultimate ball of the innings as he sought another six. India's total of 6-373 was beyond the Sri Lankans, who fell 158 runs shy of the target.

Glenn McGrath 8.4-3-14-5: Australia v West Indies at Old Trafford (Manchester), 30 May

West Indies managed only 110 before going on to lose by six wickets against Australia, following some wonderful bowling from Glenn McGrath. Warne had exceptional figures of 3-11 from 10 overs but it was McGrath who did the most damage. He reduced the West Indians from 0-7 to 2-7 with successive balls, as Sherwin Campbell edged a catch to second slip before Jimmy Adams was lbw. The next wicket fell at 20 when a sensational McGrath delivery pitched around middle and leg-stump before moving away from the left-handed Brian Lara's defensive push and hitting off-stump. McGrath had 3-12 from six overs in his first spell before he captured two of the last three wickets, as he claimed another lbw and another bowled.

Neil Johnson 8-0-43-2 and 132 not out off 144 balls: Zimbabwe v Australia at Lord's (London), 9 June

Despite an outstanding all-round effort from its opening bowler and opening batter Neil Johnson, Zimbabwe went down by 44 runs against Australia. Had Johnson found better support in the run chase, the African nation could well have won the match and changed the fortunes of both teams in the tournament.

Johnson dismissed Australia's openers, although his second wicket did not occur until Mark Waugh had posted a century which set up a commanding total of 4-303. In reply, Zimbabwe was 1-39 after the 11th over was a wicket maiden, before Johnson hammered four fours off Warne in the following over. With Moody bowling the 22nd over, Johnson struck the last three balls for four, two and six. The Africans were 1-153 after 28 overs but then faltered to 6-200 in the next 11 overs, and any hope of an upset was quashed. Johnson kept going, however, and he finished unbeaten on 132 which included 14 fours and two sixes.

Saqlain Mushtaq hat-trick: Pakistan v Zimbabwe at The Oval (London), 11 June

Pakistani off-spinner Saqlain Mushtaq claimed the second hat-trick in World Cup cricket history as Pakistan crushed Zimbabwe by 148 runs. Saqlain finished with 3-16 from 6.3 overs as he claimed the final three wickets in the 41st over.

Henry Olonga and Adam Huckle were stumped, with Olonga leaving his crease and swinging wildly before Huckle moved down the wicket and sought to drive. 'Pommie' Mbangwa then prodded half-heartedly at an arm ball, which trapped him plumb in front of the stumps.

India's Rahul Dravid steers the ball through the legside during his innings of 61 in a Super Six victory against Pakistan.

HEADLINE MOMENT

'Go-slow' tactics from Australia in run chase against West Indies

Australia's 'go-slow' tactics against West Indies were bizarre but not hard to explain, after there was also extremely slow batting from West Indies. The team from the Caribbean lasted 46.4 overs but totalled only 110, including 18 runs in wides. West Indies crashed from 3-64 to 8-71 before having partnerships of 17 and 22. Ridley Jacobs carried his bat as he made a painstaking 49 not out from 142 balls, and Reon King scored a single off 30 balls in the ninth-wicket partnership.

While Jacobs and the tail-enders could be excused for slow scoring as they tried to bat out as many overs as possible, the subsequent scenario was much different for the Australians. They wanted to boost the net run rate of the West Indians at the expense of New Zealand's. This would enable West Indies to progress to the Super Sixes while the Australians would gain two points for the Super Sixes, whereas Australia would gain no points for the Super Sixes if New Zealand finished ahead. It was therefore in Australia's interests to score the runs slowly rather than quickly. The day after Australia accounted for West Indies, a convincing win for the Kiwis against Scotland meant Australia's tactics were to no avail in any case.

Australia was 4-62 in the 20th over when Bevan joined Steve Waugh in the centre. Bevan hit a boundary in each of the 21st and 22nd overs before Waugh edged the first ball of the 25th over for four. Two ensuing no-balls increased the total to 4-83, and nothing seemed amiss at this stage. But it took another 16.3 overs for the batting duo to score the remaining 28 runs. At one stage there were 21 dot balls on the trot, followed by a four to Waugh. After successive wides took the total to 4-104, there were another 21 dot balls in succession.

The fifth ball of the 41st over was a wide, and the next was a no-ball which produced the winning run. Waugh finished on 19 from 73 balls while Bevan had 20 off 69.

PLAYER OF THE TOURNAMENT

Lance Klusener was a match-winner on numerous occasions in the 1999 World Cup. The hard-hitting lower order left-handed batter was dismissed only twice in his eight visits to the crease while he had a strike rate of 122.17. As a right-arm fast-medium bowler, he was the equal-fourth highest wicket-taker in the tournament. Unfortunately for Klusener, he was also the central figure in a catastrophic run-out that ultimately ended South Africa's campaign when a spot in the final was all but secure.

Klusener took 3-66 and scored 12 not out as the Proteas began the tournament with a four-wicket win over India. Against Sri Lanka, Klusener struck 22 runs in the final over to reach 52 not out and help the Proteas to a still disappointing 9-199 before he claimed 3-21 in an 89-run triumph. It was the first of three successive player of the match performances from the man known as 'Zulu'. The second occasion was against England, as he made 48 not out and took one wicket in a 122-run drubbing. In a seven-wicket victory against Kenya, Klusener bagged 5-21 and was not required to bat. Against Zimbabwe, Klusener made an unbeaten 52 for the second time in the tournament, but this time it was not enough to prevent a 48-run defeat. In his next outing, he earned another player of the match award after taking a wicket and scoring 46 not out in a three-wicket win over Pakistan.

Promoted to number three against New Zealand, Klusener was bowled for just four before capturing two wickets in a 74-run triumph. Against Australia, Klusener was left to wonder what might have been. On the first occasion, he smashed a quickfire 36 and took 1-53 before Australia scraped home in the last over thanks to an unbeaten Steve Waugh century. Klusener should have dismissed Waugh for 56, but the usually reliable Gibbs botched an easy catch. In the second semi-final, Klusener's bowling was ineffective before he bludgeoned 31 not out off 16 balls. He creamed two fours in the last over to level the scores with four balls remaining, but what happened two balls later could be described as panicking, choking, a brain explosion or a rush of blood. With the Proteas needing one run for a spot in the World Cup final, Klusener miscued his shot and scurried frantically down the wicket for a suicidal single which resulted in a run-out. He was only human after all. The pressure became too much. But without Klusener, the Proteas would surely not have gone as far as they did in the tournament.

Lance Klusener (South Africa)

Matches	Innings	Not outs	Runs	Highest score	Average	50s	100s	Catches
9	8	6	281	52*	140.50	2	-	1
Overs	**Maidens**	**Runs**	**Wickets**	**Average**	**Best figures**			
75.5	5	350	17	20.58	5-21			

Australia's 'go-slow' tactics against West Indies were bizarre but not hard to explain.

FIRST SEMI-FINAL

New Zealand v Pakistan at Old Trafford (Manchester), 16 June

It appeared that the Pakistanis might have spoilt their chances of reaching the World Cup decider after bowling first and conceding 29 runs in illegitimate bowling. But in the end, the margin was so decisive that the sundries count was virtually forgotten.

New Zealand was 2-38 after Nathan Astle and Craig McMillan made no impression, and the third wicket fell at 58 when Matthew Horne exited for 35. Stephen Fleming, Roger Twose and Chris Cairns all made 40s, as New Zealand's total comprised 194 runs off the bat and 47 sundries. The 34th over was entertaining, with Akhtar the bowler. Fleming hit two fours and a two from successive balls, with misfields occurring from the latter two of those three deliveries. The next ball dislodged the leg-stump, and then drinks were taken before the bowler forgot to release the ball from the first delivery after the resumption. Ijaz Ahmed held a classic one-handed catch to account for Twose in the 40th over, before Shoaib's slower ball hit Chris Harris's leg-stump in the 46th over.

New Zealand failed to take a wicket until the 41st over of the run chase, with Pakistan just 48 runs away from victory. Wajahatullah Wasti faced 123 balls for his 84 before skying a catch to mid-off. Saeed Anwar finished with 113 not out from 148 balls, while Ijaz made an unbeaten 28 from just 21 balls as Pakistan won with 2.3 overs to spare. There was a delay of several minutes in the dying stages due to a pitch invasion, with security appearing to have little interest in curbing the intrusive behaviour.

Pakistan 1-242 (Saeed Anwar 113 not out, Wajahatullah Wasti 84; Chris Cairns 1-33) beat New Zealand 7-241 (Roger Twose 46, Chris Cairns 44 not out; Shoaib Akhtar 3-55, Abdul Razzaq 2-28) by nine wickets.

SECOND SEMI-FINAL

Australia v South Africa at Edgbaston (Birmingham), 17 June

Nobody could have predicted how this match would pan out as there were countless pendulum swings. Each team looked sure to win at various times – South Africa more often – before a thrilling tie enabled Australia to reach the final and leave the Proteas shaking their heads and wondering how a World Cup final berth slipped from their grasp.

Australia welcomed back Darren Lehmann while South Africa welcomed back Jacques Kallis following the encounter four days earlier. Sent in, Australia was quickly in trouble as Pollock had Mark Waugh caught behind without scoring in the first over. A second-wicket stand of 51 put the game in the balance before Australia slipped to 4-68, with Gilchrist slashing the last ball of the 17th over straight to third man. Steve Waugh and Bevan added 90 before Pollock struck twice in three balls to leave Australia 6-158 with 10 overs left. Warne helped Bevan add 49 before the last four wickets fell in nine balls, leaving South Africa a modest target of 214.

Scotland's Gavin Hamilton is joyful as he dismisses Pakistan's Saleem Malik without scoring at Chester-le-Street. Scotland was temporarily on top in this match before Pakistan recorded a 94-run triumph.

With Gibbs finding the boundary regularly, the Proteas reached 0-48 in 12 overs before a Warne delivery spun viciously and clipped Gibbs's off-stump. South Africa fell to 3-53 in Warne's next over, with Gary Kirsten bowled attempting a slog-sweep before Cronje was ruled caught at slip when it appeared the ball hit his toe and missed his bat. The run-out of Cullinan left the Proteas 4-61, before Kallis combined with Rhodes for a vital partnership. The run rate remained sedate, although Rhodes hit a six in the 40th over which cost nine runs. He perished to a slog in the next over which yielded just two runs, meaning South Africa needed 68 from nine overs. Warne's last over cost 15 runs but also included the vital wicket of Kallis, before the next over yielded eight runs and the wicket of Pollock to leave the Proteas wobbling at 7-184 with four overs left. The dismissals of Mark Boucher (bowled middle-stump) and Steve Elworthy (run out) left the last-wicket pair needing 16 runs from eight balls. Klusener slammed a low full-toss to long-on, only for Paul Reiffel to spill an overhead catch which resulted in a six. An ensuing single gave Klusener the strike for the final over, with nine runs needed. Damien Fleming came around the wicket and overpitched twice, with Klusener belting two successive fours through the off side to level the score. A tie was not enough for the Proteas, however, as they had finished lower than Australia on the Super Six ladder. With Fleming changing to over the wicket, Klusener pulled the third delivery to mid-on where Lehmann fielded the ball and sought to run out the non-striker who had backed up too far, but the throw missed the stumps. The next ball was a yorker, with the left-handed batter backing away and trying to smack it but succeeding only in dribbling it towards mid-off. Klusener tore down the wicket but Donald, who had earlier taken four wickets, dropped his bat as he did not think a run was on. Mark Waugh flicked the ball to the bowler who underarmed it to the wicketkeeper, who broke the wicket with Donald well out of his crease. The Australians were ecstatic while the South Africans were left shaking their heads. With Cronje looking shattered, nobody could have imagined the tragedy that awaited South Africa's captain. The following year he was found guilty of match-fixing (although the 1999 World Cup semi-final was not among the matches in question) and was rubbed out of the game, before his life ended in a plane crash in 2002.

Australia 213 (Michael Bevan 65, Steve Waugh 56; Shaun Pollock 5-36, Allan Donald 4-32) tied with South Africa 213 (Jacques Kallis 53, Jonty Rhodes 43; Shane Warne 4-29).

FINAL

Australia v Pakistan at Lord's (London), 20 June

The World Cup final turned into a fizzer as it was easily the most lopsided of all of the World Cup deciders comprising 50 or 60 overs per side. Having reached 0-21 from four overs after winning the toss, Pakistan was simply never in the game from that point on.

The game began 30 minutes late due to a shower. The saying 'catches win matches' was never more evident as Mark Waugh flew from second slip to bring about the first dismissal in the fifth over, after the previous over cost 14 runs. When Anwar was bowled off a deflection just three balls after the loss of his opening partner, Pakistan had suddenly slipped to 2-21.

There was hope of a recovery as 47 runs were added for the third wicket. With the total on 58, Razzaq skied the final ball of the 17th over to deep mid-off where McGrath spilled a straightforward catch. It mattered little, as Razzaq fell to a sharp catch by Steve Waugh in the covers during the 20th over. Warne picked up the vital wickets of Ijaz and Moin, before Inzamam appeared unlucky to be adjudged caught behind off Reiffel. The collapse continued as Shahid Afridi was lbw while trying to sweep, before the Pakistanis fell from 7-129 to 132 all out. Even more embarrassing for the Pakistanis was that sundries was the top-scorer with 25. The innings ended after 39 overs as Ponting dived from third slip to hold a sensational one-handed catch.

Gilchrist took a heavy toll on the quick bowlers as the left-hander raced to a half-century in just 33 balls. He exited soon afterwards as he slammed Saqlain's first ball to mid-off, with Australia just 58 runs shy of victory. Another 37 runs were added before Ponting edged behind, and Lehmann had the honour of hitting the winning runs when he cut the first ball of the 21st over to the boundary.

Pakistan

Pakistan		R	B
Saeed Anwar	b Fleming	15	17
Wajahatullah Wasti	c Mark Waugh b McGrath	1	14
Abdul Razzaq	c Steve Waugh b Moody	17	51
Ijaz Ahmed	b Warne	22	46
Inzamam-ul-Haq	c Gilchrist b Reiffel	15	33
Moin Khan (+)	c Gilchrist b Warne	6	12
Shahid Afridi	lbw b Warne	13	16
Azhar Mahmood	c & b Moody	8	17
Wasim Akram (c)	c Steve Waugh b Warne	8	20
Saqlain Mushtaq	c Ponting b McGrath	0	4
Shoaib Akhtar	not out	2	6
Sundries	(lb 10, nb 2, w 13)	25	
TOTAL	**(39 overs) 132**		

FALL: 21, 21, 68, 77, 91, 104, 113, 129, 129, 132

McGrath 9-3-13-2, Fleming 6-0-30-1, Reiffel 10-1-29-1, Moody 5-0-17-2, Warne 9-1-33-4

Australia

Australia		R	B
Mark Waugh	not out	37	52
Adam Gilchrist (+)	c Inzamam b Saqlain	54	36
Ricky Ponting	c Moin b Akram	24	27
Darren Lehmann	not out	13	9
Sundries	(lb 1, nb 3, w 1)	5	
TOTAL	**(20.1 overs) 2-133**		

DID NOT BAT: Steve Waugh (c), Michael Bevan, Tom Moody, Shane Warne, Paul Reiffel, Damien Fleming, Glenn McGrath

FALL: 75, 112

Wasim Akram 8-1-41-1, Shoaib Akhtar 4-0-37-0, Abdul Razzaq 2-0-13-0, Azhar Mahmood 2-0-20-0, Saqlain Mushtaq 4.1-0-21-1

UMPIRES: Steve Bucknor, David Shepherd (TV: Srinivas Venkataraghavan)

TOSS: Pakistan

PLAYER OF THE MATCH: Shane Warne

AUSTRALIA WON BY EIGHT WICKETS

2003

No Warne, no Waughs, no worries for Aussies as Ponting's team finishes unbeaten

- Australia overcomes the absence of a suspended Shane Warne to go through the tournament without a defeat
- Australia's standout performers include Andrew Symonds with 143 not out against Pakistan, Andy Bichel with seven wickets and crucial runs against England, and captain Ricky Ponting with a wonderful century in the final
- A tied result again proves fatal for South Africa, this time in a rain-affected clash with Sri Lanka
- Sri Lanka's Chaminda Vaas captures four wickets in the first over of one match, including a hat-trick to start proceedings
- The Netherlands all-rounder Feiko Kloppenburg sets a World Cup record

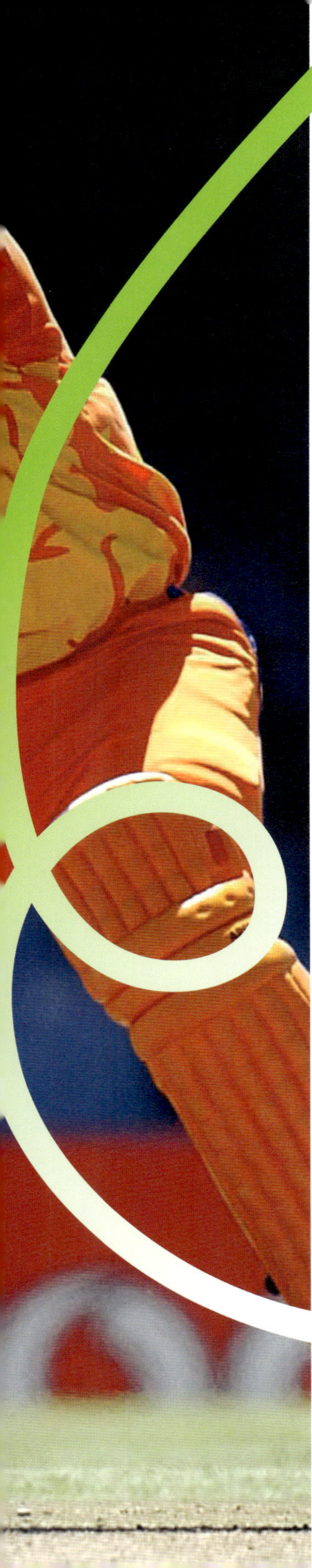

The Cricket World Cup went to Africa for the first time as South Africa, Zimbabwe and Kenya hosted the 2003 tournament, while the tally of 14 teams was a record at the time. Canada and the Netherlands were involved for the second time, with Canada previously appearing back in 1979 while the Netherlands previously appeared in 1996. Namibia made its World Cup debut, and Scotland was the only nation from 1999 to drop out. The format resembled that of 1999 as there were two groups – now known as pools – while the top-three teams in each pool qualified for the 'Super Sixes'.

While the Netherlands, Namibia, Canada and Bangladesh were never likely to push for a finals berth, it was notable that England, Pakistan, West Indies and South Africa also failed to qualify. South Africa was desperately unlucky once again when another tied result was detrimental. While it must have been pleasing for competition organisers that Zimbabwe placed in the top-three in Pool A while Kenya was second only to Sri Lanka in Pool B, there were a couple of unsatisfactory factors. England forfeited its clash with Zimbabwe due to political unrest in Zimbabwe, and this eventually enabled Zimbabwe to reach the Super Sixes at England's expense as two points separated the teams on the ladder. New Zealand meanwhile finished third in Pool B after being level with Kenya on 16 points while West Indies and South Africa were on 14, yet the ladder would have been totally different had the Kiwis not forfeited their contest with Kenya due to security concerns. Ultimately, Kenya became the first non-Test-playing nation to reach the World Cup finals series.

The political situation in Zimbabwe also affected the cricketing nation, as Andy Flower and Henry Olonga temporarily wore black armbands in protest against the regime of President Robert Mugabe. It proved to be the beginning of the end of their cricketing careers for their home country.

In spite of everything, Australia won back-to-back titles following an undefeated campaign. Ironically, Australia was rocked shortly before the tournament started as Shane Warne earned a 12-month suspension after testing positive to a banned diuretic while Steve and Mark Waugh were no longer in the team. Australia was in deep trouble against England and New Zealand before overcoming these two nations, and then struggled for a while against Sri Lanka in a semi-final. In the decider, there were no such concerns.

Tim de Leede on his way to 58 not out for the Netherlands against England.

A HAT-TRICK OF CLASSICS: Three great contests

West Indies v South Africa at Newlands Cricket Ground (Cape Town), 9 February

While there were many pendulum swings during this thriller, South Africa was vitally penalised for a slow over rate. The outcome could have been different had the Proteas been allotted the standard 50 overs rather than 49, but nonetheless they had enough chances to win.

The West Indians were 2-7 in the seventh over after Shaun Pollock dismissed the openers, before Brian Lara produced a splendid 116 from 134 balls. Lara was on 81 while the total was a modest 3-146 after 38 overs, before the final 12 overs yielded 132 runs. An unbroken sixth-wicket stand of 63 came from the final 28 balls, following Lara's departure. Ricardo Powell creamed 40 not out from 18 balls while Ramnaresh Sarwan clubbed 32 not out from 15 balls.

Gary Kirsten played an anchoring role in the run chase, but no lengthy partnerships developed. Kirsten departed in the 32nd over before Pollock's dismissal in the next over left the Proteas in disarray at 6-160. Mark Boucher scored a run-a-ball 49, before his departure left South Africa needing 75 runs off 49 balls. Fifty-four were needed from five overs before Lance Klusener hit three sixes in the 45th over, and was lucky not to be out caught on the boundary from the last of them. Another six from Klusener reduced the task to only 14 runs from 12 balls. Pedro Collins conceded five runs in the penultimate over, before Vasbert Drakes bowled a brilliant final over. With three fielders on the mid-wicket boundary, Klusener was caught in this region from the third ball. With eight runs needed from two balls, Makhaya Ntini holed out to extra cover where Sarwan held a fine running catch, before a last-ball boundary to Nicky Boje proved inconsequential.

West Indies 5-278 (Brian Lara 116, Ricardo Powell 40 not out, Carl Hooper 40; Makhaya Ntini 2-37) beat South Africa 9-275 (Gary Kirsten 69, Lance Klusener 57; Vasbert Drakes 2-33) by three runs.

England v Australia at St George's Park Cricket Ground (Port Elizabeth), 2 March

Outstanding contributions from Andy Bichel and Michael Bevan helped Australia to a narrow victory, and England was left to wonder how a winnable situation slipped away while its World Cup chances also evaporated.

Nasser Hussain's decision to bat appeared vindicated as openers Marcus Trescothick and Nick Knight put on 66 runs, until Bichel struck in the 10th over. The innings fell apart, thanks largely to Bichel, as England tumbled to 5-87 just eight overs after the fall of the first wicket. Alec Stewart and Andrew Flintoff made 40s but were tied down before they too fell to Bichel, who finished with seven wickets. England was restricted to 204 runs in its 50 overs despite having two wickets in hand.

Despite a brief flurry of runs from Adam Gilchrist and Ricky Ponting, Australia fell to 4-48 as three indiscreet strokes and a successful lbw shout enabled Andy Caddick to make four breakthroughs. Left-handers Darren Lehmann and Bevan added 63 runs before Lehmann was caught behind off his brother-in-law Craig White, and then Ashley Giles dismissed Andrew Symonds and Brad Hogg cheaply to have Australia 7-114. When Brett Lee was run out, the Australians needed 70 runs from 74 balls as Bichel joined Bevan, with only Glenn McGrath yet to come.

Bevan reached a half-century from 101 balls, but there was much more work to do as 48 runs were needed from nine overs. The batting duo methodically reduced the requirement, before Bichel hit a six and a four from successive balls in the 49th over. Only two runs were needed from the final over, and a hot return catch was dropped from the second ball before a misfield from the third ball resulted in a single to level the score. Bevan dispatched a full-toss wide of mid-on for the winning boundary with two balls remaining.

Australia 8-208 (Michael Bevan 74 not out, Andy Bichel 34 not out; Andy Caddick 4-35) beat England 8-204 (Alec Stewart 46, Andrew Flintoff 45; Andy Bichel 7-20) by two wickets.

India's Ashish Nehra appeals for a wicket.

Sri Lanka v South Africa at Kingsmead Cricket Ground (Durban), 3 March

For the second successive World Cup, a tied result worked against South Africa. Had there not been a misunderstanding of the rules, the result could easily have been different and affected the make-up of the finals.

A fourth wicket partnership of 152 provided the backbone of Sri Lanka's 9-268. Sri Lankan opener Marvan Atapattu scored 124 off 129 balls while Aravinda de Silva made 73 off 78, before they departed in the space of three balls. Sri Lanka's lower order faltered as only 25 runs were added in the final five overs, before South African openers Graeme Smith and Herschelle Gibbs made a flying start. They put on 65 runs in 11 overs before Smith succumbed to de Silva's first delivery as the left-hander was caught in the deep off a half-tracker. When Gibbs and Boeta Dippenaar departed from successive balls, the Proteas were 5-149 in the 30th over. Boucher and Pollock added 63 before the latter was crucially run out as light rain arrived. Klusener was uncharacteristically tied down as the rain became heavier, and then the batters were informed that the target was 229 after 45 overs under the Duckworth-Lewis formula. Muttiah Muralidaran subsequently bowled the 45th over which began with the total reading 6-216. A single and two dot balls were virtually cancelled out as a wide went to the boundary, before Klusener managed a single. Boucher clubbed the fifth legitimate ball over the mid-wicket boundary to take the total to 229, and then pushed the following delivery to mid-wicket for no run as it appeared that no more runs were required. With no further play possible as the players were forced from the field, the cruel reality for South Africa was that 229 was only enough to tie the game rather than win it. As the Proteas needed a victory in order to progress to the Super Sixes, their World Cup tournament was suddenly over.

Sri Lanka 9-268 (Marvan Atapattu 124, Aravinda de Silva 73; Jacques Kallis 3-41) tied with South Africa 6-229 (Herschelle Gibbs 73, Mark Boucher 45 not out; Aravinda de Silva 2-36) under Duckworth-Lewis method.

SIX OF THE BEST: Individual performances

(excluding player of the tournament, and the finals)

Andrew Symonds 143 not out off 125 balls: Australia v Pakistan at Wanderers Stadium (Johannesburg), 11 February

The stars had to align for Andrew Symonds to be included in the Australian team for its first match. An injury to Bevan and a suspension for Lehmann provided opportunities for Symonds and his Queensland teammate Jimmy Maher, after Ponting had pushed hard for Symonds's inclusion in the touring squad.

Andy Bichel and Michael Bevan are buoyant after their unbroken partnership guided Australia to a two-wicket win against England.

Symonds strode to the wicket in the 16th over as Maher's dismissal left the Australians 4-86. Thirty-four overs later, Symonds virtually secured his place in the team for the foreseeable future. He received a first-up bouncer from Waqar Younis, before opening his account with a boundary from the seventh ball he faced. Two balls later, a great cover drive produced another four runs.

Symonds had 28 runs from 46 balls before lifting the tempo. His eighth four took him to 52 from 60 balls. Some slipshod fielding enabled Symonds to register four fours off a luckless Shahid Afridi in the 35th over, before Symonds crunched the same bowler through the off side in the 41st over to raise his maiden ODI ton from 92 balls. The very next delivery produced Symonds's 16th four.

Symonds hit Wasim Akram for two consecutive fours in the 48th over, before the following over proved eventful. Waqar bowled a beamer before Symonds smashed the next ball wide of long-on for six. Brett Lee was dismissed two balls later, and then Symonds evaded another beamer which resulted in a heated exchange before veteran umpire David Shepherd removed Waqar from the attack. Symonds struck Akram for six with the first ball of the final over, before a single from the final ball took Symonds to 143 not out. Symonds later held a great catch as Pakistan tumbled to 228 all out in response to Australia's 8-310.

Chaminda Vaas 9.1-2-25-6: Sri Lanka v Bangladesh at City Oval (Pietermaritzburg), 14 February

The opening over of the Sri Lanka versus Bangladesh contest was extraordinary, as wickets from the first three balls were followed by a boundary, an illegal delivery and another wicket.

Bangladesh's Hannan Sarkar was bowled as he drove at the first ball, before Mohammad Ashraful pushed an easy return catch. Sri Lanka's left-arm pace bowler Chaminda Vaas achieved his hat-trick as Ehsanul Haque edged a prod to second slip, before Sanuar Hossain drove the fourth ball of the match through the off side for four. A wide followed, and then Hossain was adjudged lbw before the final ball of the remarkable over was a dot ball.

Vaas had a five-wicket haul as Al Sahariar lofted the fourth ball of his third over to mid-off. Vaas's first spell produced figures of 6-1-14-5, before he returned for the 24th over. He claimed the final wicket from the first ball of the 32nd over as Mashrafe Mortaza presented an easy catch to point. Sri Lanka passed the target of 125 in 21.1 overs, without losing a wicket.

Brett Lee also took a hat-trick, as he captured the first three wickets in Australia's win against Kenya. Lee struck with the final three balls of the fourth over of the match as Kenya crashed to 3-3. A vicious rising delivery cannoned into Kennedy Otieno's elbow and dropped onto the stumps, and then Brijal Patel was caught in the slips before David Obuya was yorked.

John Davison 111 off 76 balls: Canada v West Indies at Centurion Park (Centurion), 23 February

At first glance, the West Indies versus Canada match appears to have been heavily one-sided while the victorious team from the Caribbean had four standout performers. Drakes claimed five wickets while Wavell Hinds chipped in with two, as Canada was dismissed for 202 in 42.5 overs. Hinds followed up with 64 off just 31 balls, and Lara made 73 off 40 before Sarwan made 42 not out off 32. The West Indians reached the target in a mere 20.3 overs, after losing their second wicket at 134 in just the 12th over.

Yet the player of the match was Canada's opening batter and part-time off-spinner John Davison, who set the game alight in the first 20 overs. He reached

50 in 30 balls, and required another 37 balls to reach triple figures. When he departed for 111, he had registered eight fours and six sixes.

Facing Pedro Collins, Davison hit his first four in the fourth over when an attacking shot flew behind point, before he backed away from the next ball and slammed it over cover for six. Davison struck three successive fours off Mervyn Dillon in the next over, before Dillon's next over featured a pull for four and a six over point. Davison went from 39 to 49 with successive deliveries in Drakes's first over, as an uncontrolled hook shot cleared the fine leg boundary, before a no-ball was dispatched through the slips. Davison took 16 runs off Drakes's second over, including 10 from the first two balls as a pull through square leg was followed by a pull which soared into the crowd.

The momentum slowed temporarily, before Davison hoicked Chris Gayle for six. Davison reached his ton when he skied Dillon wide of long-on for another six, before his final boundary took the total to 1-149 after 20 overs. Desmond Chumney departed with the total at 155, and then the match changed irrevocably as Davison was spectacularly caught one-handed by Drakes at deep mid-wicket from the first ball of the 23rd over. Davison later took 1-36 off five overs and accounted for Hinds, who was stumped from the off-spinner's third delivery after hitting the previous one to the boundary.

Eight days later, Davison earned another player of the match award in a losing cause. He blasted nine fours and four sixes in his 75 off 62 balls in a total of 196, before claiming 3-61 in 10 overs as the second opening bowler while New Zealand raced to a five-wicket win.

Glenn McGrath 7-4-15-7: Australia v Namibia at Senwes Park (Potchefstroom), 27 February

Glenn McGrath achieved the best bowling figures in World Cup history as Australia opposed Namibia. Facing a target of 302, Namibia tallied 45 in just 14 overs. Gilchrist, meanwhile, became the first wicketkeeper to complete six dismissals in a World Cup contest.

Bizarrely, Namibia was 1-12 after the first over, bowled by McGrath. Two dot balls were followed by a boundary to Jan-Berrie Burger, and then a wide. Burger then edged a catch to second slip, before a legside wide reached the boundary. A subsequent dot ball was followed by two runs off an inside edge.

Morne Karg was McGrath's second victim as he tried to evade an awkward short-pitched delivery and was caught behind. McGrath's next victim was lbw, before the following three were caught by Gilchrist. Danie Keulder was caught behind off an inside edge, and Louis Burger lobbed a pull shot behind the wicket, before an outside edge from Deon Kotzé was brilliantly caught one-handed in front of first slip. Björn Kotzé was McGrath's final victim when a fast and straight delivery crashed into the stumps.

Andy Bichel 10-0-20-7 and 34 not out off 36 balls: Australia v England at St George's Park Cricket Ground (Port Elizabeth), 2 March

Everything Andy Bichel did turned to gold on 2 March, remarkably, after he was a late inclusion for this contest due to an injury to Jason Gillespie.

England was ominously placed at 0-66 after nine overs when Bichel came on to bowl. With his fifth ball, he began a top-order collapse as the left-handed Nick Knight steered a catch to Damien Martyn in the gully. Michael Vaughan feathered a catch behind with the first delivery of Bichel's second over, before Nasser Hussain had his off-stump bent back from the final ball of the over. Paul Collingwood was Bichel's fourth victim as a slash outside off-stump produced another snick to the wicketkeeper, before Bichel was taken off after a spell of 6-0-12-4. England did not lose another wicket until Bichel returned for his second spell, which reaped figures of 4-0-8-3. Flintoff skied a slog and was caught by the wicketkeeper, before Stewart swung across the line and had his middle-stump knocked back. Giles was Bichel's final scalp when Bevan held a fine catch at mid-off.

Bichel's day was far from over, as Australia was on the verge of defeat at 8-135 and needing a further 70 runs when Bichel joined Bevan in the 38th over. Bichel worked his way to 12 and then had a swing-and-a-miss, before driving the next ball to the long-off boundary. Australia required 13 runs from 11 balls before Bichel thumped James Anderson for a huge six, and then drove the next ball for four. Two singles to Bichel brought the score level with three balls left,

Namibia's Jan-Berrie Burger raises his bat after scoring 85 against England.

before Bevan hit the winning runs. Remarkably, Bichel gave a hard caught-and-bowled chance to Flintoff when Australia was still two runs shy of victory, before the tail-ender levelled the score from the next delivery as the ball was crucially misfielded.

Feiko Kloppenburg 121 off 142 balls and 10-0-42-4: Netherlands v Namibia at Goodyear Park (Bloemfontein), 3 March

Who was the first player to score a century and take four wickets in a World Cup match?

The answer is the Netherlands all-rounder Feiko Kloppenburg, who achieved the feat against Namibia in 2003.

Kloppenburg opened the batting and scored 121 in a total of 4-314. He registered six fours and four sixes, and shared a second-wicket stand of 228 with Klaas-Jan van Noortwijk who finished unbeaten on 134 from 129 balls. Kloppenburg had only 11 runs from 34 balls, before reaching his 50 in 83 balls. He hit three sixes and one four while progressing from 50 to 100, as his century took him 126 balls. He nearly missed out on triple figures, as a throw at the stumps went astray when he took the single to move on from 99.

As second change bowler, Kloppenburg took 4-42 from 10 overs of medium-pace while Adeel Raja had the same figures from 8.5 overs as third change bowler. Kloppenburg took the first, third, fifth and sixth wickets, before Raja captured the final four as Namibia was dismissed for 250. Kloppenburg's fourth delivery produced the first breakthrough in the 14th over, as sub fielder Ruud Nijman held a catch in the deep. Kloppenburg claimed his second wicket when he bowled Keulder in the 35th over, before he was on a hat-trick in his final over; the 41st of the innings. Louis Burger was bowled, before Gerrie Snyman was caught by Tim de Leede.

HEADLINE MOMENT

Leggie bags five as Kenya upsets Sri Lanka

While not as stunning as Kenya's win over West Indies in 1996, Kenya's victory against Sri Lanka in 2003 was a huge boilover nonetheless.

Kenya was a wicket down after just two balls before the middle order batters made starts without passing 26. Kennedy Otieno struck eight fours and two sixes in his 60 at the top of the order, before his dismissal left Kenya 4-112 in the 28th over. The African nation was 8-173 after 45.1 overs when Muralidaran nabbed his fourth wicket. Peter Ongondo made a valuable 20 at number 10 as Kenya's tail boosted the total beyond 200, but it still appeared very attainable for Sri Lanka.

Atapattu struck the second and fourth balls of the run chase to the boundary, before Sanath Jayasuriya exited in the fifth over. Atapattu's dismissal left Sri Lanka 2-39, before de Silva and Hashan Tillakaratne added 32 runs. The match changed complexion as leg-spinner Collins Obuya snared five wickets to leave Sri Lanka 7-119 with 18 overs remaining. The tail-enders resisted briefly, but two wickets to Steve Tikolo and one to Maurice Odumbe – the hero of the 1996 triumph against West Indies – sealed Kenya's 53-run triumph with five overs remaining.

Kenya 9-210 (Kennedy Otieno 60; Muttiah Muralidaran 4-28, Chaminda Vaas 3-41) beat Sri Lanka 157 (Aravinda de Silva 41; Collins Obuya 5-24, Steve Tikolo 2-13) by 53 runs.

Sachin Tendulkar (India)

Matches	Innings	Not outs	Runs	Highest score	Average	50s	100s	Catches
11	11	-	673	152	61.18	6	1	4

Overs	Maidens	Runs	Wickets	Average	Best figures
18	-	77	2	38.50	2-28

ICC Cricket World Cup
SOUTH AFRICA 2003
NAMIBIA

Who was the first player to score a century and take four wickets in a World Cup match? The answer is the Netherlands all-rounder Feiko Kloppenburg.

PLAYER OF THE TOURNAMENT

The choice of Sachin Tendulkar as player of the tournament was far from difficult. His run tally was more than 200 runs higher than the second placegetter, his Indian captain Sourav Ganguly. Although Tendulkar scored only one century, he was only one shot away from reaching triple figures on two other occasions. Ironically, he entered the World Cup while recovering from a finger injury, an ankle ailment and a hamstring strain.

In India's opening match, Tendulkar made 52 and achieved economical bowling figures of 4-0-9-0 as India won by 68 runs after tallying a modest 204 against the Netherlands. Tendulkar continued his regular habit of top-scoring for India in its next fixture despite making a modest 36, and India was never in the game as Australia raced to a nine-wicket victory after routing the Indians for 125. In India's subsequent two contests, Tendulkar earned player of the match honours. His 81 helped set up a total of 7-255 in an 83-run win over Zimbabwe, before his 152 off 151 balls helped India to 2-311 against Namibia. Tendulkar shared a second-wicket stand of 244 with Ganguly, who scored an undefeated 112 in his team's 181-run win.

Against England, Tendulkar must have rued not converting a start into a big score as he made 50 off 52 balls before departing in the 16th over. India nonetheless went on to win by 82 runs. Against Pakistan, Tendulkar was in outstanding form as he registered 12 fours and a six in his 98 off 75 balls and earned another player of the match award. India won the battle of the sub-continent by six wickets with 26 balls to spare after Pakistan set a target of 274. Tendulkar drove the third ball of the opening over to the boundary before hitting Shoaib Akhtar for a six and two fours from the final three balls of the second over. Akhtar ultimately dismissed Tendulkar with a brutal short ball when a century beckoned.

India subsequently beat Kenya, Sri Lanka and New Zealand comprehensively in the lead-up to the semi-finals. Two rare failures from Tendulkar were spliced by a fine 97 against Sri Lanka, despite the 'Little Master' battling stomach cramps. With another ton within reach, Tendulkar departed when a paddle sweep resulted in a top-edge to the wicketkeeper.

In the second semi-final, Tendulkar made 83 and then returned 6-0-28-2 as India trounced Kenya. The final, however, was not Tendulkar's day. Indian supporters were no doubt counting on him to produce another special innings as the team faced a target of 360. After opening his account with a pull for four from the fourth ball of the run chase, a similar stroke from the next ball resulted in a top-edged catch. Although a title remained elusive to Tendulkar in his fourth World Cup campaign, his time would eventually come.

FIRST SEMI-FINAL

Australia v Sri Lanka at St George's Park Cricket Ground (Port Elizabeth), 18 March

Rain ended the match with 71 balls remaining, although the result was clear-cut under the Duckworth-Lewis (DL) formula.

Australia was 0-34 after five overs before de Silva struck with his second delivery, as Gilchrist sportingly walked when an appeal for caught behind was turned down. Two wickets to Vaas reduced Australia to 3-51, before Symonds and a subdued Lehmann added 93 runs. Sri Lanka regained control as Jayasuriya accounted for Lehmann, and then dismissed Bevan first ball. Australia stumbled to 7-175 before Symonds and Bichel added 37 runs from as many balls. Symonds's undefeated 91 came from 118 balls and included seven fours and a six.

The 213-run target was hardly daunting, but Sri Lanka plunged from 0-21 in the fourth over to 7-76 in the 25th over amid some faulty batting and good bowling. Left-handers Kumar Sangakkara and Vaas added 47 runs, before wet weather forced the match to be cut short as the batting team was 90 runs shy of the target. With the Sri Lankans having three wickets in hand, the DL formula revealed that they required 172 runs after 38.1 overs for victory.

Australia 7-212 (Andrew Symonds 91 not out, Darren Lehmann 36; Chaminda Vaas 3-34, Aravinda de Silva 2-36) beat Sri Lanka 7-123 (Kumar Sangakkara 39 not out; Brett Lee 3-35, Brad Hogg 2-30) by 48 runs.

SECOND SEMI-FINAL

India v Kenya at Kingsmead Cricket Ground (Durban), 20 March

Kenya's dream of a World Cup final berth was quashed as India was always destined to win the semi-final. After winning the toss, Ganguly produced his third century of the tournament.

The Kenyans kept the Indians in check for the first 25 overs, as India had 99 runs on the board for the loss of Virender Sehwag. Ganguly changed the complexion as he cleared the fence in the 26th over and smashed two massive sixes in the 29th over. The second-wicket partnership produced 103 runs before Tendulkar fell for 83, and then Ganguly did most of the damage for the rest of the innings. Ganguly struck 12 runs from the first three balls of the 46th over, before he and Yuvraj Singh combined to take 18 runs off the 49th over. Ganguly's unbeaten 111 came from 114 balls and featured five fours and five sixes.

Facing a target of 271, the Kenyans fell to 7-104 when David Obuya was run out from the first ball of the 34th over. Tikolo registered a half-century which included five fours and two sixes, while the next top-scorer was sundries as there were 16 byes, 15 wides and eight leg byes. An eighth wicket stand of 57 added a sliver of respectability to Kenya's total, before the final two wickets fell at 179.

India 4-270 (Sourav Ganguly 111 not out, Sachin Tendulkar 83) beat Kenya 179 (Steve Tikolo 56; Zaheer Khan 3-14, Ashish Nehra 2-11) by 91 runs.

FINAL

Australia v India at Wanderers Stadium (Johannesburg), 23 March

Following rain in the lead-up, it was somewhat understandable that Ganguly chose to field first. Ponting meanwhile said he would have batted first if he won the toss. It was easy to say in hindsight that Ganguly's decision backfired badly. Meanwhile, Australia's decision to recall Martyn in place of Ian Harvey was a spectacular success, after Martyn missed the semi-final with a finger injury.

The first over yielded 15 runs as Zaheer Khan sent down no-balls and wides, and also conceded a boundary. The eighth over cost 16 runs, before Harbhajan Singh's off-spin was introduced with the score 0-74 after nine overs. Gilchrist raced to 57 before falling to Harbhajan, to end a 105-run opening stand with the last ball of the 14th over. Harbhajan also accounted for Matthew Hayden, to leave Australia 2-125 in the 20th over.

No more wickets fell in Australia's innings as Ponting and Martyn produced a wonderful batting exhibition. The 200 was raised in the 33rd over which cost 13 runs, before Ponting hammered successive sixes off Harbhajan in the 39th over. Martyn and Ponting were both on 64 as the total was 2-250 after 40 overs, before 109 runs were added in the final 10 overs. Ponting had most of the strike as he scored 76 runs to Martyn's 24 in this period, to bring their unbroken partnership to 234 from 30.1 overs. Ponting's undefeated 140 off 121 balls featured eight sixes and only four fours, while Martyn's unconquered 88 came off 84 balls and included seven fours and one six. India's bowlers also conceded 23 runs in illegitimate deliveries.

Tendulkar opened India's account with a boundary from the fourth ball of the run chase, but India's hopes were crushed from the next ball as he perished to a miscued pull. Ganguly and Sehwag combined to take 19 runs off the fifth over, before the departures of Ganguly and Mohammad Kaif in quick succession left India reeling at 3-59. Sehwag slammed a series of boundaries off Australia's left-arm spinners Lehmann and Hogg, before rain halted play with the score at 3-103 after 17 overs. No overs were lost, and Sehwag quickly moved to 82 before being run out by Lehmann while chancing a single in the 24th over with the total at 147. The next partnership produced 40 runs, and then the remaining wickets fell regularly. Having hit the winning runs in the 1999 final, Lehmann held the catch to bring about the final wicket in the 2003 decider as Australia completed another landslide victory. Lehmann was one of five Australians to play in both the 1999 and 2003 World Cup deciders.

Australia		R	B
Adam Gilchrist (+)	c Sehwag b Harbhajan Singh	57	48
Matthew Hayden	c Dravid b Harbhajan Singh	37	54
Ricky Ponting (c)	not out	140	121
Damien Martyn	not out	88	84
Sundries	(b 2, lb 12, nb 7, w 16)	37	
TOTAL	**(50 overs) 2-359**		

DID NOT BAT: Darren Lehmann, Michael Bevan, Andrew Symonds, Brad Hogg, Andy Bichel, Brett Lee, Glenn McGrath

FALL: 105, 125

Khan 7-0-67-0,
Srinath 10-0-87-0,
Nehra 10-0-57-0,
Harbhajan Singh 8-0-49-2,
Sehwag 3-0-14-0,
Tendulkar 3-0-20-0,
Mongia 7-0-39-0,
Yuvraj Singh 2-0-12-0

India		R	B
Sachin Tendulkar	c & b McGrath	4	5
Virender Sehwag	run out (Lehmann)	82	81
Sourav Ganguly (c)	c Lehmann b Lee	24	25
Mohammad Kaif	c Gilchrist b McGrath	0	3
Rahul Dravid (+)	b Bichel	47	57
Yuvraj Singh	c Lee b Hogg	24	34
Dinesh Mongia	c Martyn b Symonds	12	11
Harbhajan Singh	c McGrath b Symonds	7	8
Zaheer Khan	c Lehmann b McGrath	4	8
Javagal Srinath	b Lee	1	4
Ashish Nehra	not out	8	4
Sundries	(b 4, lb 4, nb 4, w 9)	21	
TOTAL	**(39.2 overs) 234**		

FALL: 4, 58, 59, 147, 187, 208, 209, 223, 226, 234

McGrath 8.2-0-52-3,
Lee 7-1-31-2,
Hogg 10-0-61-1,
Lehmann 2-0-18-0,
Bichel 10-0-57-1,
Symonds 2-0-7-2

UMPIRES: Steve Bucknor, David Shepherd (TV: Rudi Koertzen)

TOSS: India

PLAYER OF THE MATCH: Ricky Ponting

AUSTRALIA WON BY 125 RUNS

2007

Another undefeated tournament as Aussies achieve three-peat

- Brian Lara farewells international cricket as West Indies record a one-wicket loss to England
- Ireland and Zimbabwe play out a thrilling tie
- South Africa's Herschelle Gibbs blasts six sixes in an over: the first player to do so in international cricket
- Sri Lanka's Lasith Malinga captures four wickets in four balls as he comes achingly close to stealing an extraordinary victory against South Africa
- Australia's third successive World Cup triumph and second successive unbeaten World Cup campaign ends on a crazy note in dark conditions in the final

The World Cup continued to expand as the 2007 tournament featured 16 teams, with Namibia excluded while Bermuda, Ireland and Scotland were included. It was a first for Bermuda and Ireland while Scotland returned after being omitted in 2003. Another first was the tournament hosts, as hosting rights were awarded to West Indies for the first time according to the International Cricket Council's (ICC) rotational policy. Unfortunately for West Indian fans, the days of a world champion ODI team from the Caribbean were long gone.

With the teams divided into groups of four, most of the group matches were won and lost decisively although two of Ireland's matches were an exception. One team from each group was left without a victory – Scotland, Bermuda, Canada and Zimbabwe – while there were some surprise results as the bottom two teams in each group were eliminated. Bangladesh placed second while India was third in Group B, and Ireland placed second in Group D while Pakistan was third. With the next phase of the tournament changing from Super Sixes to Super Eights, there were many solid beatings in this phase while there were also a few cliff-hangers.

In any case, it was again a matter of seeing which team would challenge Australia. The reigning titleholders enjoyed a second successive unbeaten tournament as they comprehensively won all of their matches, including the decider. While Sri Lanka earned runner-up status, realistically it was Australia first and daylight second.

A HAT-TRICK OF CLASSICS: Three great contests

Ireland v Zimbabwe at Sabina Park (Kingston), 15 March

The Zimbabweans rued their tied result with Ireland after squandering a certain victory, although the Irish also missed a golden chance to steal a miraculous triumph. Dropped catches and sloppy fielding proved costly for both teams, before Zimbabwe choked badly in the final six overs of the run chase.

The first over of the game was a wicket maiden, and then Ireland struggled to 5-89 before partnerships of 56 and 37 unfolded. After the seventh and eighth wickets fell at the same score, 39 vital runs were added for the ninth wicket. Ireland's situation would have been catastrophic without opener Jeremy Bray, who registered 10 fours and two sixes in his undefeated 115 from 137 deliveries.

Needing 222, Zimbabwe was well placed at 1-92 before stumbling to 5-133. Sean Williams batted recklessly for his 14, and opener Vusi Sibanda's 67 ended when he stepped onto his stumps. Ireland, however, bungled a vital chance to run out Stuart Matsikenyeri when the score was 3-107, just two balls after Williams

Zimbabwe's Sean Williams launches into a sweep shot while West Indies wicketkeeper Denesh Ramdin looks on.

exited. Matsikenyeri later reached 50 with a boundary from a dropped catch, during a seemingly match-winning partnership which ended when Brendan Taylor was unluckily run out at the non-striker's end. Nonetheless, two fours to Matsikenyeri in the same over meant only 15 runs were needed from six overs. Amazingly, the next four overs produced only six runs and a wicket, before the 49th over was a double-wicket maiden. Zimbabwean captain Prosper Utseya was caught off a full-toss from the first ball before the final ball of the over produced a run-out, and suddenly Zimbabwe was on the verge of defeat as nine runs were needed from the final over with one wicket remaining. Matsikenyeri struck Andrew White for two twos and a single before a single to Ed Rainsford was followed by another two to Matsikenyeri to level the scores. However, Matsikenyeri failed to make contact from the final ball, and a run-out at the bowler's end sealed the third tie in World Cup cricket history.

Ireland 9-221 (Jeremy Bray 115 not out; Elton Chigumbura 2-21) tied with Zimbabwe 221 (Stuart Matsikenyeri 73 not out, Vusi Sibanda 67; Kyle McCallan 2-56).

Sri Lanka v England at Sir Vivian Richards Stadium (North Sound), 4 April

This thrilling match went down to the very last ball, following many pendulum swings. Batting first, Sri Lanka was 2-160 with Upul Tharanga and captain Mahela Jayawardene in form, when Tharanga succumbed to a miscued pull shot in the 35th over. Jayawardene departed in the 39th over after hitting the previous ball to the boundary, and none of Sri Lanka's remaining batters could make a strong impact. The total was 5-209 after 45 overs, before the final five overs yielded five wickets for only 26 runs. The last over featured nine runs and three wickets, including a run-out from the final ball.

England was 2-11 before Ian Bell and Kevin Pietersen took the total past 100. Their partnership ended streakily as a straight drive from Pietersen was deflected by the bowler into the stumps at the non-striker's end to run out Bell. Another turning point came as a doosra from Muttiah Muralidaran found the leading edge of Pietersen's bat for a caught-and-bowled. Two wickets in three balls to Dilhara Fernando left England 6-133 in the 34th over, before Ravi Bopara and Paul Nixon halted the collapse. They struggled to score against some disciplined bowling, and 66 runs were needed from the last seven overs before Bopara finally found the boundary. Twenty-nine runs were needed from 15 balls before Nixon reverse-swept a six and a four in the space of three balls. Nixon was caught from the fifth ball of the 49th over before a subsequent boundary to Bopara meant 12 runs were needed from the final six balls. Bopara paddled the second ball of the final over for four, before a two was followed by successive singles, meaning Bopara needed three runs from the last delivery to snatch victory. Fernando failed to release the ball at first, before his second attempt was slightly short of a length, and crashed into the off-stump as Bopara gave himself room and tried to whack the ball through the off side.

Sri Lanka 235 (Upul Tharanga 62, Mahela Jayawardene 56; Sajid Mahmood 4-50, Andrew Flintoff 3-35) beat England 8-233 (Kevin Pietersen 58, Ravi Bopara 52; Dilhara Fernando 3-41) by two runs.

West Indies v England at Kensington Oval (Bridgetown), 21 April

With 601 runs scored and 19 wickets falling, the West Indies versus England match was a beauty. It was also Brian Lara's farewell to international cricket.

Lara was treated to a guard of honour from the England players when he arrived at the crease in the 24th over, with the score 1-131 after Chris Gayle had slammed 79 from 58 balls. In the eighth over, Gayle went from 25 to 45 in four balls as consecutive fours were followed by consecutive sixes. Lara scored a quickfire 18 before being run out, as Marlon Samuels called for a single and then changed his mind. Samuels compensated as he hit 19 runs in the 36th over, which cost 24 runs. The West Indians were 4-250 with 10 overs remaining, but added just 50 more runs before being all out with one ball to spare. Having won the toss, England's captain Michael Vaughan was the pick of the bowlers with 3-39 from 10 overs as fifth change bowler.

Vaughan subsequently scored 79 off 68 balls, before becoming the second of three run-out victims in the run chase after there had also been three run-outs in the West Indian innings. The last of the run-outs left England in trouble at 6-189 in the 36th over. England needed 88 runs from the final 10 overs, and then a series of fours to Pietersen reduced the requirement to 38 from four overs. A run-out chance was butchered before a six took Pietersen to a century, but he was bowled next ball. When Liam Plunkett departed three balls later, England needed 30 from 19 deliveries with only two wickets left. Nixon struck three fours in four balls in the 48th over, before four byes meant 13 runs were needed from 13 balls. The equation was just three runs from five balls, before a slower ball from Dwayne Bravo dismissed Nixon. Amid great tension, a leg bye was followed by a dot ball before Stuart Broad struck the penultimate delivery over cover for the winning runs. It wasn't the farewell Lara wanted, but he still walked a lap of honour.

England 9-301 (Kevin Pietersen 100, Michael Vaughan 79; Dwayne Bravo 2-47) beat West Indies 300 (Chris Gayle 79, Devon Smith 61; Michael Vaughan 3-39) by one wicket.

Scotland's Dougie Brown hits out.

SIX OF THE BEST: Individual performances

(excluding player of the tournament, and the finals)

Herschelle Gibbs six sixes in an over: South Africa v Netherlands at Warner Park Stadium (Basseterre), 16 March

Herschelle Gibbs became the first player to hit six sixes in an over in an international cricket match; incidentally in the 2007 World Cup.

Gibbs achieved the feat in the 30th over of South Africa's clash with the Netherlands, as Daan van Bunge was the bowler. Gibbs charged the first ball of the over and sent it over the long-on boundary, before he lofted the next two balls over long-off. The fourth ball was a low full-toss which Gibbs dispatched over mid-wicket, before he swatted the fifth ball over long-off as this delivery was short of a length and around off-stump. The final ball of the over was pitched up and outside off-stump, with Gibbs crunching it over mid-wicket for another maximum.

After hitting a four in the following over, Gibbs was caught at long-on from the next ball as he sought another boundary. He finished with 72 off 40 balls before Mark Boucher smashed 75 not out from 31 balls as the Proteas amassed 3-353 in 40 overs, and then restricted the Netherlands to 9-132.

Herschelle Gibbs became the first player to hit six sixes in an over in an international cricket match; incidentally in the 2007 World Cup.

Matthew Hayden 158 off 143 balls: Australia v West Indies at Sir Vivian Richards Stadium (North Sound), 27–28 March

Anand Vasu succinctly described Matthew Hayden's century in Australia's win against West Indies as 'an innings of tremendous control and power'.

After scoring a splendid 101 off 68 balls against South Africa only three days earlier, Hayden began slowly against West Indies as he opened his account with a single from the 18th ball he faced. Following another two dot balls, Hayden crunched two successive deliveries wide of mid-off for four. From the final ball of the subsequent over, Hayden charged Daren Powell and brazenly belted the ball over the bowler's head for another four. When Hayden twice advanced him in the 21st over, Powell dropped short but was dispatched for four both times.

Hayden's sixth four took him to 51 from 72 balls, before he reached his ton from 110 balls despite only two fours and a six as he moved from 51 to 100. With the six, Hayden was deceived in flight by Marlon Samuels's off-spin but still cleared the boundary despite one hand coming off the bat. After reaching 120, Hayden clubbed Jerome Taylor for six, four and six from successive balls before hitting Samuels for two fours and a six in the space of four balls. When he holed out to long-off, Hayden had registered 14 fours and four sixes in his 158. With the rain-affected match played over two days, Australia won by 103 runs after compiling 6-322.

Lasith Malinga four wickets in four balls: Sri Lanka v South Africa at Providence Stadium (Guyana), 28 March

Chasing a target of 210, South Africa was cruising towards victory against Sri Lanka before incredibly crashing from 5-206 to 9-207. Lasith Malinga captured wickets from the final two balls of one over before striking with the first two balls of his next over, making him the first bowler to capture four wickets in as many balls in a World Cup cricket match.

Shaun Pollock was Malinga's first victim as a slower ball hit the leg-stump. The next ball was nearly a yorker, with Andrew Hall lobbing an easy catch to cover. Jacques Kallis edged an attempted drive to the wicketkeeper, before a yorker crashed into Makhaya Ntini's middle-stump. Malinga nearly had five in five balls which would have won the game for Sri Lanka, but the third ball of his ninth over just missed Charl Langeveldt's off-stump. With the second ball of his next over, Malinga found the outside edge of Robin Peterson's bat but the ball flew to the third man boundary to seal a thrilling one-wicket win for the Proteas. Malinga's record-breaking feat couldn't be ignored, even if it wasn't rewarded with a Sri Lankan victory.

Sanath Jayasuriya 115 off 101 balls and 8.3-0-38-3: Sri Lanka v West Indies at Providence Stadium (Guyana), 1 April

In Sri Lanka's 113-run thrashing of West Indies, the 37-year-old Sanath Jayasuriya was every bit as destructive as he had been in his prime some 11 years earlier.

After striking his first boundary from the 16th ball he faced, Jayasuriya moved unconvincingly to 14 off 33 balls before hitting his straps with two successive fours – a hook to the fine leg boundary followed by a sliced shot over mid-off. Jayasuriya slammed three fours and a straight six in the ensuing over, before his next boundary took him to 45 in the 20th over. Soon he reached his 50 off 47 balls, and it took him only 39 more deliveries to reach triple figures. In the 31st over, Jayasuriya played a remarkable shot as he flicked a six wide of mid-wicket with a minimum of effort. He soon belted another six to reach 94, as Shivnarine Chanderpaul nearly pulled off a spectacular one-handed catch.

After reaching 115 which included 10 fours and four sixes, Jayasuriya was bowled off an inside edge as he attempted another forceful shot. His day was far from over, however, as he was Sri Lanka's seventh bowler while the team defended a total of 303. West Indies progressed from 3-42 to 3-134, until Ramnaresh Sarwan heaved at a Jayasuriya delivery and was stumped. The score slid to 7-158 as Denesh Ramdin slogged a catch to deep mid-wicket off Jayasuriya, who finished the match as he bowled Powell who had earlier dismissed the century-maker. Jayasuriya finished as the pick of Sri Lanka's bowlers with his left-arm spinners.

AB de Villiers 146 off 130 balls: South Africa v West Indies at Queen's Park (Grenada), 10 April

AB de Villiers registered his maiden ODI ton when the Proteas contested West Indies in the 2007 World Cup. It was a memorable knock, as he battled cramps and hamstring troubles during the latter half of his innings.

De Villiers struck only one boundary in the first nine overs as South Africa ambled to 1-27, before he found the boundary twice in the 10th over. On 34, de Villiers was somewhat lucky not to be bowled as an Ian Bradshaw delivery narrowly missed the off-stump. De Villiers nearly ran himself out in Bradshaw's next over, before reaching 40 as he belted a four over the bowler's head. With Dwayne Bravo bowling the following over, de Villiers went from 40 to 50 in consecutive deliveries as he cut a four and drove a slower ball over mid-on for six.

The boundaries dried up for a little while, before three fours helped de Villiers progress from 74 to 90. A single brought up his hundred and took the total to 2-199 in the 38th over, before he struck sixes off Chris Gayle from the first and last balls of the 40th over. De Villiers clutched his hamstring after the latter six, and then in the next over he savaged Sarwan. Two successive slog-sweeps for six were followed by a single, and then he squirted a four behind point and limped away as cramping took a toll. With Bravo back on for the next over, de Villiers crunched two boundaries to the deep cover region despite his hamstring appearing to shut down completely.

De Villiers's sensational innings brought 12 fours and five sixes before he flicked an easy catch to backward square leg to leave the Proteas 3-261. A further 95 runs were added in less than seven overs, before South Africa restricted West Indies to 9-289.

West Indies captain Brian Lara is given a round of applause by the England team as he prepares for his final innings in international cricket.

Andrew Hall 10-2-18-5: South Africa v England at Kensington Oval (Bridgetown), 17 April

Andrew Hall's fast-medium bowling was outstanding as South Africa routed England for 154 on the way to a nine-wicket drubbing. Hall bowled three spells, with 0-10 from five overs followed by 4-6 from three and 1-2 from two. He swung and cut the ball, while his victims were stuck on the crease.

Hall's first victim was Paul Collingwood, who was lbw from a ball which swung in. Hall struck twice in his next over, with a great off-cutter bowling Andrew Flintoff through the gate before the left-handed Paul Nixon fished outside off-stump and snicked a catch behind. Hall's fourth victim was Sajid Mahmood, who prodded at an inswinger and played it onto the stumps. The final ball of Hall's 10-over allotment

Glenn McGrath (Australia)

Matches	Innings	Not outs	Runs	Highest score	Average	50s	100s	Catches
11	-	-	-	-	-	-	-	1
Overs	**Maidens**	**Runs**	**Wickets**	**Average**	**Best figures**			
80.5	5	357	26	13.73	3-14			

brought about his fifth wicket, as a full-pitched delivery rapped left-hander James Anderson on the pad to produce another lbw.

HEADLINE MOMENT

Irish boilover sinks Pakistan

Two days after their tied result against Zimbabwe, the Irish caused a huge boilover as they ended Pakistan's semi-final chances.

Sent in, Pakistan sank to 2-15 and then recovered temporarily as a 41-run partnership unfolded, but then wickets tumbled regularly. A 25-run ninth-wicket stand occupied more than 12 overs, before Pakistan was all out for a miserable 132 in the 46th over. Only two batters passed 15 while none reached 30, and sundries top-scored as the 29 extras included 23 runs from wides and three from no-balls. All six of Ireland's bowlers snared at least one wicket each, with Andre Botha having sensational figures of 8-4-5-2.

Ireland also lost its first two wickets at seven and 15, before recovering. Ireland reached 2-62 before falling to 4-70, with Botha wrongly given out caught at short leg. Ireland was 4-81 after 27.3 overs when a rain break reduced the target to 128 off 47 overs. The standout batter in the game, Niall O'Brien, reached 72 with a six before he was stumped next ball, leaving Ireland 5-108. Wickets with successive balls in the next over left Ireland shakily placed at 7-113, before O'Brien's brother Kevin provided solidity. With one run needed for an Irish victory, captain Trent Johnston clubbed a giant six over long-on to ensure Ireland finished ahead of Pakistan's total.

Ireland 7-133 (Niall O'Brien 72; Mohammad Sami 3-29, Iftikhar Anjum 2-29) beat Pakistan 132 (Sundries 29, Kamran Akmal 27; Boyd Rankin 3-32, Andre Botha 2-5, Kyle McCallan 2-12) by three wickets.

PLAYER OF THE TOURNAMENT

For the first time, the award went to a specialist bowler. Such was Australia's dominance with the bat, none of Australia's frontline bowlers – Glenn McGrath, Nathan Bracken and Shaun Tait – were even required to use the willow at all.

Having opened the bowling in Tests and ODIs for many years, McGrath was often used as the first change bowler in the 2007 World Cup. In the Group A matches, his figures were 6-1-14-3, 8-0-33-2 and 9-0-62-1 respectively, as Australia topped 300 each time before winning by big margins against Scotland, the Netherlands and South Africa. In the Super Eights matches, McGrath captured three wickets in four successive matches. Against West Indies, Australia again passed 300 and won comprehensively. Australia's clash with Bangladesh was reduced to 22 overs per team, with McGrath claiming player of the match honours after being the second opening bowler. He took 3-16 in his five overs as Bangladesh made 6-104, before Australia won by 10 wickets. Back to being first change bowler in the clash with England, McGrath was expensive as his 9.5 overs cost 62 runs, but England's total of 247 looked small as Australia passed it with 16 balls to spare for the loss of just three wickets.

Opening the bowling against Ireland, McGrath bowled Jeremy Bray with the sixth ball of the match and went on to return figures of 7-1-17-3 to earn another player of the match award. Ireland was all out for 91, before Australia won by nine wickets. After reverting to first change bowler, McGrath was a little wayward against Sri Lanka and New Zealand as his figures were 9-1-48-2 and 4-0-25-2. In both cases, nonetheless, the Australians recorded crushing victories.

In a semi-final, McGrath bowled the second over and finished with player of the match figures of 8-1-18-3 as South Africa was all out for 149. After bowling Kallis in the sixth over, McGrath had Ashwell Prince caught behind and Boucher caught at first slip from consecutive balls in the 10th over to render the Proteas 5-27. After winning this match by seven wickets, Australia went on to win the final by 53 runs against Sri Lanka as McGrath bade farewell to international cricket. Having reverted to first change, he took 1-31 from seven overs and claimed a wicket from his second-last delivery as Russel Arnold was caught by the wicketkeeper from a full-toss.

FIRST SEMI-FINAL

Sri Lanka v New Zealand at Sabina Park (Kingston), 24 April

A superbly paced century from Jayawardene was the highlight as his team cruised to a big win over New Zealand. There was some controversy as two Sri Lankans and one Kiwi were unfortunate to be ruled lbw, but there was little doubt that Sri Lanka was much too good overall.

Tharanga starred in the first half of Sri Lanka's innings, whereas opening partner Jayasuriya fell cheaply before Kumar Sangakkara scored a sluggish 18. When Tharanga fell from the first ball of the 26th over, Sri Lanka was 3-111 while Jayawardene had just nine runs from 33 balls. After 37 overs, Jayawardene had 31 runs from 64 balls while the score was 4-164. In the final 13 overs, Sri Lanka's skipper scored 84 runs from 45 balls while his team amassed 125 runs, with Tillakaratne Dilshan and Russel Arnold making useful contributions. Jayawardene went from 70 to 76 as a crucial catch was fumbled over the boundary, before Dilshan was controversially given out in the following over.

New Zealand was 2-32 after two lbw appeals were upheld, with Ross Taylor unluckily sent packing in the 11th over. Peter Fulton and Scott Styris took the total to 105, but then an astonishing collapse of 5-11 virtually ensured a Sri Lankan victory. James Franklin and Jeetan Patel put on a final wicket partnership of 59 to lift the total to 208, before Patel departed in the 42nd over.

Sri Lanka 5-289 (Mahela Jayawardene 115 not out, Upul Tharanga 73) beat New Zealand 208 (Peter Fulton 46; Muttiah Muralidaran 4-31) by 81 runs.

SECOND SEMI-FINAL

Australia v South Africa at Beausejour Stadium (Gros Islet), 25 April

The second semi-final was anti-climactic and heavily one-sided, with the Proteas scraping together only 149 runs in 43.5 overs before the Australians passed the target in the 32nd over. After electing to bat, the Proteas crashed to 5-27 when Boucher was out for a golden duck in the 10th over. They should have been 6-27 just moments later, but umpire Steve Bucknor failed to detect an inside edge to the wicketkeeper from Gibbs's bat. It appeared that this could turn the game, as Gibbs hit the next two balls for four. Sixty runs were added for the sixth wicket before Gibbs was belatedly out caught behind, oddly, off a thinner edge than the one that was earlier given not out. The eighth wicket fell at 103 before partnerships of 27 and 19 meant Australia's target was a little higher than it might otherwise have been. All five Australian bowlers shared the wickets, with Shane Watson the only disappointment as he had 1-49 in 8.5 overs after capturing the final wicket.

South Africa had a brief hope of causing a miracle as Adam Gilchrist was bowled with just one run on the board. Australian skipper Ricky Ponting found the boundary five times before falling for 22, and then Matthew Hayden and Michael Clarke took the total to 110 before Hayden exited in the 25th over. There were no more wickets as Clarke advanced to 60 not out, before Andrew Symonds swished the winning boundary off a legside full-toss.

Australia 3-153 (Michael Clarke 60 not out, Matthew Hayden 41) beat South Africa 149 (Justin Kemp 49 not out; Shaun Tait 4-39, Glenn McGrath 3-18) by seven wickets.

FINAL

Australia v Sri Lanka at Kensington Oval (Bridgetown), 28 April

The result was as clear-cut as the previous two World Cup deciders, but unfortunately the conclusion was beyond farcical after unsatisfactory weather intervened.

For the first time, a World Cup cricket decider involved two countries which had previously faced off in a World Cup final. Sri Lankan trio Jayasuriya, Vaas and Muralidaran backed up from the 1996 decider, as did Australian duo Ponting and McGrath. Australia's 2007 World Cup final team also had three survivors from the 1999 winning team (Ponting, McGrath and Gilchrist) and six from the 2003 winning team (Ponting, McGrath, Gilchrist, Hayden, Symonds and Brad Hogg).

The 2007 decider was reduced to 38 overs per side, after the start was delayed because of rain. With Australia batting first after Ponting won the toss, it was one of those occasions when Gilchrist was simply unstoppable. Hayden made only 38 while Gilchrist raced to 119, after the latter had more of the strike in an opening stand of 172 which ended in the 23rd over. Without being reckless, Gilchrist recorded 13 fours and eight sixes in his majestic 149 from 104 balls. He exited in the 31st over with the total at 224, and a further 57 runs were added in the final seven-and-a-half overs for the loss of two wickets as Ponting and Symonds did most of the scoring. None of Sri Lanka's six bowlers conceded fewer than six runs per over.

Tharanga hit the first ball of the run chase for four but didn't last much longer, before speedy half-centuries to Jayasuriya and Sangakkara gave Sri Lanka a chance. It was the second century stand involving two left-handers in the match. The Sri Lankans faltered, however, and rain returned. The players exited the field in the 25th over with the total at 3-149, and two overs were deducted from the run chase while the target was reduced from 282 to 269. When the score moved to 7-206 after 33 overs, Vaas and Malinga accepted an offer to leave the field for bad light which seemingly concluded proceedings. As the presentations were being set up, Australia's celebrations were put on hold as the umpires absurdly ruled that the final three overs needed to be bowled the following day. Common sense prevailed as Sri Lanka's captain agreed to finish the game as quickly as possible, but the farce meant a worker had to place the 30-yard circles back on the field. Symonds gently bowled two of the final three overs while fellow spinner Clarke bowled the other one as conditions grew darker, with the vision from stumpcam suggesting it was pitch black. Malinga was stumped with two overs remaining, and eventually the Australians were able to celebrate their second successive undefeated World Cup campaign in addition to becoming the first nation to win three successive World Cups.

Adam Gilchrist scored a scintillating 149 for Australia in the World Cup final. Australia won the World Cup in all three campaigns which Gilchrist played in, while he scored a half-century in two deciders and a century in the third.

Australia		R	B
Adam Gilchrist (+)	c Silva b Fernando	149	104
Matthew Hayden	c Jayawardene b Malinga	38	55
Ricky Ponting (c)	run out (Jayawardene)	37	42
Andrew Symonds	not out	23	21
Shane Watson	b Malinga	3	3
Michael Clarke	not out	8	6
Sundries	(lb 4, nb 3, w 16)	23	
TOTAL	**(38 overs) 4-281**		

DID NOT BAT: Michael Hussey, Brad Hogg, Nathan Bracken, Shaun Tait, Glenn McGrath

FALL: 172, 224, 261, 266

Vaas 8-0-54-0, Malinga 8-1-49-2, Fernando 8-0-74-1, Muralidaran 7-0-44-0, Dilshan 2-0-23-0, Jayasuriya 5-0-33-0

Sri Lanka		R	B
Upul Tharanga	c Gilchrist b Bracken	6	8
Sanath Jayasuriya	b Clarke	63	67
Kumar Sangakkara (+)	c Ponting b Hogg	54	52
Mahela Jayawardene (c)	lbw b Watson	19	19
Chamara Silva	b Clarke	21	22
Tillakaratne Dilshan	run out (Clarke/McGrath)	14	13
Russel Arnold	c Gilchrist b McGrath	1	2
Chaminda Vaas	not out	11	21
Lasith Malinga	st Gilchrist b Symonds	10	6
Dilhara Fernando	not out	1	6
Sundries	(lb 1, w 14)	15	
TOTAL	**(36 overs) 8-215**		

DID NOT BAT: Muttiah Muralidaran

FALL: 7, 123, 145, 156, 188, 190, 194, 211

Bracken 6-1-34-1, Tait 6-0-42-0, McGrath 7-0-31-1, Watson 7-0-49-1, Hogg 3-0-19-1, Clarke 5-0-33-2, Symonds 2-0-6-1

UMPIRES: Steve Bucknor, Aleem Dar (TV: Rudi Koertzen)

TOSS: Australia

PLAYER OF THE MATCH: Adam Gilchrist

AUSTRALIA WON BY 53 RUNS

2011

Tendulkar's glorious swansong

- India and England play out a thrilling tie in a match involving 676 runs
- Kemar Roach and Lasith Malinga claim a hat-trick each
- Two World Cup records are broken as Ireland achieves a stunning victory in a huge run chase against England
- For the first time in nearly 20 years, Australia misses the finals series
- Sachin Tendulkar bows out a winner in his sixth and final World Cup as co-hosts India and Sri Lanka contest the final, with India becoming the first nation to win a World Cup final on home soil

Bangladesh became one of the competition hosts for the first time as this country co-hosted the 2011 tournament along with India and Sri Lanka, with the latter two ultimately battling out the decider. Fourteen matches were originally scheduled for Pakistan, but the ICC cancelled Pakistan's co-hosting status following a terrorist attack on the Sri Lankan team in Lahore in 2009. Of those 14 matches, eight were rescheduled for India while four were awarded to Sri Lanka, and two to Bangladesh.

While the number of teams reverted from 16 to 14 as Bermuda and Scotland dropped out since the 2007 tournament, the format underwent a shake-up as it resembled the 1996 itinerary. The teams were divided into Group A and Group B, before the group matches were followed by quarter-finals.

Australia's dominance ended as the reigning three-time titleholders didn't even make the semi-finals, while it was the first time in nearly 20 years that Australia didn't reach the decider. After four victories and a no-result, Australia's unbeaten streak in the World Cup had stretched to 34 matches. An ensuing loss to Pakistan was Australia's first World Cup loss since its defeat against none other than Pakistan in 1999. Pakistan subsequently topped the Group A ladder while Australia was relegated to third after being equal with Sri Lanka on points. South Africa and India were the front-runners in Group B before the Proteas, like Australia, faltered in the quarter-finals. New Zealand meanwhile reached the semi-finals after placing fourth in Group A.

The final was significant in a number of ways. It was the first time that two Asian countries and two tournament co-hosts contested a World Cup decider, while it was also the first time that a World Cup decider was won by the host team.

A HAT-TRICK OF CLASSICS: Three great contests

India v England at M. Chinnaswamy Stadium (Bengaluru), 27 February

Andrew Miller wrote that this contest 'twisted and turned like an insomniac in a mosquito-pit', and that for the first 39 and final seven overs, 'the Bangalore crowd was as raucous as a monsoon wedding'.

An incredible first over set the tone. Graeme Swann dropped a tough catch at second slip from the first ball which cost four runs, before Virender Sehwag miscued two more strokes in the same over and narrowly escaped being caught both times. Sehwag raced to 35 before departing in the eighth over, but the top order kept the runs flowing as Sachin Tendulkar made a splendid century while

Cometh the hour, cometh the man. Sachin Tendulkar hammers the ball during his century in the tied match against England. In his sixth and final World Cup, Tendulkar was finally able to hold the main prize.

England captain Andrew Strauss strikes the ball through the off side during a quarter-final, won by Sri Lanka. Strauss played some brilliant knocks, none better than his 158 against India.

Gautam Gambhir and Yuvraj Singh made quality half-centuries. India was 3-305 with 4.1 overs left before being all out for 338 with one ball to spare, having lost its last five wickets for 11 runs in 11 balls. Tim Bresnan finished with five wickets after taking three in the 49th over before James Anderson finished with 1-91, having been out of luck in the first over. The final wicket could have made a huge difference in the final washup, as a run-out occurred when the last pair sought a second run after Munaf Patel failed to touch down properly and therefore did not register a run. Later, Patel bowled the final over of the match.

England captain and opener Andrew Strauss led the reply with an outstanding 158, although his innings was by no means chanceless. He added 170 runs with Ian Bell for the third wicket before Zaheer Khan dismissed the duo from successive balls with the total on 281. England lost its way and appeared gone at 7-307 with 15 balls left, before the 49th over yielded 15 runs from five balls and a wicket from the final ball. England needed 14 runs from the final over for victory, and then a straight six from Ajmal Shahzad meant five runs were needed from three balls. The batters scrambled a bye before Swann scored a two, and then managed a single from the final ball to secure a thrilling tie. 'We're happy and devastated at the same time but privileged to play in a game like this,' Strauss said in a post-match discussion.

India 338 (Sachin Tendulkar 120, Yuvraj Singh 58; Tim Bresnan 5-48) tied with England 8-338 (Andrew Strauss 158, Ian Bell 69; Zaheer Khan 3-64).

England v South Africa at M.A. Chidambaram Stadium (Chennai), 6 March

On a tricky pitch in Chennai, the scoring in the England versus South Africa fixture resembled a contest from the 1970s. Evidently, a low-scoring tussle could be just as riveting as a high-scoring one.

England lost both openers in the first over before falling to 3-15 in the fifth over, but half-centuries to Jonathan Trott and Ravi Bopara provided some stability. After the 99-run fourth wicket stand was broken, however, the innings fell apart again. The eighth and ninth wickets fell at 161 before a last-wicket stand of 10 proved vital in the long run. Leg-spinner Imran Tahir had the best figures, after taking the final three wickets.

A South African victory appeared a formality as the openers put on 63 in 14 overs before captain Graeme Smith departed. The Proteas stumbled to 3-82 before progressing to 3-124, and then crashing to 7-127. A 33-run stand had them back on track for victory, only for the eighth wicket to fall in the 47th over. With the Proteas needing eight runs in the final three overs, Stuart Broad scuttled their hopes as he struck twice in four balls, with Dale Steyn lbw before Morne Morkel attempted a big hit and feathered a catch behind.

England 171 (Ravi Bopara 60, Jonathan Trott 52; Imran Tahir 4-38, Robin Peterson 3-22) beat South Africa 165 (Hashim Amla 42, AB de Villiers 25; Stuart Broad 4-15, James Anderson 2-16) by six runs.

India v South Africa at Vidarbha Cricket Association Stadium (Nagpur), 12 March

Despite making a healthy total of 296, the Indians lamented wasting the chance to set a target around the 350 mark. The host nation had 142 runs on the board when Sehwag was first to depart in the 18th over, before Tendulkar went on to make another attractive hundred. His dismissal in the 40th over with the total at 267 sparked an extraordinary collapse, as India lost 9-29 and was all out with eight balls to spare. Steyn finished with five wickets after Morkel, Jacques Kallis and Robin Peterson also made crucial breakthroughs.

Kallis, Hashim Amla and AB de Villiers made half-centuries in the run chase while there were five scores between 16 and 25. The score was 3-173 when Kallis was run out in the 36th over, before the dismissal of Morne van Wyk left the Proteas needing 50 from the final six overs with four wickets in hand. The 48th over yielded 14 runs and the wicket of Johan Botha, before a mere four runs in the following over meant 13 were needed from the final one. The first ball of the 50th over was a sliding doors moment as a thick inside edge produced a boundary, before Peterson belted the next ball over cow corner for six. The third ball was a good yorker but Peterson squirted it to fine leg and tied the scores, before hammering the fourth ball to the cover boundary for the winning runs.

South Africa 7-300 (Jacques Kallis 69, Hashim Amla 61; Harbhajan Singh 3-53) beat India 296 (Sachin Tendulkar 111, Virender Sehwag 73, Gautam Gambhir 69; Dale Steyn 5-50) by three wickets.

SIX OF THE BEST: Individual performances

(excluding player of the tournament, and the finals)

Ryan ten Doeschate 119 off 110 balls and 10-0-47-2: Netherlands v England at Vidarbha Cricket Association Stadium (Nagpur), 22 February

It was a pity for Ryan ten Doeschate that his tremendous all-round display wasn't enough for the Dutch to beat England. He earned player of the match honours in any case.

The Netherlands was 2-58 when ten Doeschate arrived in the 12th over. He faced 11 dot balls before opening his account with a boundary to fine leg off Paul Collingwood. Nearly 10 overs later, ten Doeschate struck two fours in three balls off the same bowler before smacking a Kevin Pietersen full-toss for six in the subsequent over. Ten Doeschate went from 47 to 49 as a skied shot fell safely when two fielders made a mess of the catching opportunity. Soon the batter reached his 50 off 59 balls, before he reached 62 with a great shot over the mid-wicket boundary off the economical Swann. Ten Doeschate's third six came when he sent Collingwood's slower ball over long-on. Two successive fours off Bresnan took ten Doeschate to 95, before he bizarrely reached triple figures with a five as he completed a single while a throw hit the stumps and ricocheted to the boundary.

Ten Doeschate soon dispatched a couple of loose balls, including a high full-toss from Anderson. After reaching 119 which included 54 runs in boundaries, ten Doeschate holed out to deep square leg to leave the Netherlands 6-274 with 11 balls left.

Ten Doeschate came on to bowl as England was 0-85 after 14 overs, chasing 293. He returned 0-36 in an eight-over spell, before coming back on to bowl as England needed just 71 runs in the final 10 overs. Ten Doeschate's second ball of his second spell brought the wicket of Trott who was smartly stumped off a wide, before ten Doeschate finished with 2-47 as he bowled Bell with his final delivery. England ultimately won by six wickets with eight balls to spare.

Andrew Strauss 158 off 145 balls: England v India at M. Chinnaswamy Stadium (Bengaluru), 27 February

Andrew Strauss's 158 in England's tied match against India was a gem, starting from the first ball of the innings when a half-volley from Zaheer drifted into his pads. Strauss flicked the opening delivery in front of square leg for four before punching the sixth ball in front of point for another boundary. Strauss's third scoring shot was similar to the previous one, before he had a stroke of luck as his score was 17. He appeared to feather a catch to the wicketkeeper, but nobody appealed. Strauss had another scare as a botched catch at mid-on enabled him to go from 22

‘We’re happy and devastated at the same time but privileged to play in a game like this.’

– England captain Andrew Strauss after a tied game.

to 26, before he went from 43 to 47 as he was beaten by a googly and edged the ball wide of slip.

After Strauss reached 50 from as many balls, an unusually poor piece of fielding from Tendulkar resulted in another boundary. A reverse sweep took Strauss to 88, before his 13th boundary took him to 99. Strauss brought up his hundred from 99 balls, before advancing Yuvraj and lofting a majestic six over long-on to reach 118. Strauss's 18th and final four came as he smashed a long-hop to bring up 150 from 135 balls. A brilliant yorker from Zaheer ended his brilliant innings, as a brilliant contest continued to unfold.

Kemar Roach hat-trick: West Indies v Netherlands at Feroz Shah Kotla Stadium (Delhi), 28 February

West Indies recorded a 215-run thumping of the Netherlands as Kemar Roach captured a hat-trick. He already had good figures of 3-27 from eight overs, before he claimed the final three wickets with the first three balls of his ninth over. With the ability to move the ball into the right-handers, Roach trapped Pieter Seelaar and Bernard Loots lbw before Berend Westdijk was bowled middle-stump.

For the record, Roach's first victim was caught in the slips before the next two had their stumps wrecked.

Lasith Malinga hat-trick: Sri Lanka v Kenya at R. Premadasa Stadium (Colombo), 1 March

Kenya improved from 2-8 to 2-102 before succumbing for 142 in a nine-wicket loss to Sri Lanka. Lasith Malinga's inswinging yorker was lethal as he captured 6-38 in 7.4 overs, with four of his victims bowled while two were lbw. He captured a hat-trick across two overs in the process.

Malinga struck in the third over before breaking the 94-run stand in the 32nd over. From the final ball of the 42nd over, a yorker crashed into Tanmay Mishra's boot to bring about Malinga's second lbw victim. The first two balls of Malinga's next over also found the blockhole, with Peter Ongondo and Shem Ngoche having their stumps rattled. Malinga's hopes of a double hat-trick were dashed when a stray delivery went to the boundary for five wides, but two balls later he found the target again as he bowled Elijah Otieno to end Kenya's innings.

Kevin O'Brien 113 off 63 balls: Ireland v England at M. Chinnaswamy Stadium (Bengaluru), 2 March

With Ireland chasing a massive target of 328 against England, the score was 4-106 when Kevin O'Brien arrived at the centre. He edged a speculative four from the second ball he faced, before he lost Gary Wilson in the 25th over with the total at 111. O'Brien refused to surrender, however, as he hit two fours in three balls off Michael Yardy in the next over before heaving two sixes in three balls off Swann.

O'Brien's third six took him to 51 off 30 balls, and in the next over he hit Bresnan for four before battering the same bowler over cover for six. In the following over, an inside-edged four off Anderson was immediately followed by a cracking four through the covers, and then two balls later the Irishman whacked a six over mid-wicket. When O'Brien smacked Bresnan for four and six from the final two balls of the 37th over, he had 90 runs off 42 balls while Ireland needed only 85 more runs. The final ball of the 38th over was match-turning as a skied catch was grassed and enabled O'Brien to score two runs. Another two runs from the final ball of the 41st over brought up O'Brien's century from 50 balls, while the team needed 56 more runs.

O'Brien's heroic knock ended with the first ball of the 49th over as he chanced a suicidal second run and was run out. He had registered 13 fours and six sixes, and taken his team to within 11 runs of victory. Trent Johnston and John Mooney polished off the remaining runs as Ireland won by three wickets.

Tillakaratne Dilshan 144 off 131 balls and 3-1-4-4: Sri Lanka v Zimbabwe at Pallekele International Cricket Stadium (Kandy), 10 March

Tillakaratne Dilshan became the second player to score a ton and capture four wickets in a World Cup ODI, while he was also involved in the first double-century opening partnership in World Cup cricket history.

Dilshan took a single from the only ball he faced in the first over, before thumping 18 runs from the first four balls of the second over. Another boundary in the next over took him to 23 from eight balls. Although he was understandably unable to maintain this scoring rate, Dilshan reached his 50 in 43 balls before racking up his 100 in 95 balls.

Trent Johnston and John Mooney rejoice as Ireland records an astonishing victory against England.

Upul Tharanga's departure for 133 left Sri Lanka 1-282 in the 45th over, before Dilshan lofted a catch to deep mid-wicket in the following over. His 144 included 16 fours and a six.

In reply to Sri Lanka's 6-327, Zimbabwe's openers put on 116 runs before being separated in the 20th over. When Kumar Sangakkara produced a scrappy stumping from Dilshan's third ball, the African nation slipped to 4-150 in the 28th over. In his next over, Dilshan trapped Craig Ervine lbw and then had Greg Lamb brilliantly caught one-handed by Mahela Jayawardene next ball. A hat-trick beckoned as Graeme Cremer edged the following delivery to slip, but Jayawardene couldn't hold the low chance. Dilshan was taken off despite having 3-4 from two overs, before he bowled a wicket maiden in the 38th over. Dilshan's final victim was lbw, before his hopes of a five-wicket haul were dashed as Muttiah Muralidaran snared the final wicket.

HEADLINE MOMENT

Records tumble as Ireland stuns England

Ireland was at long odds to beat England before the game started, let alone when England amassed 8-327 batting first. A wicket from the first ball of Ireland's innings would have lengthened the odds even more, and Ireland's task appeared impossible when the score became 5-111 in the 25th over. Incredibly, Kevin O'Brien subsequently smashed what was then the fastest century in World Cup history to help Ireland to what was then the highest successful run chase in World Cup history. He registered triple figures in 50 balls, and was later out for 113 before Ireland sealed a staggering three-wicket win with five balls to spare. The standout player was easy to notice as his hair was dyed purple and bleach blonde.

Ireland 7-329 (Kevin O'Brien 113, Alex Cusack 47; Graeme Swann 3-47) beat England 8-327 (Jonathan Trott 92, Ian Bell 81; John Mooney 4-63) by three wickets.

PLAYER OF THE TOURNAMENT

With Yuvraj Singh winning player of the match honours on four occasions, his selection as player of the tournament was easily vindicated. He could excel with bat and ball in the same game, and his statistics were very strong as he was not out in half of his stints at the crease while his 15 wickets included a five-wicket haul. Although Yuvraj was India's fourth highest run-scorer, his batting average towered above India's top-three run-getters while he was India's second leading wicket-taker and, intriguingly, the competition's equal-fourth leading wicket-taker. It would have been fitting if Yuvraj had hit the winning runs in the final, but he had to settle for being at the non-striker's end after he had registered the winning runs in two previous fixtures.

Yuvraj didn't bat in India's first fixture, as centuries to Virender Sehwag and Virat Kohli set up the match-winning total of 4-370 against Bangladesh. Yuvraj held a catch and had untidy bowling figures of 7-0-42-0 in the 87-run win. In the thrilling high-scoring tie against England, Yuvraj made 58 off 50 balls before conceding 46 runs in seven wicketless overs. He then hit a purple patch as he won player of the match honours against Ireland and the Netherlands, before having a quiet game against South Africa and then winning the individual prize against West Indies and Australia.

Yuvraj Singh (India)

Matches	Innings	Not outs	Runs	Highest score	Average	50s	100s	Catches
9	8	4	362	113	90.50	4	1	3

Overs	Maidens	Runs	Wickets	Average	Best figures
75	2	377	15	25.13	5-31

JOHNSTON
23
IRELAND

In the match against Ireland, Yuvraj became the first player to achieve a five-wicket haul and a half-century in the same World Cup match. Ireland was 2-122 before a run-out triggered a collapse, with Yuvraj taking five consecutive scalps. A catch behind the wicket was followed by a caught-and-bowled, before a bad ball resulted in a catch at cover. Yuvraj's final two victims were lbw, and he finished his 10 overs with 5-31 as Ireland folded for 207. India was 3-87 when Yuvraj arrived at the crease, and he reached his 50 in the 46th over before Yusuf Pathan hit the winning boundary from the next ball. Against the Dutch, Yuvraj took the second and third wickets as the batting side slipped to 3-99 before tumbling to 189 all out. After taking 2-43 from nine overs, Yuvraj struck the winning four in the 37th over to reach 51 not out as India achieved its second successive five-wicket triumph.

Yuvraj hit a six against the Proteas but his impact was minimal, as he fell for 12 off nine balls before having figures of 8-0-47-0 as South Africa overhauled

'Life, to be honest, seemed complete. It was the greatest moment of my cricketing journey.'
– Sachin Tendulkar, in his autobiography

India's total of 296. Against West Indies, Yuvraj began his innings with the score at 2-51 before his 113 set up a total of 268. Having hit 10 fours and two sixes in his 123-ball knock, Yuvraj later took 2-18 in four overs as West Indies collapsed to 188 all out after being 2-154. In the quarter-final against the three-time defending World Cup champions, Yuvraj claimed the key wickets of Brad Haddin and Michael Clarke. Yuvraj's figures of 2-44 from 10 overs would have been even better had Ricky Ponting not hit a six and a four in his final three deliveries. India was 3-143 in the 29th over when Yuvraj came to the crease, and he received a first-ball full-toss which he slammed for four. India stumbled to 5-187 and needed 74 more runs, but Yuvraj stepped up along with Suresh Raina who belted a quickfire 34 not out. Yuvraj sealed another five-wicket victory when he blazed a Brett Lee delivery to the boundary in the 48th over to reach 57, and he rejoiced as Australia's domination had ended.

Yuvraj showed he was only human when he was bowled first ball in the semi-final against Pakistan, before conceding 57 runs in his 10 overs. Nonetheless he held a catch to bring about the first wicket in the run chase, before nabbing the third and fourth wickets as he bowled Asad Shafiq and had Younis Khan caught at cover.

In the final, Yuvraj had Sangakkara caught behind for 48 and later trapped Thilan Samaraweera for 21 to leave Sri Lanka 4-179 in the 39th over. Yuvraj had respectable figures of 2-49 in 10 overs before coming to the crease as the game was there to be won. India needed to score at a run-a-ball as 52 runs were needed with six wickets in hand, and Yuvraj worked his way to an undefeated 21 off 24 balls while his skipper MS Dhoni took control.

FIRST SEMI-FINAL

New Zealand v Sri Lanka at R. Premadasa Stadium (Colombo), 29 March

With Sri Lanka winning by five wickets and with 13 balls remaining, the New Zealanders had only themselves to blame for not setting a bigger target than 218. It was particularly frustrating for the Kiwis that their top-six batters reached double figures without making a big score. A total of 240 or 250 looked possible when New Zealand was 3-161 with 11 overs remaining, but then the dismissal of Ross Taylor was a big setback. A brisk 31-run stand followed before the innings crashed, with the final four wickets falling for a miserable four runs as the Kiwis were all out with seven balls remaining. In his final international appearance on Sri Lankan soil, Muralidaran claimed a wicket with his final delivery when he trapped Scott Styris lbw.

Sri Lanka cruised to 1-160 as Dilshan and Sangakkara scored half-centuries, before the loss of

3-9 threw a little scare through the home side. Only seven runs were scored in the following 31 balls, before successive fours to Chamara Silva eased the pressure. Silva departed soon afterwards with 33 runs still needed as 46 balls remained, but there were no further hiccups. Muralidaran walked a lap of honour and was chaired by teammates, while the result set up an all-Asian final regardless of the result in the second semi-final.

Sri Lanka 5-220 (Tillakaratne Dilshan 73, Kumar Sangakkara 54; Tim Southee 3-57) beat New Zealand 217 (Scott Styris 57; Ajantha Mendis 3-35, Lasith Malinga 3-55) by five wickets.

SECOND SEMI-FINAL

India v Pakistan at Punjab Cricket Association Stadium (Mohali), 30 March

The second semi-final was guaranteed to have millions of followers as arch-rivals India and Pakistan faced off to decide which team would face another Asian nation in the decider. As it turned out, Pakistan rued repeatedly reprieving Tendulkar and later losing wickets at vital times.

The match came to life in the third over as Sehwag struck five boundaries off Umar Gul, with the last one coming from a no-ball. Sehwag raced to 38 before departing in the sixth over, as Tendulkar's score was only eight. Tendulkar had close shaves from successive balls with his score on 23, as he was adjudged lbw before having the decision overturned upon review, and then narrowly escaping being stumped. Tendulkar was subsequently dropped on 27, 45, 70 and 81, with Shahid Afridi the bowler on the first three occasions.

India was 2-116 when Gambhir exited in the 19th over, before Wahab Riaz struck with consecutive balls in the 26th over with the total at 141. When Afridi, incidentally, finally held a chance which Tendulkar offered, the score was 5-187 with 13 overs left. A sub-250 total looked possible when Dhoni fell at 205, but Suresh Raina made an unbeaten 36 while Harbhajan Singh and Zaheer offered valuable support to help the total towards its eventual 9-260.

Pakistan's top-order batters made starts without making substantial progress. After getting bogged down, Younis Khan spooned a catch to cover which made the score 4-106 in the 26th over. Umar Akmal looked threatening until a bowling change instantly brought him undone, as Harbhajan came around the wicket and bowled him. A slower ball from Patel wrecked Abdul Razzaq's stumps, and suddenly the score was 6-150. Afridi was virtually Pakistan's last hope, and he departed at 184 when he mishit a full-toss and was comfortably caught. Mathematically, Pakistan was still in the match until the start of the final over when 30 runs were needed. Four dot balls ensued, before Misbah-ul-Haq hoisted a catch to long-on. Interestingly, Tendulkar earned player of the match honours against Pakistan in a World Cup match for the third time. This time it was certainly not one of his best knocks. Regardless, Tendulkar and his teammates were set to play in a World Cup final on home soil.

India 9-260 (Sachin Tendulkar 85; Wahab Riaz 5-46) beat Pakistan 231 (Misbah-ul-Haq 56; Ashish Nehra 2-33) by 29 runs.

Sri Lanka's Lasith Malinga celebrates a wicket.

FINAL

India v Sri Lanka at Wankhede Stadium
(Mumbai), 2 April

While the 2011 World Cup final was Muralidaran's final ODI appearance, he was also the only player in the match who had previously been in a World Cup title-winning side. He was Sri Lanka's sole survivor from the 1996 final, while he was among six survivors from the 2007 final. India meanwhile had five players backing up from the 2003 final, as both nations were seeking their second World Cup title. Interestingly, both captains were wicketkeepers.

The toss needed to be done twice due to some confusion amid the crowd noise. With Sri Lanka electing to bat, Tharanga scored just two before he was caught at slip from the first ball of the seventh over. Zaheer's opening spell produced remarkable figures of 5-3-6-1, and his second spell produced 2-0-10-1 before he was hammered for 44 runs in his final three overs. Following Tharanga's departure, Dilshan and captain Sangakkara staged a recovery before both were back in the pavilion with the total on 122 in the 28th over. Jayawardene, who had 33 runs from as many balls when the third wicket fell, went on to score a magnificent 103 not out from 88 balls. He lost two partners when he was in his 60s, before Nuwan Kulasekara proved a worthy ally. Only 28 runs were scored from the 41st over to the end of the 45th, before 63 runs in the final five overs boosted the total to a respectable 6-274. After Kulasekara was run out, Thisara Perera smashed 22 not out from nine balls including four, four, two and six from the final four balls of the innings.

Malinga trapped Sehwag lbw for a duck with the second ball of the run chase, before Gambhir registered a boundary from the next delivery. A few irresistible shots took Tendulkar to 18, but then he edged the first ball of Malinga's fourth over to the diving wicketkeeper. The crowd was stunned into silence, before giving Tendulkar a standing ovation as his dismissal left India wobbling at 2-31.

A turning point came in the 14th over when a catch at long-off went begging. India could have been 3-68 with Gambhir out for 30. As he approached 50, Gambhir had another scare as he narrowly avoided being run out. Dilshan, however, took a superb one-handed return catch to dismiss Kohli in the 22nd over with the total at 114.

Dhoni promoted himself to number five and steered his team back on track while Gambhir kept the runs flowing. Dhoni raced to 50 at nearly a run per ball, and Gambhir was just three runs short of a century as he played a reckless shot and was bowled. India needed 52 runs from as many balls as Yuvraj joined his captain, and the duo had little trouble. Dhoni cut the first ball of the 44th over for six, before he and his batting partner creamed a four each in the 47th over. Dhoni hammered two successive fours in the 48th over, before finishing the match memorably with 10 balls to spare as he clubbed a huge six over long-on. Tendulkar was held aloft in his World Cup farewell. 'Being carried by my teammates, waving the tricolour at my home ground, having won the World Cup – what more could I ask for? Life, to be honest, seemed complete. It was the greatest moment of my cricketing journey,' Tendulkar said in his autobiography *Playing It My Way*.

Sri Lanka

Sri Lanka		R	B
Upul Tharanga	c Sehwag b Khan	2	20
Tillakaratne Dilshan	b Harbhajan Singh	33	49
Kumar Sangakkara (c+)	c Dhoni b Yuvraj Singh	48	67
Mahela Jayawardene	not out	103	88
Thilan Samaraweera	lbw b Yuvraj Singh	21	34
Chamara Kapugedera	c Raina b Khan	1	5
Nuwan Kulasekara	run out (Dhoni)	32	30
Thisara Perera	not out	22	9
Sundries	(b 1, lb 3, nb 2, w 6)	12	
TOTAL	**(50 overs) 6-274**		

DID NOT BAT: Lasith Malinga, Suraj Randiv, Muttiah Muralidaran

FALL: 17, 60, 122, 179, 182, 248

Khan 10-3-60-2, Sreesanth 8-0-52-0, Patel 9-0-41-0, Harbhajan Singh 10-0-50-1, Yuvraj Singh 10-0-49-2, Tendulkar 2-0-12-0, Kohli 1-0-6-0

India

India		R	B
Virender Sehwag	lbw b Malinga	0	2
Sachin Tendulkar	c Sangakkara b Malinga	18	14
Gautam Gambhir	b Perera	97	122
Virat Kohli	c & b Dilshan	35	49
MS Dhoni (c+)	not out	91	79
Yuvraj Singh	not out	21	24
Sundries	(b 1, lb 6, w 8)	15	
TOTAL	**(48.2 overs) 4-277**		

DID NOT BAT: Suresh Raina, Harbhajan Singh, Zaheer Khan, Munaf Patel, Sreesanth

FALL: 0, 31, 114, 223

Malinga 9-0-42-2, Kulasekara 8.2-0-64-0, Perera 9-0-55-1, Randiv 9-0-43-0, Dilshan 5-0-27-1, Muralidaran 8-0-39-0

UMPIRES: Aleem Dar, Simon Taufel (TV: Ian Gould)

TOSS: Sri Lanka

PLAYER OF THE MATCH: MS Dhoni

INDIA WON BY SIX WICKETS

2015

Battle of the Trans-Tasman rivals

- Competition co-hosts New Zealand and Australia engage in a thrilling round-robin match, with the Kiwis winning by one wicket
- New Zealand wins all of its matches on its home turf, before losing the final to Australia in Melbourne
- West Indian opener Chris Gayle registers the first double-century in World Cup cricket, while taking part in the highest partnership in limited overs internationals
- New Zealand's Martin Guptill eclipses Gayle's record for highest individual World Cup score
- South Africa again falls narrowly short of a berth in the final

As was the case four years earlier, the tournament co-hosts contested the decider while the host of the final emerged triumphant. In 2015 it was the Trans-Tasman rivals, as Australia and New Zealand were the tournament hosts for the second time; 23 years since the first occasion.

Another resemblance to 2011 was 14 teams being split into two groups (known in 2015 as pools). Canada, Kenya and the Netherlands missed the cut in 2015 while Afghanistan was a newcomer. Scotland and United Arab Emirates (UAE) returned, with Scotland having previously competed in 1999 and 2007 while UAE had taken part in 1996.

There were no great surprises on the points tables, apart from perhaps Bangladesh reaching the top-four while England placed fifth in Pool A. Sri Lanka, West Indies, Pakistan and Bangladesh were thrashed in the quarter-finals before India and South Africa were knocked out in the semi-finals after they were the top-two teams in Pool B. India won its first seven games convincingly before being crushed by Australia, which had narrowly lost one round-robin match but did not lose again (although Australia's clash with Bangladesh was a washout). The Kiwis meanwhile won their first eight matches – all on home soil – only to lose the one which mattered the most, as the final was the only time in the tournament that they played on Australian soil. It was notable nonetheless that New Zealand reached a World Cup decider for the first time.

A HAT-TRICK OF CLASSICS: Three great contests

United Arab Emirates v Ireland at The Gabba (Brisbane), 25 February

A then World Cup record seventh wicket partnership set up a thrilling match which went down to the wire. Despite 45 from opener Amjad Ali and 36 from number four Khurram Khan, UAE was in trouble at 6-131 with 15 overs remaining after being 0-49 in the 12th over.

Twelve runs in the 37th over were followed by 16 in the 39th, and the runs kept flowing as the seventh wicket stand produced 107 runs in just 11.5 overs. Amjad Javed's dismissal for 42 didn't halt UAE's momentum, as Shaiman Anwar went from 87 to 103 during the 48th over which cost 19 runs. The final two overs were less spectacular as two wickets fell for 13 runs.

Australia's World Cup-winning captain Michael Clarke holds the trophy while being chaired by teammates David Warner and Aaron Finch.

Brendon McCullum gave New Zealand some explosive starts, before he was dismissed without scoring in the first over of the final.

Needing 279, Ireland lost a wicket in the second over and was a little sluggish when the fourth wicket fell at 97 in the 26th over. Gary Wilson settled in before showing more urgency, and a 74-run partnership unfolded before Andy Balbirnie exited in the 39th over. With Ireland needing 95 runs in the final 10 overs, Kevin O'Brien hammered 50 off just 25 balls before being caught as he sought his third six in four balls. He had fortuitously gone from 24 to 28 as a catch was dropped in the deep.

Thirteen runs in the 46th over were followed by three runs and a wicket in the next over. Wilson belted the first two balls of the 48th over to the boundary but was well caught from the next ball, and only two wickets remained as 12 runs were needed. When George Dockrell smashed a slower ball for four, only three runs were required from seven balls. A throw missed the stumps as a run-out beckoned from the first ball of the final over, before Dockrell sealed Ireland's two-wicket victory with two runs from the next ball.

Ireland 8-279 (Gary Wilson 80, Kevin O'Brien 50; Amjad Javed 3-60, Mohammad Tauqir 2-38) beat United Arab Emirates 9-278 (Shaiman Anwar 106; Paul Stirling 2-27) by two wickets.

Scotland v Afghanistan at University Oval (Dunedin), 26 February

Both teams were in danger of being skittled for a miserable total before vital lower order partnerships led to a nail-biting finish.

Seven batters passed 14 but none passed 31 in Scotland's 210 all out, which occupied the full 50 overs. Scotland was 3-40 before Matt Machan and captain Preston Mommsen added 53 for the fourth wicket, and then further stutters left the team 8-144 before a 62-run ninth-wicket stand unfolded.

Afghanistan opener Javed Ahmadi scored a fluent half-century before his departure triggered a collapse, as Afghanistan plunged from 2-85 to 7-97. However, with the score at 4-88, a regulation slips catch went begging to reprieve Samiullah Shinwari who was on 20.

The eighth wicket fell at 132 as a wild shot and a fine catch led to Dawlat Zadran's demise. Shinwari posted his half-century from 113 balls, and carefully chose which balls to attack while number 10 Hamid Hassan held firm. Shinwari struck successive balls for six and four in the 39th over, but then things slowed down. Thirty-eight runs were needed from four overs, before Shinwari clouted three sixes in the 47th over. But then he struck a catch to deep mid-wicket and was out for 96 which left the final pair needing 19 runs from 19 balls. A boundary to Shapoor Zadran reduced the equation to five runs from the final over, and Shapoor settled the issue with the third ball as he struck a legside full-toss for four.

Afghanistan 9-211 (Samiullah Shinwari 96, Javed Ahmadi 51; Richie Berrington 4-40) beat Scotland 210 (Matt Machan 31, Majid Haq 31; Shapoor Zadran 4-38, Dawlat Zadran 3-29) by one wicket.

New Zealand v Australia at Eden Park (Auckland), 28 February

A riveting round-robin contest involving the competition co-hosts finished two hours early and was 'one hell of a game' in the words of Kiwi captain Brendon McCullum.

After Australia won the toss and batted, the opening over cost 15 runs after the final ball went for four byes. David Warner hit a six in the second over before Aaron Finch did likewise in the third over, only for the subsequent delivery to deck his off-stump. A 50-run stand ensued before Shane Watson and Warner departed from successive balls to make the score 3-80. Five wickets to Trent Boult left Australia 9-106 after 22 overs, before a crucial last-wicket stand produced 45 runs in 10.2 overs. Brad Haddin's second six took the total past 150, and he was caught at short third man next ball.

New Zealand was 0-11 after one ball, with Martin Guptill glancing a no-ball for four before smashing the free hit for a massive six. McCullum belted 50 off just 21 deliveries, before departing without adding to his score. When Mitchell Starc struck with consecutive balls, the Kiwis had lost three wickets in five balls and were 4-79 in the ninth over.

Corey Anderson took 16 runs off the 15th over, before he succumbed to a wild shot in the 20th over. With Luke Ronchi opening his account with a six, the Kiwis needed only 15 more runs. But Ronchi soon fell to Starc before Daniel Vettori

NEW ZEALAND
SS
SS
LG
RELIANCE
Bluebird
MRF TYRES
Reebok

was caught off a full-toss from Pat Cummins, and then Starc bowled Adam Milne and Tim Southee with spectacular back-to-back deliveries to leave the Kiwis 9-146. Amid incredible tension, Boult survived the final two balls of Starc's over before Kane Williamson sealed the deal from the ensuing ball as he creamed a full-pitched delivery from Cummins over the long-on boundary.

New Zealand 9-152 (Brendon McCullum 50, Kane Williamson 45 not out; Mitchell Starc 6-28, Pat Cummins 2-38) beat Australia 151 (Brad Haddin 43, David Warner 34; Trent Boult 5-27, Daniel Vettori 2-41) by one wicket

SIX OF THE BEST: Individual performances

(excluding player of the tournament, and the finals)

Tim Southee 9-0-33-7: New Zealand v England at Wellington Regional Stadium (Wellington), 20 February

New Zealand's opening bowler Tim Southee returned spells of 2-23 from five overs and 5-10 from four overs as England crumbled for 123 in 33.2 overs.

Southee's first wicket came as a brilliant delivery angled in before swinging away and hitting Ian Bell's off-stump. Moeen Ali hit three successive fours later in the over, before succumbing in Southee's next over. A bouncer which was called wide was followed by two full deliveries, with the latter swinging in and rattling the left-hander's off-stick.

Southee again struck the off-peg with the second ball of his second spell, this time with an out-swinging yorker to James Taylor. In Southee's following over, an out-swinger produced an edge to the wicketkeeper before another out-swinger again hit the off-stump. Stuart Broad was caught at mid-off in Southee's eighth over, and Steven Finn was Southee's final victim when he edged a catch to first slip.

McCullum subsequently registered the fastest 50 in World Cup history as he took just 18 balls to reach a half-century. The opener's thunderous hitting set up an eight-wicket victory in just 12.2 overs. McCullum smashed eight fours and seven sixes in his 77 off 25 balls, having cleared the boundary from four successive balls to go from 48 to 72.

Chris Gayle 215 off 147 balls and 6-0-35-2: West Indies v Zimbabwe at Manuka Oval (Canberra), 24 February

West Indian opener Chris Gayle scored the first double-century in World Cup history, while he and Marlon Samuels produced the highest partnership for any wicket in ODI history. After Dwayne Smith was bowled for zero from the second ball of the match, 372 runs were added for the second wicket. The left-handed Gayle scored 215 off just 147 balls, including 10 fours and 16 sixes. Marlon Samuels overcame a slow start as he registered 11 fours and three sixes in an undefeated 133 from 156 deliveries.

The story could easily have been much different. Two balls after Smith's demise, Gayle survived a close call for lbw from the first ball he faced. And from the final ball of the 17th over, Samuels was dropped at backward point as the score was a modest 1-73.

Gayle reached 50 from 51 balls before raising his ton off 105 balls with workmanlike rather than dominant batting, despite many aggressive shots. He even faced a maiden over. The score was 1-177 after 37 overs, before the final 13 overs yielded an unbelievable 195 runs. Gayle blasted 10 sixes and five fours in nine overs and needed only seven balls to go from 151 to 189. While most of Gayle's runs came from powerful on side strokes and straight hits, he reached his double-century from 138 balls when he crunched a full-toss to the extra cover boundary. Gayle scored only 10 runs in the final four overs as Samuels had most of the strike, before Gayle sliced the final ball of the innings high over point for a catch.

Following some drizzle during the West Indian innings, play was halted early in the run chase as the rain became heavier. Facing a revised target of 363 in 48 overs, the Zimbabweans were all out for a respectable 289 in 44.3 overs. Gayle took 2-5 in his first 10 deliveries as he captured the sixth and seventh wickets with his off-breaks, before finishing with 2-35 from six overs. Craig Ervine was bowled, and Stuart Matsikenyeri was adjudged lbw.

AB de Villiers 162 not out off 66 balls: South Africa v West Indies at Sydney Cricket Ground (Sydney), 27 February

AB de Villiers recorded the fastest 150 in ODI history as South Africa amassed 5-408 against West Indies. After being 1-30 at the 10-over mark, the Proteas stumbled from 1-145 to 3-146 in the 30th over before their captain produced a breathtaking onslaught.

After scoring 19 runs from 18 balls without a boundary, de Villiers straight-drove a slower ball from Jerome Taylor to the fence. In the next over, de Villiers slammed a full-toss from opposing skipper Jason Holder down the ground before cover-driving the following delivery for another four. De Villiers soon turned his attention to Sulieman Benn's left-arm spin, with a six followed by back-to-back fours to raise the batter's half-century.

De Villiers repeatedly swept Benn for four, before producing an astonishing lap sweep over the long leg boundary from a fast Andre Russell delivery outside off-stump. Holder conceded a whopping 34 runs in the 48th over as de Villiers motored from 95 to 127. A four was followed by a six off a no-ball, and then a two was followed by a four from another no-ball. De Villiers then creamed another two fours and a two before swinging the final ball over the fence. The four off the illegitimate delivery was sensational as de Villiers swept a low full-toss to fine leg from well outside off-stump. The last of the fours in this over came as de Villiers produced an incredible lofted reverse paddle. Holder also bowled the final over, with de Villiers smashing 30 runs as a two was followed by two sixes, a four and two more sixes.

Having reached his half-century in 30 balls before achieving his century in 52 balls and his 150 in 64 balls, de Villiers had hammered 17 fours and eight sixes as he faced just 66 balls. In reply, the whole West Indian team fell 11 runs shy of de Villiers' score.

Trent Boult 10-3-27-5: New Zealand v Australia at Eden Park (Auckland), 28 February

Trent Boult was wicketless when Australia was 4-96 in the battle of the Trans-Tasman rivals on New Zealand soil, before he had a five-wicket haul as the score became 9-106. His first five overs cost 24 runs before his second spell produced spectacular figures of 5-3 in five overs, including three maidens and a wide.

New Zealand's Tim Southee bagged seven wickets against England.

From the second ball of Boult's second spell, Glenn Maxwell slashed outside off-stump and chopped the ball onto his middle-stump. Mitchell Marsh fell for a second-ball duck as he also played the ball into his middle-stump, albeit as he attempted a back foot defensive shot.

Michael Clarke and the left-handed Johnson were caught at short cover, with Williamson not having to move on the first occasion before he dived to his right on the second occasion. Starc was Boult's fifth victim as the ball uprooted the middle-stump.

Glenn Maxwell 102 off 53 balls: Australia v Sri Lanka at Sydney Cricket Ground (Sydney), 8 March

Glenn Maxwell's first international ton prompted Sidharth Monga to report that 'A young punk scored a punkish first century'. It was the second fastest in World Cup history at the time.

After scoring three runs from six balls, Maxwell lofted a four to long-off to make the score 4-182 in

A riveting round-robin contest involving the competition co-hosts finished two hours early and was ‘one hell of a game’.

the 34th over. In the following over, Maxwell chipped a four over extra cover before lofting the next ball beyond the long-off boundary. After the drinks break, Maxwell slog-swept a six and then clipped a two to deep mid-wicket before a reverse paddle-flick bounced once on its way to the boundary.

Maxwell raised his half-century from 26 balls as he smashed a full-toss for six. After hitting three fours in four balls off Seekkuge Prasanna, Maxwell executed a switch-hit off Angelo Mathews. Maxwell also rode his luck as a couple of skied shots produced difficult catching opportunities which went begging.

Maxwell's staggering innings featured 10 fours and four sixes. He had 98 off 48 balls before a single and a leg bye ensured O'Brien's record remained. Maxwell chipped a two to reach his breakthrough hundred from 51 balls, before he miscued a full-toss and was caught at mid-on. Maxwell's 53-ball knock helped the total towards its eventual 9-376, before he took 0-35 from six overs as Australia won by 64 runs despite 104 off 107 balls from Kumar Sangakkara.

Martin Guptill 237 not out off 163 balls: New Zealand v West Indies at Wellington Regional Stadium (Wellington), 21 March

New Zealand opener Martin Guptill amassed the highest individual World Cup score, as Gayle's record figure lasted just 25 days. Incidentally, Gayle was fielding as his score of 215 was surpassed in the fourth quarter-final. Following their heroics against Zimbabwe, Gayle and Samuels realised cricket could be a great leveller.

As was the case with Gayle, Guptill had a narrow escape in the first over before taking more than 100 balls to crack three figures and then upping the ante. Neither Gayle nor Guptill played ramp shots or reverse sweeps, as both struck the ball cleanly without being reckless. Incidentally, Guptill didn't hit a six until after he posted his ton.

In hindsight, the first and third balls of the game were very telling. Guptill produced a lovely on-drive from the opening delivery, with slack chasing allowing the ball to reach the boundary. Two balls later, Guptill clipped a half-volley to square leg where Samuels spilled a low catch.

The first two deliveries of the third over were also half-volleys, with Guptill finding the boundary as he drove each side of the bowler. Guptill faced a maiden over, before reaching his 50 from 64 balls. After Guptill punished loose balls from Benn and Samuels, there were no boundaries for seven overs before Guptill found the gap between mid-on and mid-wicket. A single in the 35th over brought up Guptill's hundred from 111 balls, before he raced from 100 to 150 in 23 balls. Guptill had 199 from 151 balls before crunching the next three balls for four, six and four.

The first ball of the final over was a full-toss which Guptill deposited onto the roof of the Cake Tin. The over cost 20 runs, with Guptill finishing unbeaten on 237 with 24 fours and 11 sixes in a total of 6-393.

In the chase, Gayle smashed eight sixes and two fours before falling for 61 off 33, and Samuels hit 27 off 15 as the West Indians succumbed for 250 in just the 31st over. Guptill held two catches.

HEADLINE MOMENT

Hat-trick for JP Duminy

South Africa's Jean-Paul 'JP' Duminy had a sound batting average of 36.81 in his 199 ODIs, while his part-time off-spin brought 69 wickets at an expensive average of 45.55. Nonetheless, he claimed a hat-trick in South Africa's nine-wicket thrashing of Sri Lanka in a quarter-final.

Duminy dismissed Angelo Mathews with the final ball of the 33rd over, before accounting for Nuwan Kulasekara and Tharindu Kaushal with the first two balls of the 35th over as the score fell to 8-116. Mathews whipped a catch to mid-wicket, and then Duminy's second victim edged behind before the third victim was lbw.

England paceman Steven Finn meanwhile claimed a hat-trick on the first day of the tournament, but this was overshadowed as Australia won easily. Finn had 5-71 after claiming wickets with the final three balls of the final over as Australia slipped from 6-342 to 9-342. A misdirected slog from Haddin was caught by a tumbling Broad at third man, before Glenn Maxwell was splendidly caught by a running and diving Joe Root at long-off. Finn's hat-trick ball was slightly short of a good length, with Mitchell Johnson backing away and flat-batting it to James Anderson at mid-off.

Mitchell Starc (Australia)

Matches	Innings	Not outs	Runs	Highest score	Average	50s	100s	Catches
8	3	1	0	0	0	-	-	5

Overs	Maidens	Runs	Wickets	Average	Best figures
63.5	3	224	22	10.18	6-28

PLAYER OF THE TOURNAMENT

The player of the tournament earned player of the match honours only once, but was a valuable contributor every time he bowled. Ironically, Mitchell Starc's best figures of 6-28 came on the one occasion which Australia lost, while this was also the only time he bowled the second over rather than the first over. He claimed four wickets in an innings on another occasion, and otherwise he invariably nabbed two wickets per game. In addition to being a consistent wicket-taker, he was also consistently economical as he conceded only 3.51 runs per over.

Starc's most expensive figures were in Australia's first outing, as he took 2-47 in nine overs in a 111-run drubbing of England. Starc came desperately close to snatching victory against New Zealand after Australia tallied only 151. This match featured the only time Starc took strike at the crease during the tournament, and he was bowled by opposing left-arm paceman Boult for a third-ball duck as Boult nabbed 5-27. (Incidentally, Starc and Boult finished joint leading wicket-takers in the tournament). Starc's teammate and fellow left-arm paceman Mitchell Johnson was carted for 68 runs in six overs, while Starc's fortunes changed markedly after his opening over cost 14 runs. In Starc's second over, Guptill spooned a catch to mid-off. Starc took a catch at mid-off in the eighth over, and was on a hat-trick in the next over as Ross Taylor and Grant Elliott were bowled through the gate. Taylor lost his off-stump as he played across the line, before Elliott lost his middle-stump as he sought to defend. Starc had figures of 6-0-24-3 as New Zealand was 4-90, and returned when the Kiwis needed only 23 more runs. Ten runs were added before Ronchi swayed to evade a Starc bouncer and gloved it to the wicketkeeper. In Starc's next over, two pinpoint yorkers wrecked the stumps from successive balls to leave Australia one wicket shy of victory while New Zealand needed six runs. Boult survived the hat-trick ball and the final ball of Starc's ninth over, before Williamson hit the winning runs.

Both of Starc's victims were yorked as he claimed 2-18 from six overs in a 275-run annihilation of Afghanistan, before he had figures of 8.2-0-29-2 in a 64-run win against Sri Lanka. In the latter match, he was run out without facing a ball in the final over of Australia's innings as the total neared its eventual 376. In Australia's final pool match, Starc was player of the match after taking 4-14 in 4.4 overs in a seven-wicket triumph against Scotland. Both of Scotland's openers were caught off Starc, with the second wicket coming from the final ball of his fourth over. Starc later polished off the innings in the space of four balls, as full-pitched balls again sent the bails flying.

In the quarter-final, Starc had 10-1-40-2 but was outshone by fellow opening bowler Josh Hazlewood, who claimed 10-1-35-4 as Pakistan fell for 213. Australia beat Pakistan by six wickets before trouncing India by 95 runs in a semi-final, with Starc taking 2-28 from 8.5 overs. He ended a fifth wicket stand of 70 as Ajinkya Rahane edged a catch behind, before ending the contest in familiar fashion.

Starc played a huge role in the final as one of his swinging full-pitched deliveries bowled McCullum for a duck in the first over. Starc's opening four-over spell cost just eight runs, before his next spell comprised two overs including a top-edged six. His final two-over spell yielded 1-3, with former Australian player Luke Ronchi caught at slip as Australia maintained the upper hand.

FIRST SEMI-FINAL

New Zealand v South Africa at Eden Park (Auckland), 24 March

The first semi-final was a heart-stopper as the Kiwis and Proteas strived to reach a World Cup decider for the first time. To top it off, New Zealand's hero was the South African-born Grant Elliott.

The Proteas fell to 2-31 before 83 runs were added for the third wicket. The subsequent arrival of de Villiers spelt danger for the Kiwis while Faf du Plessis was well set. Six successive overs contained at least one boundary, with the 36th over involving a dropped catch and then 14 runs in the next three balls as de Villiers raced beyond 50. South Africa was 3-216 after 38 overs when a rain delay reduced the match to 43 overs per side. Du Plessis departed for 82 from the second ball after the resumption, before David Miller walloped six fours and three sixes in a whirlwind knock of 49 from 18 balls. Miller departed in the final over which featured 15 runs, including a four from a dropped catch. De Villiers was unbeaten on 65 off 45 balls, with South Africa compiling 5-281 which meant New Zealand's target was 298 under the Duckworth-Lewis-Stern method.

McCullum smashed 59 runs in the first 4.5 overs, including 24 off Dale Steyn in the fifth over to take the total to 0-71. The next 17 balls yielded just two runs for the loss of McCullum, caught by Steyn at mid-on. Morne Morkel struck again as Williamson edged a pull onto his stumps, before the run-out of Guptill left the Kiwis 3-128 after 17.1 overs.

Elliott paddle-swept his first delivery for four, before Ross Taylor exited with the total on 149. The momentum shifted back-and-forth, and a golden chance to run out Anderson was butchered with the score at 4-204 in the 32nd over. Anderson's eventual exit from a skyscraping hit left New Zealand needing 46 from five overs, and the equation was 29 from 17 balls when Ronchi departed. Elliott nailed a boundary from the fifth ball of the penultimate over, and luckily gained a two from the next ball as two fielders messed up a possible catch.

With the Kiwis needing 12 runs from the last over, a bye and a single were followed by Vettori squeezing a yorker to the third man boundary. Another bye ensued, before Elliott crunched a full-pitched ball from Steyn over the long-on boundary to send the host nation into raptures.

New Zealand 6-299 (Grant Elliott 84 not out, Brendon McCullum 59, Corey Anderson 58; Morne Morkel 3-59) beat South Africa 5-281 (Faf du Plessis 82, AB de Villiers 65 not out; Corey Anderson 3-72) by four wickets.

South Africa's Rilee Rossouw bats against New Zealand at Eden Park.

The Kiwis had reached the final undefeated, but playing on Melbourne soil in front of a crowd of 93,013 was a far-removed situation from any of their preceding fixtures.

SECOND SEMI-FINAL

Australia v India at Sydney Cricket Ground (Sydney), 26 March

India's hopes of back-to-back titles were dashed as Australia's total of 7-328 proved well beyond the reach of the reigning champions. Following the loss of Warner for 12, Steve Smith scored a splendid 105 off 93 balls in a second-wicket partnership of 182 before he exited from the first ball of the 35th over. Finch scored a steady 81 at the top of the order, and a few teammates chipped in with 20s. After losing their sixth wicket at 284, the hosts lost one more wicket while adding 44 runs in the final 19 balls as Johnson slogged an undefeated 27 from nine deliveries.

India was sitting well at 0-76 in the 13th over before faltering to 4-108 after 23 overs. A 70-run fifth wicket partnership ended in the 37th over, leaving captain MS Dhoni with the task of getting his team out of the mire. He scored 65 at a run per ball before becoming the second run-out victim, and the final four wickets fell for a miserable two runs to ensure a landslide margin.

Australia 7-328 (Steve Smith 105, Aaron Finch 81; Umesh Yadav 4-72) beat India 233 (MS Dhoni 65; James Faulkner 3-59, Mitchell Starc 2-28) by 95 runs.

FINAL

Australia v New Zealand at Melbourne Cricket Ground (Melbourne), 29 March

Although a World Cup final involving the co-hosts could be considered a promoter's dream, the outcome was something of a fizzer. The Kiwis had reached the final undefeated, but playing on Melbourne soil in front of a crowd of 93,013 was a far-removed situation from any of their preceding fixtures. New Zealand's total of 183 in 45 overs was simply nowhere near enough to mount a decent challenge.

After winning the toss, McCullum was out for a duck from the fifth ball of the game as he was no match for a brilliant Starc delivery. The introduction of Maxwell for the 12th over quickly produced the vital wicket of Guptill, before Johnson's dismissal of Williamson in the next over left the Kiwis 3-39. A 111-run fourth wicket stand revived their fortunes before another bowling change worked wonders as James Faulkner bowled a double-wicket maiden. He began with a slower ball which Ross Taylor edged to a flying Haddin, before Anderson was bowled for a second-ball duck. New Zealand never recovered despite 83 from Elliott, who was caught behind from another Faulkner slower ball to leave the Kiwis 8-171. Southee hit the first ball he faced for six, before he was last to go as he was run out by a great bit of fielding from Maxwell.

Australia was 1-2 as Boult took a return catch to dismiss Finch, before Warner and Smith added 61 runs. Warner registered three successive fours in the fifth over, with the last one from an edge. He raced to 45 with his seventh four before he perished next ball to a top-edged pull. In his final ODI, Clarke began a little uncertainly before two edgy fours from consecutive deliveries took Australia's total into the 90s. Clarke hit a six on his way to a half-century in 56 balls, before striking four consecutive fours off Southee. Clarke played the ball onto his stumps in the next over and was given a standing ovation as his team needed just nine more runs. Smith passed 50 later in the 32nd over, and pulled a Matt Henry delivery for four from the first ball of the 34th over to secure victory. It was the second time Clarke and Watson had been in a World Cup title win, while umpire Kumar Dharmasena had played in Sri Lanka's 1996 triumph.

New Zealand

		R	B
Martin Guptill	b Maxwell	15	34
Brendon McCullum (c)	b Starc	0	3
Kane Williamson	c & b Johnson	12	33
Ross Taylor	c Haddin b Faulkner	40	72
Grant Elliott	c Haddin b Faulkner	83	82
Corey Anderson	b Faulkner	0	2
Luke Ronchi (+)	c Clarke b Starc	0	4
Daniel Vettori	b Johnson	9	21
Tim Southee	run out (Maxwell)	11	11
Matt Henry	c Starc b Johnson	0	7
Trent Boult	not out	0	1
Sundries	(lb 7, w 6)	13	
TOTAL	**(45 overs) 183**		

FALL: 1, 33, 39, 150, 150, 151, 167, 171, 182, 183

Starc 8-0-20-2, Hazlewood 8-2-30-0, Johnson 9-0-30-3, Maxwell 7-0-37-1, Faulkner 9-1-36-3, Watson 4-0-23-0

Australia

		R	B
David Warner	c Elliott b Henry	45	46
Aaron Finch	c & b Boult	0	5
Steve Smith	not out	56	71
Michael Clarke (c)	b Henry	74	72
Shane Watson	not out	2	5
Sundries	(lb 3, w 6)	9	
TOTAL	**(33.1 overs) 3-186**		

DID NOT BAT: Glenn Maxwell, James Faulkner, Brad Haddin (+), Mitchell Johnson, Mitchell Starc, Josh Hazlewood

FALL: 2, 63, 175

Southee 8-0-65-0, Boult 10-0-40-1, Vettori 5-0-25-0, Henry 9.1-0-46-2, Anderson 1-0-7-0

UMPIRES: Kumar Dharmasena, Richard Kettleborough (TV: Marais Erasmus)

TOSS: New Zealand

PLAYER OF THE MATCH: James Faulkner

AUSTRALIA WON BY SEVEN WICKETS

2019

Stoking the fire as finalists can't be separated

- Nineteen-year-old Pakistan bowler Shaheen Shah Afridi is the only player to capture six wickets in an innings
- England captain Eoin Morgan strikes just four fours and an astonishing 17 sixes in one innings
- England trounces Australia in a semi-final after Australia's Steve Smith is freakishly run out
- England wins the World Cup for the first time, following a tied final against New Zealand featuring many twists and turns and a bit of controversy, while England's hero is the New Zealand-born Ben Stokes
- The decider goes to Super Over which is also tied, with England declared the victor after hitting more boundaries during the decider

After it seemed to take forever for a World Cup final to be won by the team hosting the final, England became the third successive nation to achieve the honour. It was the first time England won the World Cup, while New Zealand was desperately unlucky to finish runner-up for the second successive time after an unbelievable finish to the 2019 decider which ended in a pulsating tie.

It was the fifth time England had hosting rights while it was the third time Wales was a co-host, with Wales having previously staged World Cup fixtures in 1983 and 1999. The 2019 World Cup underwent a considerable makeover from 2015 as Zimbabwe, Ireland, Scotland and United Arab Emirates dropped out. It was the first time since 1979 that Zimbabwe failed to qualify, and it was the first time since 2003 that Ireland would not feature. With the number of nations down to 10, the structure resembled that of 1992 as the teams opposed each other once in a round-robin format before the top-four contested the semi-finals. New Zealand and Pakistan finished equal-fourth on points, with the Kiwis reaching the semi-finals due to a superior net run rate. India and Australia were the top-two teams and competition front-runners, only for both to falter in the semi-finals as the third- and fourth-placed teams progressed.

A HAT-TRICK OF CLASSICS: Three great contests

New Zealand v West Indies at Old Trafford (Manchester), 22 June

An incredible opening over featuring 10 runs and two wickets heralded an incredible contest. Sheldon Cottrell trapped Martin Guptill lbw with a first-ball yorker, before fellow opener Colin Munro also registered a golden duck as he was yorked with the fifth ball.

A wonderful 148 from captain Kane Williamson and a more sedate 69 from Ross Taylor laid a strong platform for the Kiwis. This duo added 160 for the third wicket, and the score was 6-291 when Mitchell Santner slogged the fourth ball of the 50th over for six. The remaining two balls produced catches to mid-off from Carlos Brathwaite's bowling while the fielder, Cottrell, was involved in seven of the eight dismissals which included a run-out and a skied caught-and-bowled.

Trent Boult struck twice in the first seven overs of the West Indian innings, before regular boundaries to Chris Gayle and Shimron Hetmyer helped the score to 2-142 after 22 overs. Gayle was dropped twice in the 18th over, before clubbing

England captain Eoin Morgan holds the competition trophy after England won a thrilling tied World Cup decider against New Zealand on a count back.

successive sixes in the 20th over. Lockie Ferguson dismissed Hetmyer and Jason Holder from the first two deliveries of the 23rd over, before Gayle hoisted a catch in the next over as he sought his seventh six. When the return of Boult brought two quick wickets, the West Indians appeared gone at 7-164 with 23 overs left.

Brathwaite progressed to 60 while the tail-enders supported him, before Cottrell's demise meant 47 runs were needed from five overs. Incredibly, number 11 Oshane Thomas faced just four balls without scoring as Brathwaite pursued an apparently impossible victory. In the 48th over, Brathwaite followed up a two with three spectacular sixes, a four and a single to reach 99 from 76 balls and take the total to 9-284. He passed 100 from the fourth ball of the 49th over, but failed to score from the other deliveries. With six runs needed from seven balls, Brathwaite pulled James Neesham's final delivery to the right of long-on where Boult held a fine catch and kept his footing just inside the boundary line. Brathwaite was distraught but his heroic effort could not be faulted, while his dismissal was merely one of many key moments.

New Zealand 8-291 (Kane Williamson 148, Ross Taylor 69; Sheldon Cottrell 4-56, Carlos Brathwaite 2-58) beat West Indies 286 (Carlos Brathwaite 101, Chris Gayle 87, Shimron Hetmyer 54; Trent Boult 4-30, Lockie Ferguson 3-59) by five runs.

Pakistan v Afghanistan at Headingley (Leeds), 29 June

The batting from both teams stumbled along in fits and starts before the game was decided with two balls to spare. Nobody made a half-century, despite numerous batters making a sound start.

Afghanistan went from 0-27 to 2-27 in two balls before opener Rahmat Shah exited for 35 with the total at 57. The next partnership produced 64 runs before Asghar Afghan crucially exited for a 35-ball 42 which included three fours and two sixes. Further partnerships ended when they were building nicely, with Najibullah Zadran making equal top score before falling in the 45th over to leave the score 7-202. The final 10 overs yielded three wickets for only 43 runs, leaving Pakistan a target of 228.

The second-ball dismissal of Fakhar Zaman was followed by a 72-run second-wicket stand, before the departures of Imam-ul-Haq and Babar Azam left Pakistan 3-81. Pakistan needed 72 runs from 11 overs when the sixth wicket fell, and the next six overs cost only 26 runs before Afghanistan captain Gulbadin Naib's return to the bowling crease was a risk which backfired. Imad Wasim dispatched three boundaries in the 46th over which cost 18 runs, and then the next over featured an edgy boundary, a run-out and an authoritative boundary. Just two runs in the 48th over meant 16 more were needed, and then Wahab Riaz smashed the second ball of the 49th over for six. With six runs required from the final over, two singles were followed by sloppy fielding from the third ball which brought about two runs. Imad subsequently hammered a full-toss through the covers for four to end proceedings. Unfortunately, unruly crowd behaviour marred this great contest.

Pakistan 7-230 (Imad Wasim 49 not out, Babar Azam 45; Mohammad Nabi 2-23, Mujeeb Ur Rahman 2-34) beat Afghanistan 9-227 (Asghar Afghan 42, Najibullah Zadran 42; Shaheen Shah Afridi 4-47, Wahab Riaz 2-29) by three wickets.

South Africa v Australia at Old Trafford (Manchester), 6 July

The last match before the finals was a cliff-hanger as the second-placed Australia sought to leapfrog India, while South Africa pursued a consolation victory.

The first over could have cost Australia dearly in the long run, with Mitchell Starc conceding five runs in wides from the opening delivery before Aiden Markram hit two fours. The first wicket came in the 12th over with the total at 79, and Quinton de Kock departed in the 18th over after posting a half-century in the previous over. Proteas skipper Faf du Plessis combined with Rassie van der Dussen for a 151-run partnership before the former fell for 100 with seven overs remaining. Van der Dussen was frustratingly caught at deep mid-wicket from the final ball of the innings as he sought his fifth six which would have brought him a century.

Cricket was the real winner (after the tied decider).

Shakib Al Hasan sends down a delivery for Bangladesh.

Imran Tahir's leg-spin induced a wicket in the third over as Australia chased a 326-run target. Usman Khawaja soon retired hurt with a hamstring injury, before Steve Smith fell cheaply. Marcus Stoinis and Glenn Maxwell made little impact, but a speedy century to David Warner kept Australia in the hunt. Alex Carey meanwhile raced to 50, before Warner was superbly caught in the 40th over which was a wicket maiden as Australia needed 99 runs. Twenty-nine runs in two overs were followed by only eight in the next two for the loss of two wickets, including Carey. Starc and Khawaja combined to take 17 runs off the 48th over, but both departed in the second-last over. The last pair needed 18 runs in the final over, and Nathan Lyon hoicked a catch to deep mid-wicket when the task was 11 runs from two balls.

South Africa 6-325 (Faf du Plessis 100, Rassie van der Dussen 95; Nathan Lyon 2-53, Mitchell Starc 2-59) beat Australia 315 (David Warner 122, Alex Carey 85; Kagiso Rabada 3-56, Andile Phehlukwayo 2-22) by 10 runs.

SIX OF THE BEST: Individual performances

(excluding player of the tournament, and the finals)

Rohit Sharma 140 off 113 balls: India v Pakistan at Old Trafford (Manchester), 16 June

Indian opener Rohit Sharma was visibly annoyed after being dismissed for 140 against arch-rival Pakistan, as he may have felt a double-century was achievable.

Sharma opened India's account with a streaky boundary to fine leg as he inside-edged a Hasan Ali delivery wide of the stumps. A splendid off drive off the same bowler produced Sharma's second boundary, before he hammered Hasan for four and six in the bowler's next over. Sharma gave two run-out chances in his 30s, but sloppy fielding cost Pakistan.

Sharma dispatched a full-toss from Shadab Khan into the crowd before driving the next ball to the point boundary to reach 50 in 34 balls. Hasan again rued bad luck as Sharma went from 76 to 80 similarly to his first scoring shot. Sharma reached 91 with a brilliant cut for six off Hasan, before raising his hundred off 85 balls with a single off Shadab.

Sharma recorded his 14th four from the first ball of the 39th over, but Hasan finally had his man next ball as Sharma intercepted the ball outside off-stump and scooped it straight to short fine leg.

Another 102 runs boosted India's total to 5-336, before the Indians won by 89 runs after Pakistan's target was changed to 302 in 40 overs due to a rain interruption.

Shakib Al Hasan 8-0-54-2 and 124 not out off 99 balls: Bangladesh v West Indies at County Ground (Taunton), 17 June

Shakib Al Hasan became the second player to achieve both a half-century and a five-wicket haul in a World Cup match. Shakib's 51 and 5-29 helped Bangladesh to a 62-run win against Afghanistan, yet his display against West Indies a week earlier was at least as commendable.

As the fourth change bowler, Shakib took 2-54 in eight overs as the West Indians tallied 8-321. After striding to the wicket at 1-52 in the ninth over, Shakib helped Bangladesh to a seven-wicket win with 8.3 overs to spare as he made an undefeated 124. Shakib relished batting with Litton Das, who hammered 94 not out off 69 balls while Shakib scored 80 in an unbroken 189-run partnership. Luck ran Bangladesh's way as a number of miscued strokes fell safely.

Shakib's 50 came off 40 balls, before he brought up triple figures from 83 balls with a wondrous cover drive for four. It was one of 16 fours for Shakib.

Eoin Morgan 148 off 71 balls: England v Afghanistan at Old Trafford (Manchester), 18 June

England captain Eoin Morgan was unstoppable as he blasted 148 at better than two runs per ball against Afghanistan. He cleared the boundary an astonishing 17 times and hit only four fours.

Having come to the crease at 2-164 in the 30th over, Morgan scored just a single in his first seven balls but it was the seventh ball which instigated his vicious form. It was a no-ball which gave him a free hit, and Morgan spanked the ensuing half-tracker over the mid-wicket boundary. He clubbed the next ball over long-on for another six, and in the next over he produced a bizarre reverse chip over short third man for four.

Morgan could have been out for 28 off 26 deliveries, but a catch went begging and enabled him to go to 32. He hit a six from the next ball and followed up with another six just three balls later off the luckless Rashid Khan. Morgan's fifth six took him to 54 off 36 balls, before he went from 67 to 79 in two deliveries. After raising his ton from 57 balls with his 11th six, Morgan cleared the boundary six more times and also hit a four as he spectacularly sped from 104 to 148 in 10 balls. The carnage ended immediately after his final six as he flat-batted a catch to long-off, leaving England 4-359 with three overs left. England finished on 6-397, before Afghanistan managed 8-247.

David Warner 166 off 147 balls: Australia v Bangladesh at Trent Bridge (Nottingham), 20 June

Australian opener David Warner made the highest individual score in the tournament as he smoked 166 against Bangladesh.

Bangladesh could ill-afford to reprieve Warner, who cut a catch which was missed at backward point from the final ball of the fifth over. Warner moved from 10 to 12 in the process, and the score became 0-27 instead of 1-25. The first wicket belatedly fell at 121, and the next partnership produced 192 runs before Warner departed in the 45th over.

Warner punished anything too short or too full, as his innings yielded 14 fours and five sixes. His first 50 took 55 balls and included four fours and two sixes, and he also scored 50 runs in his next 55 balls while hitting only three boundaries in this period. Another four fours and three sixes helped Warner to 150 off 139 balls, and three quick fours followed. Immediately after slapping a wide full-toss to the fence, Warner was caught at short third man as he mistimed his cut shot to a short slower ball. Australia totalled 5-381, before Bangladesh replied with a gallant 8-333. Warner held two catches.

Mohammed Shami hat-trick: India v Afghanistan at The Rose Bowl (Southampton), 22 June

At 7-209, Afghanistan needed 16 runs from the final over to upset India. The equation became 12 runs from four balls, and then right-arm paceman Mohammed Shami finished the game with a hat-trick.

With the third ball of the over, Mohammad Nabi picked out Hardik Pandya at long-on. Aftab Alam was bowled first ball as he swished across the line, and then a yorker crashed into Mujeeb Ur Rahman's leg-stump as the batter backed away and swung desperately. Shami finished with 4-40 from 9.5 overs.

Boult meanwhile claimed a hat-trick seven days later, coincidentally also with the third, fourth and fifth balls of the final over of an innings. Unfortunately for the left-arm paceman, his milestone was in vain as Australia beat New Zealand by 86 runs after tallying 9-243. Boult's victims succumbed to yorkers, with Khawaja departing for 88 before Mitchell Starc and Jason Behrendorff made golden ducks. Khawaja moved across his stumps and had his leg-stump rattled, before the next ball cannoned into fellow left-hander Starc's middle-stump. The third victim was right-handed, with the ball hitting him on the right foot in front of middle and leg stumps. Boult finished with 4-51 from 10 overs.

PAKISTAN

Shaheen Shah Afridi 9.1-0-35-6: Pakistan v Bangladesh at Lord's (London), 5 July

Shaheen Shah Afridi was the only bowler to capture six wickets in an innings in the 2019 World Cup; a worthy achievement for a 19-year-old. His performance helped dismiss Bangladesh for 221 in reply to Pakistan's 9-315. Interestingly, four of the left-arm pace bowler's victims were left-handers. Just as interesting was Bangladesh left-arm paceman Mustafizur Rahman capturing 5-75 from 10 overs after he too dismissed four left-handers.

Afridi began with 1-12 in a four-over spell, followed by 2-12 in a three-over spell and 3-11 in his final 2.1 overs. He breached Tamim Iqbal's defence with his 10th delivery, and struck with the first ball of his second spell when Litton Das spooned a catch to cover. Shakib Al Hasan was Afridi's next victim as a cut was edged to the wicketkeeper, and the bowler also struck with the first ball of his third spell as Mohammad Saifuddin belted a catch to mid-off. Two balls later, the teen bagged his fifth scalp as a yorker hit Mahmudullah's off-stump.

Mashrafe Mortaza hit a six in Afridi's ninth over, before the 19-year-old began his final over with a bouncer which was called a wide. The short ball was followed by a brilliant yorker which made a mess of Rahman's stumps.

Nineteen-year-old Shaheen Shah Afridi was the only bowler to capture a six-wicket haul in the 2019 World Cup.

Shaheen Shah Afridi was the only bowler to capture six wickets in an innings in the 2019 World Cup; a worthy achievement for a 19-year-old.

HEADLINE MOMENT

A freakish run out

Steve Smith was wretchedly unfortunate to be run out in the second semi-final, but this should not detract from what England wicketkeeper Jos Buttler was able to produce.

Smith pulled at a Chris Woakes delivery which struck him on the body and rolled behind square on the legside. He chanced a leg bye when Buttler removed his right glove and shied at the bowler's end, as Smith tried to place himself in the line of the throw. Alas for Smith, the ball scattered the stumps while he was just short of his ground, with Buttler promptly saying 'it went through his legs'.

A replay from behind the stumps revealed just how freakish the dismissal was. The ball not only went between the batter's legs, but made its way through a tiny gap just below Smith's groin. Bearing in mind the distance, angle, timing and execution of the throw, combined with the minuscule amount of space between Smith's legs as the batter was running, what were the odds of Buttler's throw finding the tiny gap and hitting the stumps?

In the context of the game, the run-out was crucial as Smith's dismissal for 85 left Australia 8-217 with 17 balls left and denied Smith the chance to produce a late onslaught. Another wicket fell from the next ball, and Australia's eventual total of 223 proved far too small.

PLAYER OF THE TOURNAMENT

New Zealand's captain must have decidedly mixed feelings about the 2019 World Cup, having won the player of the tournament award while his team lost the final on a count back against England. He was also the tournament's fourth leading runmaker, having shone in the number three role after the Kiwis usually lost an early wicket. Yet he rode his luck at times as he escaped at least three blatant run-out chances, and had a few other close shaves.

New Zealand won its first four games (excluding a washout against India) after Williamson chose to field each time. The skipper wasn't required to bat in a 10-wicket slaughter of Sri Lanka, before making 40 against Bangladesh. Defending a total of 244, the Bangladeshis butchered a chance to run out Williamson for eight as the score was 2-61. New Zealand was in control at 2-160 until Williamson flicked a catch to deep mid-wicket, and the Kiwis

Kane Williamson (New Zealand)

Matches	Innings	Not outs	Runs	Highest score	Average	50s	100s	Catches
10	9	2	578	148	82.57	2	2	6

Overs	Maidens	Runs	Wickets	Average	Best figures
15	-	64	2	32	1-25

nearly threw the game away before spluttering to a two-wicket win.

After his team dismissed Afghanistan for 172, Williamson faced up after the first-ball dismissal of Guptill. This time Williamson survived a run-out chance on 22 and went on to score 79 not out including the winning single as his team prevailed by seven wickets.

Following the washed out game, Williamson was player of the match in a four-wicket win over South Africa. After Williamson arrived at 1-12 in reply to South Africa's 6-241, his team slid from 1-72 to 4-80 before he led a recovery. New Zealand's skipper had two crucial let-offs in the 70s, as a faint edge behind was undetected by the wicketkeeper and umpire before a run-out chance went begging. When Williamson delicately glided the final ball of the penultimate over for four, his team needed eight runs from six balls. The Kiwi skipper slog-swept a six to raise his ton, before another glide behind point sealed the win with three balls to spare and took his score to 106 not out.

After the Kiwis were sent in against West Indies, Williamson again faced the second ball of the match following another first-ball dismissal for Guptill. Williamson elegantly stroked the first and third balls he faced through the off side for four and three, and then witnessed a dismissal from the fifth ball. Williamson went from seven to 11 as he edged a four just wide of slip, and a little over 10 overs passed before he hit another boundary. He reached 50 in 75 balls, before dispatching a rubbish delivery to go from 99 to 103. Williamson played many sumptuous strokes, and it wasn't until he passed 130 that he finally cleared the boundary. Williamson exited for 148 in the 47th over as a skied top-edge was caught by the wicketkeeper, after Williamson registered 14 fours and a six while facing 154 balls.

Having recorded a nervous five-run win against West Indies, the Kiwis lost their final three round-robin games as their captain made 41, 40 and 27. He also used himself as fifth change bowler on two occasions. After wet conditions delayed the start against Pakistan, Williamson chose to bat first and continued to do so when he had the choice for the remainder of the tournament. After his team tallied 6-237, Williamson broke a 66-run partnership to leave Pakistan 3-110 in the 25th over. He finished with 1-39 in eight overs before Pakistan won by six wickets and with five balls to spare.

With Williamson losing the toss in the next outing, he would have been happy to see Australia 5-92 in the 22nd over. Williamson achieved good figures of 7-0-25-1 and again broke a vital partnership, but by then Australia was on track to post a total well above 200. Williamson survived a couple of tough chances and top-scored for his team, before he was again caught at the wicket. From 2-97, New Zealand crumbled for 157 in pursuit of 244.

New Zealand's skipper held two catches against England, but little else went right for him after he lost the toss. The Kiwis succumbed for 186 in pursuit of 306, and Williamson made his lowest score in the tournament after being dismissed in the unluckiest way. A straight drive from Ross Taylor was touched by the bowler before it hit the stumps to run out the non-striker as he backed up.

In the first semi-final, Williamson first took strike at 1-1 in the fourth over after he won the toss. His steady 67 ended when he was caught at point in the 36th over, leaving his team 3-134. He held two vital catches from skied shots, with the Kiwis snapping their losing streak as they won by 18 runs.

After winning the toss in the final, Williamson arrived at 1-29 in the seventh over and was next to go when he departed for 30 in the 23rd over. He took

12 balls to open his account, and wasn't at his best before he was again caught by the wicketkeeper. At the end he was realistic in addition to showing good sportsmanship, as he congratulated England and said 'it certainly wasn't just one extra run' and that 'so many small parts in that match that could have gone either way'.

FIRST SEMI-FINAL

India v New Zealand at Old Trafford (Manchester), 9–10 July

Rain forced the match to be played across two days, with both teams starting disastrously before a fine comeback from India wasn't enough to book a spot in the decider. The semi-final turned out to be MS Dhoni's farewell from the international scene.

Guptill was nearly out to the first ball of a 2019 World Cup contest for the third time, but the lbw appeal was rejected. The first run came from the 17th ball, and New Zealand was 1-1 after 3.3 overs when Guptill exited. Henry Nicholls and his captain worked hard to rebuild the innings, with Nicholls falling in the 19th over before Ross Taylor played a match-turning knock. Williamson departed for 67 in the 36th over, before Taylor and Colin de Grandhomme combined to take 18 runs off the 44th over. De Grandhomme departed soon afterwards, and New Zealand reached 5-211 after 46.1 overs when rain forced the rest of the day's play to be abandoned. The Kiwis added 28 runs from the remaining 23 balls the following morning, and lost three wickets in seven balls at one stage.

Great bowling from Henry and Boult left India in tatters at 3-5, before the fourth wicket fell at 24. Rishabh Pant and Hardik Pandya scored 32 each, but the Indians were still in strife when a skied slog from Pandya left them 6-92 in the 31st over. A subsequent 116-run stand kept the game alive, with Ravindra Jadeja taking the initiative while Dhoni supported him. Having hit four fours and four sixes, Jadeja holed out to long-off in the 48th over before a six from Dhoni reduced the equation to 25 from 11 balls. Dhoni departed two balls later as a great throw from Guptill ran him out, and India finished 19 runs shy of the target when the final wicket fell with three balls remaining.

Australian wicketkeeper-batter Alex Carey is treated with a bandage after being hit during the World Cup semi-final clash with England.

New Zealand 8-239 (Ross Taylor 74, Kane Williamson 67; Bhuvneshwar Kumar 3-43) beat India 221 (Ravindra Jadeja 77, MS Dhoni 50; Matt Henry 3-37, Mitchell Santner 2-34) by 18 runs.

SECOND SEMI-FINAL

Australia v England at Edgbaston (Birmingham), 11 July

It was unusual for Australia to be thrashed in a World Cup semi-final, while England reached the decider for the first time in 27 years.

Warner crunched the first ball of the match through the covers for four, before wickets to Jofra Archer and Chris Woakes left Australia reeling at 3-14. Promoted to number five, the in-form Carey had his helmet dislodged by a bumper from Archer. Carey received treatment but he batted on, and soon played a commanding shot for four. He reached 46 but then needlessly holed out to deep mid-wicket off Adil Rashid, who then trapped Marcus Stoinis lbw with a googly as Australia went from 3-117 to 5-118 in the 28th over. Steve Smith meanwhile reached a half-century in the same over, and desperately needed more support.

Maxwell hit two fours and a six but made only 22, and Pat Cummins fell cheaply before Smith and Starc added 51 for the eighth wicket. Smith and Starc fell in successive balls in the 48th over, with Smith bizarrely run out for 85 before the final wicket fell with an over to spare.

England was 0-50 after 10 overs before Lyon's first over cost 13 runs. Starc conceded 15 in the 15th over, and then Smith's only over cost 21 after Jason Roy clouted three consecutive sixes. Starc trapped Jonny Bairstow for 34, but then Joe Root hit three of the next four balls to the fence to take England to 1-136 after 18 overs. Roy was controversially ruled caught behind for 85 off 65 balls, before Root and Morgan quickly added 79 to seal the result with nearly 18 overs to spare.

England 2-226 (Jason Roy 85, Joe Root 49 not out, Eoin Morgan 45 not out) beat Australia 223 (Steve Smith 85, Alex Carey 46; Chris Woakes 3-20, Adil Rashid 3-54) by eight wickets.

FINAL

England v New Zealand at Lord's (London), 14 July

England finally shed the bridesmaids tag although the England and New Zealand teams couldn't be separated, as an extraordinary contest unfolded. Both teams scored the same number of runs in the regulation 100 overs and in the subsequent 'Super Over', which meant victory was awarded to the team which registered the most boundaries in the match. Gone were the days of the 'fewer wickets lost' rule, which would have resulted in a Kiwi victory.

None of New Zealand's batters took charge as the first seven made scores between 15 and 55. After the Kiwis were 0-22 after four overs, their run rate remained below five per over at the end of every subsequent over. A 74-run second-wicket partnership took the total beyond 100, but then regular wickets hampered any possible momentum. New Zealand's eventual 8-241 was nonetheless much better than its total in the previous ODI World Cup decider, while the 2019 team had five players backing up from the 2015 decider.

Roy survived an lbw appeal first ball before he was first to go with the total at 28. England struggled to 4-86 when Morgan departed in the 24th over. The fifth wicket stand produced 110 vital runs, before the contest exploded to life when Buttler was well caught off Ferguson in the 45th over. Ferguson struck again, but the runs kept coming while New Zealand-born Ben Stokes was chiefly responsible for standing in the way of a Kiwi victory. Twenty-two runs were needed from nine balls after Liam Plunkett departed, and then Stokes recorded a six as Boult took a catch and crucially stepped on the boundary before he could release the ball. Archer departed, and England needed 15 runs in the final over for victory while Stokes sought to farm the strike. Boult delivered two priceless dot balls before Stokes slog-swept a precious six, and then the fourth ball provided ample controversy. Stokes dived towards the crease for a second run when the outfield throw hit his outstretched bat and raced to the boundary. Six runs were awarded, but technically it should have been five considering the second run had not been completed when the throw hit the bat. Stokes chanced a second run from each of the next two balls but the non-striker was run out each time, meaning England was all out for 241.

Stokes and Buttler faced Boult in the first Super Over, with a three to Stokes followed by a single to Buttler, a four and a single to Stokes, and then a two and a four to Buttler. With the Kiwis needing 16 runs, Archer began with a wide before Neesham hit a two and then whipped a six over mid-wicket to reduce the task to just seven runs from four balls. Neesham managed a pair of twos before a miscue resulted in a short single, meaning Guptill needed two runs from one ball. He clipped it towards deep mid-wicket, before Roy's throw bounced once to wicketkeeper Buttler who ran out Guptill as he sought the winning run. It was an unbelievable end to an unbelievable game, which had countless sliding doors moments and key incidents.

Regardless, cricket was the real winner.

New Zealand

New Zealand		R	B
Martin Guptill	lbw b Woakes	19	18
Henry Nicholls	b Plunkett	55	77
Kane Williamson (c)	c Buttler b Plunkett	30	53
Ross Taylor	lbw b Wood	15	31
Tom Latham (+)	c sub (Vince) b Woakes	47	56
James Neesham	c Root b Plunkett	19	25
Colin de Grandhomme	c sub (Vince) b Woakes	16	28
Mitchell Santner	not out	5	9
Matt Henry	b Archer	4	2
Trent Boult	not out	1	2
Sundries	(lb 12, nb 1, w 17)	30	
TOTAL	**(50 overs) 8-241**		

DID NOT BAT: Lockie Ferguson

FALL: 29, 103, 118, 141, 173, 219, 232, 240

Woakes 9-0-37-3, Archer 10-0-42-1, Plunkett 10-0-42-3, Wood 10-1-49-1, Rashid 8-0-39-0, Stokes 3-0-20-0

England

England		R	B
Jason Roy	c Latham b Henry	17	20
Jonny Bairstow	b Ferguson	36	55
Joe Root	c Latham b de Grandhomme	7	30
Eoin Morgan (c)	c Ferguson b Neesham	9	22
Ben Stokes	not out	84	98
Jos Buttler (+)	c sub (Southee) b Ferguson	59	60
Chris Woakes	c Latham b Ferguson	2	4
Liam Plunkett	c Boult b Neesham	10	10
Jofra Archer	b Neesham	0	1
Adil Rashid	run out (Santner/Boult)	0	0
Mark Wood	run out (Neesham/Boult)	0	0
Sundries	(b 2, lb 3, w 12)	17	
TOTAL	**(50 overs) 241**		

FALL: 28, 59, 71, 86, 196, 203, 220, 227, 240, 241

Boult 10-0-67-0, Henry 10-2-40-1, de Grandhomme 10-2-25-1, Ferguson 10-0-50-3, Neesham 7-0-43-3, Santner 3-0-11-0

UMPIRES: Kumar Dharmasena, Marais Erasmus (TV: Rod Tucker)

TOSS: New Zealand

PLAYER OF THE MATCH: Ben Stokes

MATCH TIED, SUPER OVER TIED: ENGLAND WON ON BOUNDARY COUNT

2023

Final ambush foils Indian surge

- A very closely fought battle involving Australia and New Zealand contains 771 runs
- Following a reprieve on 33, Glenn Maxwell scores an unbelievable 201 not out to help Australia overhaul Afghanistan's 5-291 after Australia was 7-91 at one point
- South Africa's Aiden Markram becomes the first player to score a World Cup century in less than 50 deliveries
- Sri Lanka's Angelo Mathews becomes the first player to be dismissed 'timed out' in international cricket
- India is undefeated until the final, losing on home soil against Australia as Travis Head scores a century

The 2023 tournament was originally scheduled for February and March, before being moved to October and November. The decision occurred in July 2020 amid the global COVID-19 pandemic, which impacted the qualification schedule. The Netherlands returned after missing the cut in 2015 and 2019, while a significant change in 2023 was the absence of West Indies. Besides being the first time West Indies did not appear in the World Cup, it was also the first time that a previous winner of the tournament did not take part.

The decision to have India as the sole host was also a first, and this could be deemed a resounding success as a total of 1,250,307 spectators across the tournament was the highest in a Cricket World Cup. India appeared destined to win the tournament after winning all of its matches convincingly on the way to the final, only to fall at the final hurdle. The Australians had their backs to the wall after losing their first two matches, but they did not lose again as they ultimately triumphed from third spot. Having inflicted Australia's heaviest World Cup defeat in terms of runs (134), South Africa finished second on the ladder as the Proteas bounced back from the disappointment of 2015, but again they found a way to miss out on a berth in the final. With New Zealand snaring fourth spot while six nations had more losses than wins, it always appeared to be a case of who would contest India in the decider.

Afghanistan meanwhile was arguably a success story, as its win-loss record of 4-5 included victories against England, Pakistan and Sri Lanka. Afghanistan would also have defeated Australia, were it not for a vital dropped catch and a scarcely believable individual performance from one of the Australians. England meanwhile was never a chance of back-to-back titles, as one win from its first two matches was followed by a five-game losing sequence. Sri Lanka fared even worse, as back-to-back wins were preceded by a three-game losing streak and followed by a four-game losing stretch.

A HAT-TRICK OF CLASSICS: Three great contests

Pakistan v South Africa at M.A. Chidambaram Stadium (Chennai), 27 October

With the Proteas beating the Pakistanis by one measly wicket, there were naturally many 'what-ifs' and 'if-onlys'.

Most players from both teams made double figures without going on to a sizeable score. Pakistani captain Babar Azam's dismissal for 50 left his team 5-141, before an 84-run partnership was followed by another stutter as Shadab Khan and Saud Shakeel departed within three overs. Pakistan was all out with 20 balls remaining and had to settle for 270 after being 5-225 in the lead-up to Shadab's dismissal in the 40th over.

The Australians are all smiles after upsetting the host nation in the decider.

The run chase began with five wides, before five boundaries to Quinton de Kock helped the Proteas to 0-30 in just the second over. De Kock holed out to deep square leg in the fourth over, and Temba Bavuma also hit a flurry of boundaries before he departed next. After replacing Shadab as a concussion substitute in the 15th over, Usama Mir claimed an lbw with his fifth delivery in the 19th over before holding a catch in the 22nd over.

A 70-run partnership took the Proteas to 4-206 with 17 overs remaining, before wickets fell regularly. Marco Jansen departed in the 37th over after scoring 10 runs in the previous two balls, but there was no cause for alarm until Aiden Markram fell nine runs short of a ton. Two wickets without a run left South Africa 8-250, before a brilliant caught-and-bowled from Haris Rauf left the last pair of Keshav Maharaj and Tabraiz Shamsi needing 11 runs in 27 balls. Three runs were added before Shamsi survived a very tight lbw appeal which was reviewed by the third umpire. With the Proteas needing four runs from 17 deliveries, Mohammad Nawaz strayed down the legside which enabled Maharaj to turn the ball behind square for the winning boundary.

South Africa 9-271 (Aiden Markram 91; Shaheen Shah Afridi 3-45) beat Pakistan 270 (Saud Shakeel 52, Babar Azam 50; Tabraiz Shamsi 4-60, Marco Jansen 3-43) by one wicket.

Australia v New Zealand at HPCA Stadium (Dharamshala), 28 October

The clash of the Trans-Tasman teams produced the highest scoring game in World Cup history, while the result was not decided until the very last ball. Seven Australians made double figures while there was also a century-maker, before the Kiwis had eight players with double-figure scores along with a century-maker. Australia's innings contained 32 fours and 20 sixes, before New Zealand's run chase contained 33 fours and 12 sixes. The only bowler to concede fewer than 6.2 runs per over was New Zealand's Glenn Phillips, whose 10 overs cost only 37 runs after he captured the first three wickets.

Australia's openers recorded a century stand in just 8.5 overs, before the first wicket fell at 175 in the 20th over. In his first game of the tournament, Travis Head went on to score 109 before falling with the total on 200 in the 24th over. Further wickets did not halt the run flow, and the Kiwis rued numerous dropped catches. Four sixes were hit in the 48th over which cost 27 runs, before the loss of 4-1 in eight balls left Australia all out for 388 with four balls remaining when a 400-run total beckoned.

New Zealand was 0-60 after seven overs, and then 2-72 in the 10th over with the openers gone. Rachin Ravindra exceeded Head's score, and New Zealand was 5-292 with 10 overs remaining after Australia had the same score at the same time. The Kiwis were rocked as Ravindra fell in the 41st over, but the total kept climbing. Nineteen runs were needed in the final over with two wickets in hand, before a wild wide from Mitchell Starc went to the boundary and reduced the task to 13 runs from five balls. Three consecutive twos were followed by a full-toss, but James Neesham mistimed it and was run out as he sought a second run. An ensuing dot ball sealed a narrow win for Australia, although it was hardly fair for New Zealand's number 11 Lockie Ferguson to face only one ball and require a six to steal victory.

Australia 388 (Travis Head 109, David Warner 81; Glenn Phillips 3-37) beat New Zealand 9-383 (Rachin Ravindra 116, James Neesham 58, Daryl Mitchell 54; Adam Zampa 3-74) by five runs.

Australia v Afghanistan at Wankhede Stadium (Mumbai), 7 November

Afghanistan was well-placed to not only upset Australia, but inflict a slaughter. In the end, a performance of a lifetime from Glenn Maxwell catapulted Australia to a scarcely believable three-wicket win.

After becoming the first Afghanistan player to score a World Cup century, opener Ibrahim Zadran finished with 129 not out from 143 balls including eight fours and three sixes. Five of the other top-six batters made scores between 12 and 30, before Rashid Khan belted 35 not out from 18 balls to help Afghanistan to 5-291.

Australia recovered from 1-4 to 1-43 before slumping to 7-91. Another 21 runs were added when Maxwell, on 33, was given a let-off when a simple catch was spilled. Little did anyone know how costly this would be, as Maxwell went on to score 201 not out from 128 balls despite battling cramps. His stupendous innings contained 144 runs in boundaries. With captain Pat Cummins holding firm at the other end, Australia passed the target with 19 balls to spare after Maxwell bashed the final 22 runs in four balls. Cummins made 12 not out from 68 balls in the unbroken partnership of 202 from 170 balls.

Australia 7-293 (Glenn Maxwell 201 not out; Rashid Khan 2-44, Naveen-ul-Haq 2-47) beat Afghanistan 5-291 (Ibrahim Zadran 129 not out, Rashid Khan 35 not out; Josh Hazlewood 2-39) by three wickets.

Fakhar Zaman goes on the attack during his splendid 126 not out in Pakistan's victory against New Zealand in a rain-interrupted fixture.

SIX OF THE BEST: Individual performances

(excluding player of the tournament, and the finals)

Devon Conway 152 not out off 121 balls: New Zealand v England at Narendra Modi Stadium (Ahmedabad), 5 October

In the first match of the tournament, New Zealand made a mockery of England's 9-282 as the Kiwis won by nine wickets and with 13.4 overs to spare. Bizarrely, all of England's batters made double figures while New Zealand's batting comprised a golden duck and two centuries.

Devon Conway began the run chase in style as he drove the first ball between cover and point for four. The over cost 10 runs after the fifth ball was also driven through the off side for a boundary. The second over was a wicket maiden, and the fourth over was a maiden with Conway on strike. The runs quickly began to flow, as Ravindra posted a half-century in 36 balls before fellow left-hander Conway did likewise. Conway reached his hundred in 83 balls before Ravindra achieved the milestone in one less delivery. Conway smashed 20 runs in the 35th over and 11 in the 36th, with Ravindra also hitting five runs in the 36th over before the game finished after a single to each batter in the 37th over. Conway's unbeaten 152 from 121 balls included 19 fours and three sixes, while Ravindra's unbeaten 123 from 96 balls included 11 fours and five sixes.

Aiden Markram 106 off 54 balls: South Africa v Sri Lanka at Arun Jaitley Stadium (Delhi), 7 October

Aiden Markram became the first player to register a World Cup century in fewer than 50 balls as he reached triple figures in 49 balls for South Africa against Sri Lanka.

The Proteas were 2-214 in the 31st over when Markram arrived, following the dismissal of de Kock for 100 off 84 balls. Several overs later, Rassie van der Dussen departed for 108 off 110 balls. While those two centurions were no slouches, they looked

Virat Kohli roars with delight during one of India's victories. Unfortunately for the player of the tournament, things went pear-shaped after he reached a half-century in the final.

slow compared to Markram. After scoring five runs from nine balls, Markram drove a four over mid-off and followed up with three successive fours in the following over.

Markram's eighth four took him to 52 off 34 balls before he reverse-scooped the next ball for another four. Markram slammed 20 runs in the following over which cost 26 runs. Markram had 92 off 47 balls before scything a four through point and then pulling a six to reach his ton. Having recorded 14 fours and three sixes, Markram departed from the 54th ball he faced when he drove a low full-toss to long-off, leaving the Proteas 5-383 after 47.1 overs. South Africa won by 102 runs after tallying 5-428.

Heinrich Klaasen 109 off 67 balls: South Africa v England at Wankhede Stadium (Mumbai), 21 October

South Africa was 3-164 in the 26th over against England, before the arrival of Heinrich Klaasen led to an even larger total than what might have been expected. His speedy 109 included 12 fours and four sixes, while Marco Jansen also fired as South Africa raced to 7-399. England's paltry reply of 170 included a 70-run last-wicket stand in 5.3 overs.

Successive boundaries took Klaasen to 56 off 41 balls, before his first six took him to 64. Klaasen went from 67 to 81 and took South Africa from 5-292 to 5-306 in three balls as two fours were followed by a six over long-off. Klaasen's next six was from a no-ball full-toss, before two singles took him to 90. A yorker from Mark Wood struck Klaasen's left boot and floored him, before the delay was instantly followed by 10 runs in two balls. Klaasen thumped a low full-toss for six before pulling the next ball for four to reach 100 in 61 balls. He registered two more fours before he was bowled by a leg-stump yorker from the first ball of the final over.

Fakhar Zaman 126 not out off 81 balls: Pakistan v New Zealand at M. Chinnaswamy Stadium (Bengaluru), 4 November

Rain spoilt an extremely high-scoring Pakistan versus New Zealand contest, with Pakistan winning by 21 runs according to the DLS method. While there was little point speculating what the result would have been had the game not been weather-affected, there was also little point wondering what Pakistani opener Fakhar Zaman would have scored.

In reply to New Zealand's staggering total of 6-401, Pakistan was 1-6 after two overs before Zaman slashed the second ball of the third over to the boundary. Zaman hit the ball all over the place as he cracked triple figures in 63 deliveries after taking 39 to reach his half-century. On 43 he faced a maiden over from Phillips, before pummelling back-to-back sixes in Phillips's third over. Phillips's fourth over included a six and back-to-back fours which took Zaman to 84, before his ninth six took him to 99. With Zaman's score on 106, play was halted as Pakistan was 1-160 after 21.3 overs. After the delay reduced Pakistan's target to 342 in 41 overs, Zaman struck two giant sixes from consecutive balls in the 25th over. The third ball of the following over turned out to be the last of the game as rain returned, with Pakistan at 1-200. Zaman's innings included eight fours and 11 sixes while Babar Azam's unbeaten 66 featured six fours and two sixes.

Adam Zampa 29 off 19 balls and 10-0-21-3: Australia v England at Narendra Modi Stadium (Ahmedabad), 4 November

With economical bowling becoming a dying breed as totals around 300 became the norm in ODIs, leg-spinner Adam Zampa's figures against England were remarkable. The only runs in his 10 overs were 19 singles off the bat and two wides, while he also claimed three middle-order wickets.

Zampa made a vital 29 off 19 balls at number 10 in Australia's 286-run total, before England lost a wicket first ball. England was 2-44 after 11 overs before Zampa sent down three overs for seven runs. He returned for the 24th over and again conceded seven runs in a three-over spell, while also claiming the wicket of Jos Buttler who skewed a booming drive to long-off.

When Zampa began his third spell, England required 118 runs from 15 overs with six wickets in hand. Zampa struck a huge blow with his third delivery as Ben Stokes swept a catch to short fine leg, and the leg-spinner also broke through in his ninth over as Moeen Ali was caught at deep mid-wicket. Having slid to 7-186, England went on to lose by 33 runs.

INDIA
Genius
MRF
BETTER

South Africa's long-suffering supporters were again left scratching their heads as a World Cup final berth eluded the Proteas once more.

Virat Kohli (India)

Matches	Innings	Not outs	Runs	Highest score	Average	50s	100s	Catches
11	1	3	765	117	95.62	6	3	6
Overs	**Maidens**	**Runs**	**Wickets**	**Average**	**Best figures**			
3.3	-	15	1	15	1-13			

Glenn Maxwell 201 not out off 128 balls: Australia v Afghanistan at Wankhede Stadium (Mumbai), 7 November

Eighteen days after Aiden Markram's 49-ball century, Glenn Maxwell broke the record as he notched triple figures in just 40 balls against the Netherlands. Remarkably, he didn't take strike until the third ball of the 41st over, as the score was 5-273. Maxwell played some crazy looking shots and also feasted on some very poor bowling. After registering his half-century in 27 balls, Maxwell was on 75 with two overs remaining. In the 49th over, back-to-back fours were followed by a hat-trick of sixes, with the last coming from a no-ball full-toss. When Maxwell was caught in the final over, he had smacked nine fours and eight sixes in his 106 off 44 balls. Australia went on to win by a World Cup record-winning 309-run margin after amassing 8-399.

Maxwell reached even superior heights 13 nights later while he lived a charmed life. Chasing 292 against Afghanistan, the Australians were 4-49 in the ninth over when Maxwell faced a hat-trick ball and edged it short of the wicketkeeper. It was not the last time he survived an anxious moment.

Maxwell was involved in the run-out of Marnus Labuschagne, before further wickets left Australia in tatters at 7-91 in the 19th over. Maxwell had 22 runs at this stage, before the 22nd over proved game-changing. Maxwell was adjudged lbw but he had the decision overturned upon review, and later in the over his mistimed sweep was fumbled at short fine leg. Had the straightforward catch been taken, Australia would have been 8-112 with Maxwell out for 33.

Maxwell's seventh four took him to 50 from 51 balls, before he reached his ton in just 76 balls. As Maxwell's supposedly 'mission impossible' situation unfolded, what made his innings more incredible was that he battled cramps and virtually 'batted on one leg' at times. Many of his shots were unconventional and would not be coached or taught, particularly the shots where he swung recklessly without any foot movement. Regardless, his risks and kamikaze approach paid off and made him a hero.

Maxwell had 179 from 123 balls as Australia needed 21 runs in four overs. Following a dot ball, Maxwell smoked back-to-back sixes, a four and another six to win the match with 3.1 overs remaining. His innings included 21 fours and 10 sixes. Meanwhile, Australia's second top score was Mitchell Marsh's 24.

HEADLINE MOMENT

Sri Lankan veteran timed out due to broken helmet strap

Angelo Mathews became the first player to be dismissed 'timed out' in international cricket, as he suffered this extraordinary dismissal in Sri Lanka's three-wicket loss to Bangladesh.

An experienced campaigner, Mathews was given out as he was not ready to face his first ball within the two-minute requirement after the fall of the previous wicket. Mathews prepared to take strike but discovered his helmet strap was broken, and then called for a replacement helmet without consulting the umpires.

While the decision was technically correct, it was debatable as to whether it was in the spirit of the game for Bangladesh to appeal for the wicket. Had Mathews consulted the umpires or Bangladesh captain Shakib Al Hasan, the issue with the helmet may have been resolved amicably and enabled Mathews to start his innings.

Sri Lanka's Angelo Mathews exits the arena after being the first player in international cricket to be timed out.

PLAYER OF THE TOURNAMENT

With India reaching the decider undefeated while Indian hero and cult figure Virat Kohli was named player of the tournament, a World Cup final win on home soil would have been the icing on the cake. Sadly for Kohli and his fellow Indians, the Australians had other ideas.

Kohli's run tally was 168 runs higher than the second placegetter; his captain Rohit Sharma. Kohli's consistency was outstanding as he passed 50 in all bar two of his 11 visits to the crease. India usually enjoyed a strong start from its openers before Kohli batted at number three.

Set just 200 to win its opening clash with Australia, India was 3-2 after losing three batters without scoring. In the eighth over with his score at 12 while India was 3-20, Kohli mistimed a pull and was lucky the regulation catch was spilled. Kohli soon had another narrow escape when he inside-edged the ball wide of the stumps. A bouncer struck him on the helmet when he was on 72, but it didn't seem to faze him as he square drove the next ball to the fence. When he departed, Kohli had scored 85 and helped KL Rahul put India on track for its six-wicket triumph.

Kohli hit a winning four to finish unbeaten on 55 in an eight-wicket win against Afghanistan, after arriving at 1-156 in the 19th over while the target was 273. India subsequently beat Pakistan by seven wickets when the target was a mere 192, with Kohli scoring a quick 16 before exiting with the total at 79. India's next victory was the first of two occasions when Kohli was the player of the match. He conceded two singles in three balls as he completed an over for an injured Hardik Pandya, before starting his innings at 1-88 in the 13th over as India chased 257 against Bangladesh. His 103 not out came from 97 balls and included six fours and four sixes. Kohli raised his ton and the winning runs with a six over mid-wicket from a full-toss in the 42nd over. Kohli found himself in a similar situation against New Zealand, as his score was 95 while India was five runs shy of its 274-run target. He attempted to hit another six over mid-wicket, but this time he was caught in the deep. Two balls later, India secured a four-wicket win.

Kohli made a rare duck in his next outing as he hit a catch to mid-off. His departure left the Indians 2-27, before they tallied 9-229 and trounced England by 100 runs. Kohli returned to form with 11 fours in a fine 88 against Sri Lanka, after arriving in the first over. He had a lucky escape on 10 when a return catch was muffed, before he helped set up India's 8-357. After dismissing Sri Lanka for a miserable 55, India followed up with a 243-run demolition of South Africa. India was 1-62 in the sixth over when Kohli arrived, and he batted until the end as he made a superb 101 not out from 121 balls in the total of 5-326. He not only won the player of the match award on his 35th birthday, but also levelled Sachin Tendulkar's figure of 49 ODI centuries.

Against the Netherlands, Kohli arrived at 1-100 in the 12th over and departed for 51 in the 29th over with the total on 200. India topped 400 before Dutch captain Scott Edwards was caught behind down the legside off Kohli, who claimed 1-13 in three overs in India's 160-run win. In the semi-final, Kohli notched his 50th ODI century as he scored 117 although he was somewhat overshadowed by Shreyas Iyer whose 105 came at a notably faster rate. With India falling just shy of 400 and then beating New Zealand by 70 runs, Kohli and his teammates had stormed into the final. Kohli's departure for 54 was one of several setbacks for India in the decider, and ultimately the home side's total of 240 was insufficient.

FIRST SEMI-FINAL

India v New Zealand at Wankhede Stadium (Mumbai), 15 November

The host nation maintained its momentum as a total just below 400 proved well beyond New Zealand's reach even though the Kiwis passed 300. In such a high-scoring contest it was interesting that the player of the match award went to a bowler.

The tone was set as Rohit Sharma cracked back-to-back fours in the opening over before Shubman Gill repeated the dose in the second over. Sharma hit four fours and four sixes before falling for 47 off 29 balls as he skied a slower ball. Gill raced to 79 before retiring hurt in the 23rd over, and then Kohli and Iyer piled on the runs. Kohli scored 117 off 113 balls, and Iyer reached 100 off just 67 balls. Rahul crunched 39 not out from just 20 balls, including 14 runs from the final four balls of the innings, while Gill returned in the final over following the fall of the fourth wicket.

Conway hit the first and third balls of the run chase to the fence, but New Zealand's openers scored only 13 runs each. A 181-run stand between Daryl Mitchell and captain Kane Williamson took the Kiwis to 2-220, before the score became 4-220 in the 33rd over. The run chase fizzled despite Mitchell making 134, with his dismissal leaving the Kiwis 7-306 in the 46th over. Mohammed Shami finished the match with his seventh wicket, after Lockie Ferguson hit the previous ball for six.

India 4-397 (Virat Kohli 117, Shreyas Iyer 105, Shubman Gill 80 not out; Tim Southee 3-100) beat New Zealand 327 (Daryl Mitchell 134, Kane Williamson 69; Mohammed Shami 7-57) by 70 runs.

SECOND SEMI-FINAL

South Africa v Australia at Eden Gardens (Kolkata), 16 November

The Proteas fought back from a horror start to their own innings and Australia's innings, but alas it wasn't enough. South Africa's long-suffering supporters were again left scratching their heads as a World Cup final berth eluded the Proteas once more.

After winning the toss, Bavuma departed without scoring as he edged the final ball of the opening over to the wicketkeeper. Starc and Hazlewood wrecked the top order as South Africa fell to 4-24 in the 12th over, before the left-handed David Miller edged the final ball of the over to the boundary. The score was 4-44 after 14 overs when rain halted play, but there was no reduction in overs.

Miller and Klaasen led the revival, with the latter hitting successive sixes off Zampa in the 27th over before hitting successive fours off Head in the 31st over. But later in the 31st over, Head dislodged Klaasen's leg-stump and then trapped Jansen first ball as the Proteas went from 4-119 to 6-119. Despite Miller going on to make 101 off 116 balls, including eight fours and five sixes, South Africa was dismissed for an unimpressive 212 with two balls remaining.

With 15 runs in the fifth over and 21 in the sixth, Australia raced to 0-60 before Markram bowled Warner with his first delivery. A brilliant catch from van der Dussen snared Mitchell Marsh for a duck, but Hendricks dropped a tough chance which Head offered with the total on 77. Head subsequently slammed a hat-trick of fours in the same over, and he had another reprieve a couple of overs later before Maharaj's first ball rattled his stumps to leave Australia 3-106. Shamsi accounted for Labuschagne and Maxwell to make things interesting at 5-137, and the next wicket fell at 174 as Steve Smith played a rash shot. Josh Inglis's dismissal left Australia needing 20 runs from 61 balls, and there were a few anxious moments before Cummins hit the winning runs with 16 balls to spare.

Australia 7-215 (Travis Head 62, Steve Smith 30; Tabraiz Shamsi 2-42, Gerald Coetzee 2-47) beat South Africa 212 (David Miller 101, Heinrich Klaasen 47; Mitchell Starc 3-34, Pat Cummins 3-51) by three wickets.

FINAL

India v Australia at Narendra Modi Stadium (Ahmedabad), 19 November

The stunned silence that engulfed the crowd of 92,453 with the fall of each Indian wicket was a defining aspect of the World Cup final. It simply wasn't India's day (or night), after the Indians had not put a foot wrong throughout the tournament. The Australians meanwhile showed why they were still the envy of other cricketing nations. Warner, Smith, Maxwell, Starc and Hazlewood backed up from Australia's 2015 triumph, while Kohli was the only Indian to back up from its 2011 triumph.

The stunned silence that engulfed the crowd of 92,453 with the fall of each Indian wicket was a defining aspect of the World Cup final.

After losing the toss and being invited to bat, Sharma gave the hosts a flying start before Gill departed in the fifth over. Three successive fours from Kohli raised India's 50 in the seventh over, before the 10th over contained 14 runs and a huge wicket. After hitting Maxwell for a six and a four, Sharma sought his third boundary in as many deliveries and skewed the ball high where Head took a splendid catch. India stumbled to 3-81 in the next over as Iyer edged Cummins behind.

Kohli and Rahul produced a recovery, but Australia's fielding was sharp while there was an incredible 97-ball boundary drought following the 10th over. Kohli passed 50 before he chopped a Cummins delivery onto the stumps, leaving the hosts 4-148 in the 29th over. Rahul faced 107 balls for his 66 and was one of five batters caught by wicketkeeper Inglis. India was restricted to 240, with the last-wicket partnership of 14 ending with a run-out from the final ball as the last pair sought a second run.

Australia had an electric start as the first two overs contained 28 runs and a wicket. Warner edged the first ball through the slips cordon for four, and drove the next ball for three before Head flayed the fourth and sixth balls to the fence. Warner was caught at slip from Shami's second ball, before the remainder of the over was expensive. Mitchell Marsh thumped a six in Shami's next over which cost 12 runs, but then Jasprit Bumrah bowled a maiden which included the wicket of Marsh to a catch behind. Australia was 3-47 after seven overs as Bumrah trapped Smith lbw, although Smith would have survived had he sought a review as replays suggested he was struck outside off-stump.

There were no runs off the bat for the next 14 deliveries before Head hit two successive fours, which were followed by a boundary drought lasting six overs. Australia still reached 100 in the 20th over, and then gained control as Head produced a wonderful 137 off 120 balls. Head hit 15 fours and four sixes, while Labuschagne provided the perfect supporting role with 58 not out from 110 balls. Interestingly, Labuschagne wasn't in Australia's squad for the tournament until an injured Ashton Agar withdrew, before Head missed Australia's first five games due to injury. Another interesting fact was Richard Illingworth becoming the second person to play and umpire a World Cup final, having played for England in 1992.

Victory was just two runs away when Head pulled a catch to deep mid-wicket from the fifth ball of the 43rd over, leaving Maxwell to hit the winning runs from the following delivery.

India

India		R	B
Rohit Sharma (c)	c Head b Maxwell	47	31
Shubman Gill	c Zampa b Starc	4	7
Virat Kohli	b Cummins	54	63
Shreyas Iyer	c Inglis b Cummins	4	3
KL Rahul (+)	c Inglis b Starc	66	107
Ravindra Jadeja	c Inglis b Hazlewood	9	22
Suryakumar Yadav	c Inglis b Hazlewood	18	28
Mohammed Shami	c Inglis b Starc	6	10
Jasprit Bumrah	lbw b Zampa	1	3
Kuldeep Yadav	run out (Labuschagne/Cummins)	10	18
Mohammed Siraj	not out	9	8
Sundries	(lb 3, w 9)	12	
TOTAL	**(50 overs) 240**		

FALL: 30, 76, 81, 148, 178, 203, 211, 214, 226, 240

Starc 10-0-55-3, Hazlewood 10-0-60-2, Maxwell 6-0-35-1, Cummins 10-0-34-2, Zampa 10-0-44-1, Marsh 2-0-5-0, Head 2-0-4-0

Australia

Australia		R	B
David Warner	c Kohli b Shami	7	3
Travis Head	c Gill b Siraj	137	120
Mitchell Marsh	c Rahul b Bumrah	15	15
Steve Smith	lbw b Bumrah	4	9
Marnus Labuschagne	not out	58	110
Glenn Maxwell	not out	2	1
Sundries	(b 5, lb 2, w 11)	18	
TOTAL	**(43 overs) 4-241**		

DID NOT BAT: Josh Inglis (+), Mitchell Starc, Pat Cummins (c), Adam Zampa, Josh Hazlewood

FALL: 16, 41, 47, 239

Bumrah 9-2-43-2, Shami 7-1-47-1, Jadeja 10-0-43-0, Yadav 10-0-56-0, Siraj 7-0-45-1

UMPIRES: Richard Illingworth, Richard Kettleborough (TV: Joel Wilson)

TOSS: Australia

PLAYER OF THE MATCH: Travis Head

AUSTRALIA WON BY SIX WICKETS

T20 WORLD CUP

NOKIA
SAHARA
INDIA
2007

India pips arch-rival in inaugural T20 World Cup decider

The first T20 World Cup took place only six months after the 50 overs per side World Cup. Officially the ICC World Twenty20, the new tournament featured 12 teams which were divided into four groups. The nine Test playing nations were automatic inclusions, and Zimbabwe was also included despite its Test status being suspended from late 2005 to 2011 due to poor results. Kenya and Scotland filled the other two spots after they contested the final of the 2007 ICC World Cricket League Division One tournament.

Kenya was no match for Sri Lanka and New Zealand in Group C, while Scotland's only competition point came from a washout in Group D which also featured India and Pakistan. South Africa and Bangladesh were the top-two teams in Group A while West Indies bowed out with back-to-back losses, and Zimbabwe finished last in Group B on net run rate after Zimbabwe, Australia and England had one win apiece.

The top-two teams in each group progressed to the Super 8s, which featured two groups of four. India and New Zealand progressed while South Africa and England were eliminated in Group E, while Pakistan and Australia advanced at the expense of Sri Lanka and Bangladesh in Group F.

After winning their respective semi-finals, arch-rivals India and Pakistan contested a memorable final which went down to the wire. It was clear that World Cup cricket had a long-term future in the 20 overs per side format, regardless of the 50 overs per side format.

One distinct feature of this inaugural T20 World Cup was that a tied match would be decided by a 'bowl-out' – resembling a soccer penalty shoot-out – with bowlers required to hit the stumps.

A HAT-TRICK OF CLASSICS: Three great contests

Australia v Zimbabwe at Newlands Cricket Ground (Cape Town), 12 September

Zimbabwe's win over Australia in the first T20 World Cup was perhaps as much of a shock as the result when the countries first met in the 1983 World Cup.

Australia sank to 3-19 before an ensuing recovery hit a hurdle as Michael Hussey was superbly run out by Vusi Sibanda. Wickets continued to fall regularly, and Zimbabwe needed to score at nearly seven runs per over.

A series of boundaries took place before a skied catch left Zimbabwe 2-54 after seven overs. The Africans were 4-74 and needing 65 runs from 49 balls when rain caused a stoppage. Brendan Taylor whacked two sixes in the 15th over, reducing

The Indians celebrate winning the first World Cup in the T20 format, after holding on for a narrow victory against arch-rival Pakistan in the decider.

the requirement to 37 runs in five overs before 12 were needed from the final over. Taylor hit the first ball for four before four leg byes sealed Zimbabwe's triumph with one ball to spare.

Zimbabwe 5-139 (Brendan Taylor 60 not out; Stuart Clark 2-22) beat Australia 9-138 (Brad Hodge 35 not out, Andrew Symonds 33; Elton Chigumbura 3-20, Gary Brent 2-19) by five wickets.

India v Pakistan at Kingsmead (Durban), 14 September

A 'bowl-out' was required after India and Pakistan couldn't be separated in the first 40 overs. India flopped to 4-36 in the seventh over before the remainder of the innings was repeatedly disrupted by rain. Robin Uthappa, MS Dhoni and Irfan Pathan helped set Pakistan a target of 142, with the wet weather delaying the start of the run chase.

Two wickets in a maiden over left Pakistan 4-47 after nine overs, before the next wicket left Pakistan needing 55 runs in five overs. Following Shahid Afridi's exit, 27 runs in the next eight balls meant 12 were needed from the final over. Pakistan seemed assured of victory as the scores were level with two balls left, but a dot ball and a run-out kept the scores equal. India subsequently hit the stumps three times in the 'bowl-out' while Pakistan's bowlers were unable to find the target.

India 9-141 (Robin Uthappa 50, MS Dhoni 33; Mohammad Asif 4-18) tied with Pakistan 7-141 (Misbah-ul-Haq 53; Irfan Pathan 2-20) before India won the bowl-out.

New Zealand v England at Kingsmead (Durban), 18 September

The Kiwis were reeling at 4-31 before Craig McMillan and Scott Styris hit four sixes each as they faced 31 balls apiece. New Zealand topped 160 after registering 124 runs in the final 11 overs, before England's openers put on 62 in 7.5 overs. Regular breakthroughs left England 5-104 and needing 61 runs from 38 balls, before Owais Shah and Luke Wright reduced the task to 20 runs in two overs. The penultimate over featured three wickets and just four runs, before Chris Schofield and Stuart Broad scored only singles and twos in the final over. Nine runs were needed from two balls, with another single followed by another two despite successive full-tosses.

New Zealand 9-164 (Craig McMillan 57, Scott Styris 42; Darren Maddy 2-6) beat England 8-159 (Darren Maddy 50; Shane Bond and Daniel Vettori 2-20) by five runs.

SIX OF THE BEST: Individual performances

(excluding player of the tournament, and the finals)

Chris Gayle 117 off 57 balls: West Indies v South Africa at Wanderers Stadium (Johannesburg), 11 September

West Indian opener Chris Gayle was at his destructive best against the Proteas in the first match. He slapped the opening delivery through point for four, and went on to reach 50 in just 26 balls before raising his ton in 50 balls. Gayle's innings featured seven fours and 10 sixes, before he exited with 22 balls left to leave West Indies 3-178.

Herschelle Gibbs 90 not out off 55 balls: South Africa v West Indies at Wanderers Stadium (Johannesburg), 11 September

South Africa overhauled the West Indian total of 6-205 with 14 balls to spare, and for the loss of only two wickets. Proteas opener Herschelle Gibbs batted the whole way through as he hammered 14 fours and two sixes, after taking five balls to score his first run. Dropped at 20 and 43, Gibbs made his opponents pay the price.

Mohammad Asif 4-18 off four overs: India v Pakistan at Kingsmead (Durban), 14 September

Pakistan opening bowler Mohammad Asif's only spell in the tied match against India left the Indians reeling at 4-36 after seven overs. Asif took a brilliant return

One distinct feature of this inaugural T20 World Cup was that a tied match would be decided by a 'bowl-out'.

catch to dismiss Gautam Gambhir with the third ball of the game, before Virender Sehwag inside-edged the first ball of the third over into his stumps. Asif also struck with the first ball of the fifth over as Yuvraj Singh was caught off a leading edge, before his third-last delivery accounted for Dinesh Karthik as the ball ricocheted onto the wicket from a deflection.

Morne Morkel 4-17 off four overs: South Africa v New Zealand at Kingsmead (Durban), 19 September

Morne Morkel conceded 10 runs in his first seven balls as the Kiwis reached 0-68 in 8.1 overs, before they finished the ninth over at 2-70 after two victims edged Morkel deliveries to the wicketkeeper. Morkel later returned to bowl the 17th and 19th overs and claimed a wicket in each, with Jacob Oram bowled as he took a swing before Shane Bond became another caught-behind victim as Mark Boucher held a sharp catch. Chasing 154, the Proteas won by six wickets.

Yuvraj Singh 58 off 16 balls: India v England at Kingsmead (Durban), 19 September

Yuvraj Singh needed only 16 deliveries and 14 minutes to slam 58 runs. Three fours helped him to 14 runs off six balls before he became the first player in a T20 international to hit six sixes in an over. Stuart Broad was the unfortunate bowler. Yuvraj subsequently hit Andrew Flintoff for six in the final over before being caught at long-on. Yuvraj's heroics helped India to 4-218, before England replied with 6-200.

RP Singh 4-13 off four overs: India v South Africa at Kingsmead (Durban), 20 September

South Africa fell 38 runs shy of its 154-run target against India, largely due to RP Singh's opening spell which produced 3-11 in three overs. He reduced the Proteas to 2-12 in the second over, after 11 runs came from the first over. Singh trapped Gibbs lbw with his first ball, before his fourth ball accounted for Graeme Smith as Karthik held a superb slips catch. In Singh's third over, a cracking delivery uprooted Shaun Pollock's leg-stump to leave the Proteas 5-31. The left-arm bowler was later brought back for the 19th over, which featured the wicket of Albie Morkel who was bowled as he sought a boundary.

Shahid Afridi (Pakistan)

Matches	Innings	Not outs	Runs	Highest score	Average	50s	100s	Catches
7	6	-	91	3	15.17	-	-	2

Overs	Maidens	Runs	Wickets	Average	Best figures
28	1	188	12	15.67	4-19

PLAYER OF THE TOURNAMENT

Known as an explosive batter, Shahid Afridi had much more success with his leg-spin bowling in the first T20 World Cup as his batting average was remarkably similar to his bowling average.

Afridi was player of the match as Pakistan began with a 51-run win against Scotland. After hitting two sixes and a four in his 22 off seven balls, Afridi claimed 4-19 as Scotland's batters from four to seven were caught off his bowling. In the tied match against India, Afridi's two victims were bowled while he conceded 37 runs in his four overs, before being dismissed for seven. Against Sri Lanka, Afridi hit a quick 17 before claiming 3-18 in a 33-run victory.

Afridi's first over cost 13 runs before his last over cost 15 against Australia, but he also achieved a rare wicket maiden. Incidentally, Kamran Akmal conceded a bye as he missed the chance to stump Ricky Ponting, before Andrew Symonds was bowled next ball. Afridi wasn't required to bat as Pakistan won the match by six wickets, chasing 165.

After winning an lbw appeal and achieving tidy figures of 1-25 against Bangladesh, Afridi was promoted to open the innings as Pakistan sought a target of 141. He slammed five fours and two sixes in his 39 off 15 balls, before his exit made the score 2-66 after seven overs. The platform was laid for the four-wicket victory, before he returned to the middle order for the finals. In the semi-final against New Zealand, Afridi had another lbw appeal upheld as he claimed 1-24. He fell for just six, as the Pakistanis coasted to a six-wicket win. The final against India was certainly not Afridi's day, as he took 0-30 in his four overs before perishing for a golden duck as he skied a catch to deep mid-off. After being named 'player of the tournament' following Pakistan's narrow defeat in the decider, Afridi said: 'I struggled a bit with my batting but I concentrated on my bowling.'

FIRST SEMI-FINAL

Pakistan v New Zealand at Newlands Cricket Ground (Cape Town), 22 September

As was the case in the 1992 and 1999 World Cup semi-finals (of the 50-over type), New Zealand's bowlers could not contain the Pakistanis in a run chase. The Kiwis were 0-44 after 6.2 overs when rain caused a delay, and then the 50-run stand was raised before the first wicket fell next ball. Two wickets fell in the 14th over with the total in the 80s, and then Craig McMillan raised the 100 with a six in the next over but lofted a catch just two balls later. Ross Taylor took 14 runs from the first three balls of the final over but only three runs were scored from the final three balls, and the target of 144 was far from formidable.

Pakistani opener Imran Nazir hit five sixes in his 59, before he exited in the 13th over to make the score 2-96. There were a couple more hiccups as the Pakistanis found themselves 4-111, but the required run rate was very manageable. Shoaib Malik sealed the result with seven balls remaining as he hit a six, after a difficult catch was missed from the previous ball.

Pakistan 4-147 (Imran Nazir 59, Mohammad Hafeez 32; Scott Styris 1-14) beat New Zealand 8-143 (Ross Taylor 37 not out; Umar Gul 3-15, Fawad Alam 2-29) by six wickets.

SECOND SEMI-FINAL

India v Australia at Kingsmead (Durban), 22 September

The second semi-final was a classic contest that wasn't decided until the dying stages, while there were plenty of runs and tension throughout. India

South Africa's Justin Kemp goes on the attack against New Zealand's Jacob Oram.

INDIA
PEPSI
RbK
RbK

was 2-41 after eight overs before Yuvraj turned the game as he slammed five fours and five sixes in his 70 off 30 balls. Yuvraj shared a third-wicket stand of 84 with Uthappa and a 30-run fourth wicket stand with MS Dhoni, who went on to score 36 off 18 balls. Four leg byes from the final ball boosted Australia's target to 189.

Two leg byes were the only runs in the fourth over of the run chase, before the next over cost 17 runs. The sixth over yielded one wicket and one run, before 18 runs in the eighth over took the total to 1-64. Brad Hodge departed in the ninth over, before three sixes in five balls reduced the requirement to 63 from 41 balls. The return of Sreesanth for the 15th over was massive as he yorked Matthew Hayden, before the next two overs cost 13 and 11 runs for the loss of Symonds. With Australia needing 30 runs off three overs, Harbhajan Singh made a priceless breakthrough as he bowled Michael Clarke. Michael Hussey and Brad Haddin were unusually tied down, and dot balls from the first two deliveries in the final over left Australia needing 22 runs from four balls. Two wickets for two runs in three balls were followed by a belated boundary from the final ball.

India 5-188 (Yuvraj Singh 70, MS Dhoni 36; Mitchell Johnson 2-31) beat Australia 7-173 (Matthew Hayden 62, Andrew Symonds 43; Sreesanth 2-12, Joginder Sharma 2-37) by 15 runs.

FINAL

India v Pakistan at Wanderers Stadium
(Johannesburg), 24 September

The first T20 World Cup final was a cracker as another India and Pakistan showdown produced another thrilling spectacle. As India missed an injured Virender Sehwag, four of its top-five batters were dismissed for 15 or less while Gambhir blazed away with 75 at the top of the order. Gambhir's dismissal left India 5-130 with two overs left, before an assault from Rohit Sharma resulted in 27 runs in the final two overs.

Two of Pakistan's first three batters failed, before Imran Nazir was crucially run out after creaming 33 runs from 14 balls. The first-ball dismissal of Afridi was a savage blow to Pakistan's hopes, and the result seemed a formality when the fall of the seventh wicket left Pakistan needing 54 runs in four overs. Misbah-ul-Haq had other ideas as he cleared the rope three times in the 17th over before Sohail Tanvir hit two sixes in the 18th over, only to be bowled from the final ball of the over. A wicket from the fifth ball of the 19th over was followed by a four next ball, meaning 13 runs were needed from the final over with one wicket remaining. A six from a full-toss reduced the task to six runs from four balls, but then Misbah erred as a premeditated scoop shot lobbed straight to fine leg. The Indians were ecstatic while the Pakistanis – as it turned out – were destined to go one better next time.

India 5-157 (Gautam Gambhir 75, Rohit Sharma 30 not out; Umar Gul 3-28) beat Pakistan 152 (Misbah-ul-Haq 43, Imran Nazir 33; Irfan Pathan 3-16, RP Singh 3-26) by five runs.

Pakistan's Yasir Arafat is bowled by Irfan Pathan during the final, while India's captain and wicketkeeper MS Dhoni looks on.

2009

Pakis prevail in another all-Asian decider

Staged only two years after the inaugural T20 World Cup, the 2009 tournament had a similar format although Zimbabwe was excluded for political reasons. The groups were reshuffled while Ireland and the Netherlands were included, as Kenya dropped out in addition to Zimbabwe.

India, Ireland, England, Pakistan, Sri Lanka, West Indies, South Africa and New Zealand progressed from the group stage to the Super 8s while Bangladesh, the Netherlands, Australia and Scotland did not. Australia lost both of its matches to Sri Lanka and West Indies in Group C. India, Ireland, England and New Zealand missed the semi-finals, before South Africa and West Indies bowed out one game short of the final. Yet again the decider featured two Asian teams, with Pakistan going one better than the previous time.

The method to decide a winner in the event of a tie had changed, as the 'bowl out' was replaced with the 'Super Over'.

A HAT-TRICK OF CLASSICS: Three great contests

England v Netherlands at Lord's (London), 5 June

The final over was chaotic to say the least, while the outcome was decided from the final ball amid incredible tension.

Astonishingly there were no sixes in England's innings, but a huge total beckoned as the score was 0-100 after 11 overs. Five wickets fell for only 62 runs in the remaining overs as the Netherlands bowlers improved, before England produced sub-standard fielding as several run-out opportunities were squandered. The Netherlands lost a wicket in its first over before Darron Reekers hit a six in each of the next two overs, only to exit in the fourth. A stumping left the score 3-66 after 8.1 overs, before it motored to 3-99 after 11 overs. Rain began to fall, and it was heavy when the fifth wicket left the Netherlands needing 30 runs in four overs. Play continued uninterrupted, however, and 10 runs from the penultimate over meant just seven were needed from six balls with four wickets in hand. Five successive singles took place, albeit with a run-out chance butchered from the first ball followed by a dropped catch from the third ball and a bye from the fourth ball. Stuart Broad had the chance to win the match for England as he fielded the final ball in his follow through, but his throw missed the stumps and also enabled the batters to run an overthrow and steal victory.

Netherlands 6-163 (Tom de Grooth 49, Peter Borren 30; James Anderson 3-23) beat England 5-162 (Luke Wright 71, Ravi Bopara 46; Ryan ten Doeschate 2-35) by four wickets.

The Pakistanis celebrate winning the second instalment of the T20 World Cup.

One of the few to play international cricket for Ireland and England, Boyd Rankin, bowls for Ireland.

South Africa v New Zealand at Lord's (London), 9 June

The match was decided by the smallest margin as all three results were possible with one ball left. Batting first, South Africa was 0-49 after seven overs before stumbling to 4-65 in the 13th over. Ian Butler, Nathan McCullum and Scott Styris had combined figures of 4-41 from 10 overs, while New Zealand's other three bowlers were not so tidy as the Proteas tallied a modest 7-128.

The Kiwis were 0-19 after two overs before falling to 2-26 just nine balls later, followed by a 56-run stand. Brendon McCullum scored a half-century but New Zealand never gained control, and the dismissal of the captain left the Kiwis needing 36 runs in three overs with six wickets in hand. The 19th over cost 12 runs, including four byes from a Dale Steyn yorker which comically kicked up over the wicketkeeper. Fifteen runs were needed from the final over, with a single to Styris followed by three twos and then a streaky inside-edged four to Jacob Oram. Needing another four from the final ball, Oram could only manage two before being run out. Jacques Kallis must have been relieved, having dropped a tough chance from the fourth ball of the over.

South Africa 7-128 (Graeme Smith 33, JP Duminy 29; Ian Butler 2-13) beat New Zealand 5-127 (Brendon McCullum 57; Roelof van der Merwe 2-14) by one run.

England v India at Lord's (London), 14 June

The English held their nerve, while the Indians were left to wonder 'what if' as their hopes of back-to-back titles were shattered.

England was merely 1-4 after two overs before Kevin Pietersen hit 46 off 27 balls at number three. Pietersen's dismissal left the score 3-92 with seven overs left, before the hundred was raised two overs later. The subsequent four overs yielded 2-43, before Harbhajan Singh captured two wickets in two balls in the final over. This was followed by three runs off the bat and then five crucial runs from a wide, due to poor fielding at short fine leg. Despite an ensuing dot ball, eight runs from the final two legitimate balls had boosted England's total to 153.

India was only 2-59 at the halfway stage, before the 11th over featured the third wicket. Yuvraj Singh hit two sixes but faced only nine balls, and was one of two dismissals in one over which left India needing 67 runs from six overs with five wickets in hand. Nineteen runs were needed from the final over, before a six from Yusuf Pathan left a requirement of nine from two balls. A single killed their campaign, before a last-ball four made the result look all the more agonising for the reigning champions.

England 7-153 (Kevin Pietersen 46, Ravi Bopara 37; Harbhajan Singh 3-30, Ravindra Jadeja 2-26) beat India 5-150 (Yusuf Pathan 33 not out, MS Dhoni 30 not out; Graeme Swann 2-28, Ryan Sidebottom 2-31) by three runs.

SIX OF THE BEST: Individual performances

(excluding player of the tournament, and the finals)

Dwayne Bravo goes on the attack for West Indies against Sri Lanka.

Chris Gayle 88 off 50 balls: West Indies v Australia at The Oval (London), 6 June

Chasing 170, West Indies won by seven wickets and with 25 balls to spare after Chris Gayle blasted six fours and six sixes. He struck the first ball of the run chase wide of mid-off before cutting the third ball for another four. Brett Lee was the bowler. In Lee's third over, the left-hander smashed three sixes and two fours. After reaching his 50 off 23 balls, Gayle's remaining 38 runs included three sixes and no fours. Victory was 13 runs away while Gayle was 12 runs short of a ton, when he skied a catch off Lee. Meanwhile, Gayle's opening partner Andre Fletcher had belted 53 off 32 balls.

AB de Villiers 79 not out off 34 balls: South Africa v Scotland at The Oval (London), 7 June

South Africa was 2-88 after 10 overs when AB de Villiers arrived, before he registered five fours and six sixes to set up a match-winning total of 5-211. He had 18 off 13 balls, before turning up the heat. He tallied 10 runs from the final two balls of the 17th over, and did likewise from the second and third balls of the 19th over. In the final over, de Villiers notched 16 runs which included back-to-back sixes.

Sanath Jayasuriya 81 off 47 balls: Sri Lanka v West Indies at Trent Bridge (Nottingham), 10 June

Twenty days shy of his 40th birthday, Sanath Jayasuriya could still be as destructive as ever. After scoring two singles off four balls in the first over, Jayasuriya hit 17 runs in the second over. He posted his 50 from his 29th delivery before hitting a six, a single and three successive fours in the 10th over. Having recorded 10 fours and three sixes, Jayasuriya exited in the 13th over to leave Sri Lanka 1-124. The eventual total of 5-192 was too much for West Indies.

Dwayne Bravo 4-38 off four overs and 66 not out off 36 balls: West Indies v India at Lord's (London), 12 June

Dwayne Bravo's all-round display helped West Indies beat India by seven wickets and with eight balls to spare. Having bowled the fifth, 13th, 15th and 20th overs, he claimed a wicket with his second and seventh deliveries, before striking with the first and third balls of the final over. Bravo's figures could have been better, but a catch was dropped in his second over before his third cost 16 runs. Furthermore, Harbhajan dispatched the final three balls of the innings to the boundary to lift the total beyond 150.

Batting at number four, Bravo arrived at 2-42 in the eighth over. He raced to 28 off 20 balls before the third wicket fell at 100 in the 15th over. Undeterred, Bravo hit the next ball for a straight six. The requirement was 39 runs in four overs before the 17th over cost 16 runs, following another six from Bravo. Moments later he raised his 50 from 29 balls, before he registered the winning runs as he smoked a low full-toss over extra cover for six.

Umar Gul 5-6 off three overs: Pakistan v New Zealand at The Oval (London), 13 June

Umar Gul became the first bowler to capture a five-wicket haul in a T20 international, as New Zealand succumbed for 99 in 18.3 overs before Pakistan

South Africa's lone defeat of the tournament ended its title hopes.

Tillakaratne Dilshan (Sri Lanka)

Matches	Innings	Not outs	Runs	Highest score	Average	50s	100s	Catches
7	7	1	317	96*	52.83	3	-	3

Overs	Maidens	Runs	Wickets	Average	Best figures
1	-	11	-	-	-

prevailed by six wickets. The Kiwis were 4-72 after 12 overs before Gul, as Pakistan's sixth and final bowler, captured 2-1 in his first over. Shahid Afridi held a great running catch to remove Scott Styris, and Peter McGlashan was lbw next ball as he attempted a sweep. After changing ends, Gul uprooted Nathan McCullum's leg-stump. In his third over, Gul again struck from consecutive deliveries. James Franklin was bowled, before Kyle Mills was caught at cover off a leading edge.

Wayne Parnell 4-13 off four overs: South Africa v West Indies at The Oval (London), 13 June

Wayne Parnell had spells of 2-0-3-2 and 2-0-10-2 as the Proteas defended their total of 7-183 against West Indies. In the second over of the run chase, Parnell struck Andre Fletcher's off-stump as a wild swing failed to connect. From the first ball of his next over, Parnell claimed the prized scalp of Gayle who smacked a catch to mid-wicket. Parnell's next over was the 18th of the innings, with Kieron Pollard chipping a low full-toss to cover before a yorker removed Jerome Taylor's off-peg.

PLAYER OF THE TOURNAMENT

Sri Lankan opener Tillakaratne Dilshan was in ominous form apart from two occasions, when he was dismissed without scoring. Unfortunately for him, the latter occasion was in the final which Sri Lanka lost to Pakistan.

Dilshan began in style as his 53 off 32 balls – including 10 fours – helped Sri Lanka to a six-wicket win over Australia as the target was 160. In Sri Lanka's next game, Dilshan made 74 while opening partner Jayasuriya scored 81 as they faced 47 deliveries each against West Indies. Dilshan was on 38 off 29 when Jayasuriya departed, before Dilshan finished with 11 fours and one six in the 15-run triumph. In a 19-run win against Pakistan, Dilshan was player of the match for his 46 off 39 in Sri Lanka's total of 7-150.

Dilshan top-edged a pull shot and was out to the second ball of Sri Lanka's clash with Ireland, which went down by nine runs after Sri Lanka made 9-144. Dilshan returned to form with 48 off 37 in a 48-run thumping of New Zealand, before scoring a magnificent 96 not out in the semi-final against West Indies. Alas, Dilshan came crashing back to earth in the final.

FIRST SEMI-FINAL

Pakistan v South Africa at Trent Bridge (Nottingham), 18 June

South Africa's lone defeat of the tournament ended its title hopes, as superb batting and bowling from Shahid Afridi was hugely decisive. He slammed 51 runs off 34 balls before capturing 2-16 from four overs.

Pakistan's Kamran Akmal slashed two fours in the first over, before the second over featured a wicket and 14 runs. Akmal hit a six in the third over but was out next ball, and Pakistan moved to 2-68 at the 10-over mark before Afridi hit four successive fours. Afridi's dismissal left the team 3-95 with 47 balls left. There were no boundaries in the final five overs which yielded only 29 runs.

Twenty days shy of his 40th birthday, Sanath Jayasuriya could still be as destructive as ever.

New Zealand's James Franklin flicks the ball behind square.

Chasing 150, the Proteas were 0-40 in the sixth over before losing 2-6 in eight balls, and then stumbling further as Afridi bowled AB de Villiers for one. The requirement was 77 runs from seven overs before becoming 52 from five. Jacques Kallis's departure left South Africa needing 39 runs from 17 balls, before the second-last over merely featured six singles. The requirement of 23 runs in one over was too steep despite a six from the second ball. Sixteen runs were needed in three balls before JP Duminy hit a two, a boundary and another two to make the result appear tight.

Pakistan 4-149 (Shahid Afridi 51, Shoaib Malik 34; JP Duminy 1-14) beat South Africa 5-142 (Jacques Kallis 64, JP Duminy 44 not out; Shahid Afridi 2-16) by seven runs.

SECOND SEMI-FINAL

Sri Lanka v West Indies at The Oval (London), 19 June

An opener from each team batted brilliantly, while the rest of the batting left much to be desired. The player of the tournament, Dilshan, finished four agonising runs shy of a ton as he faced 57 balls. His opening partner, Jayasuriya, scored just 24 before Sri Lanka fell from 0-73 to 3-77. A 50-run stand was followed by another two quick wickets, before 24 runs were scored from the final nine balls while Angelo Mathews contributed 12 from four. Dilshan scored two from the last delivery when he needed a six to reach triple figures.

Incredibly, Mathews struck three times in the first over of the run chase as three batters were bowled off deflections. Gayle carried his bat as he hammered an unbeaten 63 off 50 balls, but none of his teammates passed nine as Sri Lanka's five bowlers shared the wickets. The West Indians were a long way short of the target when the match ended with 14 balls to spare.

Sri Lanka 5-158 (Tillakaratne Dilshan 96 not out; Dwayne Bravo 2-32) beat West Indies 101 (Chris Gayle 63 not out; Angelo Mathews 3-16, Muttiah Muralidaran 3-29, Ajantha Mendis 2-9) by 57 runs.

FINAL

Sri Lanka v Pakistan at Lord's (London), 21 June

Sri Lanka did well to tally 6-138 after being 6-70 with seven overs remaining. Without a run scored, Dilshan scooped the fifth ball of the contest to short fine leg, before the next wicket left Sri Lanka 2-2. Kumar Sangakkara made the match top score while Mathews also played a vital role. Fifteen runs in the 17th over and 17 in the last over gave the Sri Lankans a fighting chance, before Pakistan's openers put on 48 runs in seven overs as Akmal did most of the damage. The Pakistanis needed 76 off 65 balls after both openers had departed, and there were no further hiccups as Afridi and Shoaib Malik set up a comprehensive victory with eight balls to spare. Afridi had another terrific all-round game, taking 1-20 in four overs and scoring 54 not out off 40 balls.

Pakistan 2-139 (Shahid Afridi 54 not out, Kamran Akmal 37; Sanath Jayasuriya 1-8) beat Sri Lanka 6-138 (Kumar Sangakkara 64 not out, Angelo Mathews 35 not out; Abdul Razzaq 3-20) by eight wickets.

2010

World Cup glory for England at last

With the Netherlands and Scotland failing to qualify for the third instalment of the World Cup in the T20 format, Zimbabwe returned while Afghanistan made its first appearance in a major ICC international tournament.

Australia, New Zealand, India and West Indies were unbeaten in the group stage while Pakistan, Sri Lanka, South Africa and England also progressed to the Super 8s. Of the teams that bowed out in the group stage – Afghanistan, Bangladesh, Ireland and Zimbabwe – Ireland was desperately unlucky while England was perhaps lucky and unlucky at the same time. England made 5-191 against West Indies, which reached 2-60 in 5.5 overs and was declared the winner on the Duckworth-Lewis formula. The next day, Ireland was 1-14 after 3.3 overs in reply to England's 8-120 when the game was abandoned. With fewer than five overs bowled in the second innings, the teams gained one point each for a 'no-result' which enabled England to reach the Super 8s on net run rate.

From that moment, England never looked back. In Group E during the Super 8s, England won all three of its matches while Pakistan edged out New Zealand and South Africa on net run rate as these three teams had one win and two defeats. The standings in Group F were more clear-cut as two points separated one team from the next, with Australia followed by Sri Lanka, West Indies and India.

With convincing victories in the semi-finals and final, England won its first Cricket World Cup title.

A HAT-TRICK OF CLASSICS: Three great contests

Sri Lanka v New Zealand at Providence Stadium (Providence), 30 April

Sri Lanka built its total of 6-135 around opener Mahela Jayawardene's 81 off 51 balls, while the rest of the team's batting was largely disappointing. Dinesh Chandimal made a handy 29, but the third highest score was only 11. Chamara Kapugedera thrashed a six in the final over, but two wickets fell for no runs from the last three balls.

England's title-winning squad. Back (left to right): James Tredwell, Tim Bresnan, Michael Lumb, James Anderson, Stuart Broad, Graeme Swann, Ravi Bopara, Eoin Morgan, Kevin Pietersen. Front (left to right): Ajmal Shahzad, Craig Kieswetter, Paul Collingwood, Michael Yardy, Luke Wright, Ryan Sidebottom.

Sri Lanka's Mahela Jayawardene plays a sweep shot during his player-of-the-match display against West Indies. The wicketkeeper is Andre Fletcher.

The first over in the run chase was a wicket maiden after Brendon McCullum succumbed to a miscued pull. Fellow opener Jesse Ryder struck 42 off 27 balls, but the Kiwis struggled after he departed in the ninth over with the total at 62. Two successive sixes from Jacob Oram left New Zealand needing 26 runs in three overs, before wickets from successive balls made the score 7-117 with 10 balls left. A couple of missed run-out chances proved crucial, before a boundary reduced the task to four runs from three balls. An ensuing run-out meant three runs were needed from two balls, and Nathan McCullum settled the issue with a ball to spare as he struck a Lasith Malinga delivery over the long-off boundary.

New Zealand 8-139 (Jesse Ryder 42; Muttiah Muralidaran 2-25) beat Sri Lanka 6-135 (Mahela Jayawardene 81; Shane Bond 2-35) by two wickets.

New Zealand v Pakistan at Kensington Oval (Bridgetown), 8 May

This contest was even more thrilling than the Kiwis versus Sri Lanka battle. New Zealand raced to 0-34 in the fourth over before sliding to 4-58 in the 10th over, with the second wicket falling as Umar Akmal held a brilliant catch. Daniel Vettori and Scott Styris led a revival, before Styris departed in the 15th over after hitting a six and a four earlier in the over. A last-ball six from Nathan McCullum proved decisive in the long run as it boosted Pakistan's target to 134.

Nathan McCullum later held a blinding catch to remove Shahid Afridi and reduce Pakistan to 5-58 in the 10th over. With opener Salman Butt progressing towards a valuable half-century, Abdul Razzaq scored 16 runs in an over to reduce the task to 40 runs in five overs. Razzaq's next six was followed by his downfall five balls later, before a six from Butt reduced the requirement to 16 from 11 balls. Butt faced two dot balls and also hit two fours in the last over, before a bye left Abdur Rehman needing two runs from the final delivery for a Pakistani victory. He lofted the ball to the legside, but picked out Martin Guptill who held a comfortable catch. Unfortunately for the Kiwis, this thrilling win wasn't enough to progress to the semi-finals.

New Zealand 7-133 (Daniel Vettori 38, Brendon McCullum 33; Abdur Rehman 2-19, Mohammad Sami 2-25) beat Pakistan 7-132 (Salman Butt 67 not out, Abdul Razzaq 29; Ian Butler 3-19, Kyle Mills 2-33) by one run.

India v Sri Lanka at Beausejour Stadium (Gros Islet), 11 May

This heart-stopping contest featured a boundary from the first delivery as Dinesh Karthik carved the ball behind point. Seventeen runs in the sixth over were followed by 13 in the seventh, and India reached 1-90 at the halfway stage. The momentum stalled, however, despite Suresh Raina's 63 which ended in the 18th over. MS Dhoni made only 23 not out from

19 balls, and Yusuf Pathan was caught off a full-toss from the final ball of the innings.

Sri Lanka's innings also began with a four, only for Jayawardene to edge a catch from the third ball. Sanath Jayasuriya's dismissal for a duck left Sri Lanka 2-6, before Tillakaratne Dilshan hit five fours in two overs and then perished in the eighth over. Sri Lanka was 3-58 at the 10-over mark, and needed a further 106 runs. Four sixes were hit in the space of four overs, before Kumar Sangakkara was bowled in the 15th over. Following 11 runs from each of the 17th and 18th overs, Sri Lanka needed 30 from two overs. The 19th over cost 17 after Kapugedera creamed the final two balls for six, and then Angelo Mathews smashed the next ball for another six. The run-out of Mathews left Kapugedera needing three runs from the final delivery. He charged down the wicket and hammered the ball over cover for six, sparking euphoria among the Sri Lankans.

Sri Lanka 5-167 (Kumar Sangakkara 46, Angelo Mathews 46; Vinay Kumar 2-30) beat India 5-163 (Suresh Raina 63, Gautam Gambhir 41; Lasith Malinga 2-25) by five wickets.

SIX OF THE BEST: Individual performances

(excluding player of the tournament, and the finals)

Daren Sammy 30 off 17 balls, 3-8 off 3.4 overs and four catches: West Indies v Ireland at Providence Stadium (Providence), 30 April

Batting at seven and later being the fifth and final bowler, Daren Sammy had the highest score and best bowling figures as West Indies trounced Ireland by 70 runs. Remarkably, he also held four catches. After arriving at the crease with the score at 5-83 with seven overs left, Sammy made just three runs off seven balls before hitting two fours and two sixes in his quickfire 30.

With Ireland chasing 139, Sammy held two catches in the first two overs before his next catch left Ireland 4-16. Sammy struck with his first ball as Andre Fletcher held a catch at long-on, making the score 5-39. Sammy was taken off after bowling two overs, and then he took his final catch. It wasn't long before he returned to the bowling crease, and polished off the tail as Ireland's final two batters were caught behind.

Suresh Raina 101 off 60 balls: India v South Africa at Beausejour Stadium (Gros Islet), 2 May

Having been caught off a no-ball on five and narrowly avoiding being run out on 47, Suresh Raina made the most of his reprieves. His first boundary took him to

Kevin Pietersen (England)

Matches	Innings	Not outs	Runs	Highest score	Average	50s	100s	Catches
6	6	2	248	73*	62	2	-	3

12 off 15 balls, before he posted his 50 in 42 balls. Raina hit two sixes in the 16th over before striking 18 runs in four balls in the 18th over. His fifth six took him to 101 off 59 balls, before he lofted a catch next ball in the final over. India finished with 5-186, before South Africa managed 5-172.

Mahela Jayawardene 98 not out off 56 balls: Sri Lanka v West Indies at Kensington Oval (Bridgetown), 7 May

Having failed to make contact as he flashed at the first and sixth balls of Sri Lanka's clash with West Indies, Mahela Jayawardene played very few false shots thereafter. After Sangakkara was dropped from the first ball of the fourth over, Jayawardene whacked the next delivery over the long-on boundary before swinging a four behind square. A paddle past the wicketkeeper brought up Jayawardene's 50 from 29 balls, before he survived a stumping chance on 65. After Sangakkara fell, Jayawardene hit the next two balls for six and four to reach 97. But he finished short of triple figures as he scored a single from the only ball he faced in the final over. Jayawardene had registered nine fours and four sixes in a match-winning total of 3-195.

Cameron White 85 not out off 49 balls: Australia v Sri Lanka at Kensington Oval (Bridgetown), 9 May

Australia was 4-30 in the fifth over against Sri Lanka, when Cameron White survived a hat-trick ball from Suraj Randiv. White went on to produce a sensational knock which set up an 81-run victory. The result could have been much different, as White went from 23 to 24 as a top-edged sweep was dropped. In the next over, he reached 30 as an outside edge went to the boundary. White progressed from 39 to 49 in two balls before reaching 50 in 32 balls, and then tickling the next delivery for another boundary. White crunched the last two balls of the 17th over for six, before clearing the boundary twice more in the 19th over. He finished with six sixes and six fours.

Charl Langeveldt 4-19 off four overs: South Africa v Pakistan at Beausejour Stadium (Gros Islet), 10 May

Charl Langeveldt took 1-5 in a two-over spell and later captured 3-14 in his final two overs. He claimed an lbw to leave Pakistan 3-18 after five overs, before he returned with four overs left while the score was 4-124. Umar Akmal promptly hit him for six but was caught two balls later, and then Shahid Afridi was bowled from the final ball of the same over. From the third ball of the final over, Misbah-ul-Haq sliced a catch to long-off.

Saeed Ajmal 4-26 off four overs: Pakistan v South Africa at Beausejour Stadium (Gros Islet), 10 May

Pakistan's sixth and final bowler played a critical role as Pakistan defended its total of 7-148 against South Africa. Saeed Ajmal's first over yielded eight runs and the dismissal of Jacques Kallis, brilliantly caught at long-on. Ajmal was promptly removed from the attack as the Proteas were 3-57 after 11 overs, before he claimed 1-4 in his second over as South Africa stumbled to 5-102 with four overs left. Ajmal's second victim was AB de Villiers, who was caught behind as a paddle scoop went awry. Ajmal's third victim was Mark Boucher, trapped lbw in an over which conceded nine runs. Entrusted with the final over as the Proteas needed 17 runs, Ajmal conceded three singles before having Johan Botha stumped.

PLAYER OF THE TOURNAMENT

The tournament began sluggishly for England and its number three batter Kevin Pietersen, but things improved enormously for both the team and the player.

Pietersen began with 24 off 20 balls in a rain-shortened eight-wicket loss to West Indies, before scoring just nine off 18 in a no-result against Ireland. In the Super 8 stage, Pietersen earned successive player of the match awards as England beat Pakistan by six wickets before defeating South Africa by 39 runs. Pietersen hit eight fours and two sixes in his

Craig Kieswetter made vital contributions in England's semi-final and final success.

unconquered 73 off 52 balls against Pakistan, and struck the winning boundary with three balls to spare. He was dropped on 21, and should have been run out for 64 when victory loomed. Against his native South Africa, Pietersen recorded eight fours and a six in his 53 off 33 balls in a total of 7-168. He missed England's victory against New Zealand as he returned home to visit his wife and newborn son. Upon returning to the cricket, Pietersen scored 42 not out off 26 balls as England beat Sri Lanka by seven wickets in a semi-final, before making 47 off 31 as England also won the final by seven wickets.

FIRST SEMI-FINAL

England v Sri Lanka at Beausejour Stadium (Gros Islet), 13 May

After the first ball of the game was a loosener which Jayawardene clipped to the boundary, England held all the aces. Sri Lanka's first four batters were gone with only 47 runs on the board after nine overs, before Angelo Mathews came to the rescue with 58 off 45 balls. None of his teammates passed 16, and Sri Lanka managed only 6-128 despite 17 runs coming from the 18th over. England's openers put on 68 runs in eight overs, and from there the result was never in doubt. A six and a four to Pietersen from successive balls sealed England's triumph with four overs left.

England 3-132 (Kevin Pietersen 42 not out, Craig Kieswetter 39; Thisara Perera 2-19) beat Sri Lanka 6-128 (Angelo Mathews 58; Stuart Broad 2-21) by seven wickets.

SECOND SEMI-FINAL

Australia v Pakistan at Beausejour Stadium (Gros Islet), 14 May

Pakistan controlled this contest as much as England controlled the other semi-final, only for Australia to snatch a miraculous victory with one ball to spare.

The first over was a maiden before the second contained three runs, but the pendulum changed as the third and fourth cost 11 and 13 each. Kamran Akmal hit 17 runs in the ninth over to reach 50, before falling to a great catch by David Warner in the 10th over. Pakistan was 3-114 with 34 balls left when Afridi fell, before a flurry of boundaries ensued. There were two run-outs in the final three balls when a 200-run total beckoned.

After Australia quickly lost Warner for a duck, several batters made a brief impact and then departed. White smacked five sixes in his 43, before his exit was soon followed by Steve Smith's to leave Australia needing 48 runs from 17 balls with only three wickets remaining. The 18th over cost 14 runs before the 19th cost 16, with Michael Hussey hitting the first and last balls of the 19th over to the boundary. With Australia needing 18 runs in the final over, Mitchell Johnson squeezed out a single before Hussey thumped back-to-back sixes and a four to level the scores, and then blasted another six.

Australia 7-197 (Michael Hussey 60 not out, Cameron White 43; Mohammad Amir 3-35) beat Pakistan 6-191 (Umar Akmal 56 not out, Kamran Akmal 50) by three wickets.

FINAL

Australia v England at Kensington Oval (Bridgetown), 16 May

There was no miracle from Australia this time, as England replicated its winning margin from the semi-final. The run-out of Warner was critical as Australia slumped to 3-8, before the dismissal of captain Michael Clarke for a run-a-ball 27 left his team 4-45 in the 10th over. Twenty-one runs in the 13th over boosted the score to 4-80, before 50 runs in the final four overs took the total towards 150. England was 1-7 after 2.3 overs before aggressive batting from Pietersen and opener Craig Kieswetter took the total beyond 100 in the 12th over. England was 3-121 after the duo departed in quick succession, before Eoin Morgan and captain Paul Collingwood saw England home with three overs left.

England 3-148 (Craig Kieswetter 63, Kevin Pietersen 47) beat Australia 6-147 (David Hussey 59, Cameron White 30; Ryan Sidebottom 2-26) by seven wickets.

England won its first Cricket World Cup title.

2012

Watto wins battle but Windies win the war

Sri Lanka was the sole host of the 2012 tournament after South Africa, England and West Indies were the previous hosts. The same 12 countries competed in 2012 as in 2010, although the teams in each group were reshuffled as usual.

Progressing to the Super 8s was clear-cut in three of the four groups as there was an undefeated team (India in Group A, South Africa in Group C and Pakistan in Group D), a team with a win and a loss (England, Sri Lanka and New Zealand) and a team with two losses (Afghanistan, Zimbabwe and Bangladesh). Group B also had a team with two wins (Australia), but the other teams had a loss and a no-result.

Unfortunately for the Irish, they copped the short end of the stick as they again missed the Super 8s on net run rate. After being denied the chance to beat the eventual titleholder in 2010, the same fate befell them in 2012! On the latter occasion, Ireland made 6-129 in 19 overs before rain prevented a West Indian run chase.

Having sneaked into the Super 8s, West Indies had a bit more luck on the way to winning the tournament. Sri Lanka and West Indies progressed from Group E to the semi-finals at the expense of England and New Zealand, with West Indies having beaten England by 15 runs before being thrashed by Sri Lanka, and then winning the Super Over following a tie with New Zealand. The Kiwis, meanwhile, were totally out of luck after they also lost to Sri Lanka in a Super Over during the Super 8s!

Australia and Pakistan progressed from Group F to the semi-finals after being tied on points with India, which had an inferior net run rate while South Africa lost all three of its Super 8s contests.

The West Indians were ultimately too strong in the finals series, as they won their first T20 World Cup just over 33 years after previously winning the limited overs World Cup. Technically, their 2012 title was their first in a 'white ball' World Cup.

A HAT-TRICK OF CLASSICS: Three great contests

New Zealand v Sri Lanka at Pallekele International Cricket Stadium (Pallekele), 27 September

A Super Over decided the winner after the teams had a thrilling tie. Sri Lanka's Tillakaratne Dilshan was the hero after scoring 76 and holding the winning catch.

Batting first, New Zealand was 0-4 after two overs before the third over contained 13 runs and a difficult catch that went begging. Akila Dananjaya required treatment in the 12th over after being hit in the face from a hot caught-

Player of the tournament, Shane Watson.

As if capturing six wickets (in one match) wasn't spectacular enough, Ajantha Mendis also delivered two maidens.

and-bowled chance. Rob Nicol slammed three sixes in the 15th over which cost 24 runs, before he exited in the next over. New Zealand's 174-run total included 94 in the latter 10 overs, before the first over of the run chase contained 17 runs. Sri Lanka needed only 62 from the final nine overs with nine wickets in hand, but lost momentum. The 19th over yielded 2-13, before a ramp shot from Lahiru Thirimanne produced a four to level the scores with one ball left. An ensuing run-out prompted the Super Over, with the Sri Lankans receiving three runs in wides as they made 1-13 without finding the boundary. Despite faulty glovework from Kumar Sangakkara from successive balls, Sri Lanka was safe when Dilshan held a splendid catch on the boundary from the fifth ball as the Kiwis needed eight more runs.

Sri Lanka 6-174 (Tillakaratne Dilshan 76, Mahela Jayawardene 44; James Franklin 2-34) tied with New Zealand 7-174 (Rob Nicol 58, Martin Guptill 38; Akila Dananjaya 2-32, Nuwan Kulasekara 2-33) before Sri Lanka won the Super Over.

West Indies v New Zealand at Pallekele International Cricket Stadium (Pallekele), 1 October

Another contest required a Super Over to split two teams, and the upshot was that New Zealand was unluckily eliminated from the competition.

Opening batter Chris Gayle smacked 30 off 14 balls before his exit left West Indies 3-61 in the seventh over. With the final six wickets falling in the space of seven overs, the West Indians were all out with three balls to spare. Needing seven runs per over, the Kiwis were 3-52 after nine overs when Martin Guptill departed. Ross Taylor, who finished with 62 not out off 40 balls, kept New Zealand in contention but had unreliable support. The Kiwis needed 14 off the last over and then nine off three balls, with Taylor scooping a full-toss for six and then managing a single which left Doug Bracewell on strike. Bracewell completed one, before a direct hit ran him out as he sought a winning second run. Marlon Samuels bowled the Super Over for West Indies, with Taylor dispatching consecutive full-tosses for four and six before finishing with a two to take New Zealand's total to 17. Tim Southee could ill-afford to begin with a no-ball, which Gayle clouted for six. With West Indies 0-13 with two balls left, Samuels thumped a low full-toss over the mid-wicket boundary to clinch victory.

West Indies 139 (Chris Gayle 30; Tim Southee 3-21, Doug Bracewell 3-31) tied with New Zealand 7-139 (Ross Taylor 62 not out; Sunil Narine 3-20) before West Indies won the Super Over.

India v South Africa at R. Premadasa Stadium (Colombo), 2 October

Victory by a solitary run wasn't enough to keep India in finals contention, while South Africa's hopes had already disappeared.

Gautam Gambhir drove the first ball of the game for four, before India stumbled to 4-68 at the 10-over mark when Yuvraj Singh exited. Suresh Raina and MS Dhoni added 40 runs in the final four overs before Raina was run out from the final ball, leaving the Proteas a target of 153. The second-ball dismissal of Hashim Amla was followed by the dismissal of Jacques Kallis in the fourth over, and AB de Villiers in the seventh. Wickets from successive balls in the 18th over left South Africa needing 26 runs from 15 balls with three wickets in hand, before the task became 14 from six balls with two wickets remaining. Albie Morkel cleared the rope but was bowled next ball, and then his brother Morne failed to score from one ball before thumping the next for six. Lakshmipathy Balaji was up to the task, as a full-pitched ball rearranged Morne Morkel's stumps while a desperate swing failed to connect.

India's Rohit Sharma bats during the nail-biting clash with South Africa. The wicketkeeper is Proteas skipper AB de Villiers.

India 6-152 (Suresh Raina 45; Robin Peterson 2-25, Morne Morkel 2-28) beat South Africa 151 (Faf du Plessis 65; Zaheer Khan 3-22, Lakshmipathy Balaji 3-37) by one run.

SIX OF THE BEST: Individual performances

(excluding player of the tournament, and the finals)

Ajantha Mendis 6-8 off four overs: Sri Lanka v Zimbabwe at Mahinda Rajapaksa International Cricket Stadium (Sooriyawewa), 18 September

As if capturing six wickets wasn't spectacular enough, Ajantha Mendis also delivered two maidens. In reply to Sri Lanka's 4-182, Zimbabwe was 0-36 after five overs before Mendis struck with his third and fourth balls, with Vusi Sibanda bowled before Brendan Taylor was stumped. Mendis's second over was a wicket maiden, with Hamilton Masakadza bowled through the gate. Mendis's third over was the 14th of the innings, with Elton Chigumbura bowled from the final ball. Mendis's final over was a double-wicket maiden, featuring a catch at slip from the first ball and an lbw from the fourth ball.

Brendon McCullum 123 off 58 balls: New Zealand v Bangladesh at Pallekele International Cricket Stadium (Pallekele), 21 September

Brendon McCullum faced nearly half of New Zealand's 20 overs against Bangladesh, and made 64.39 percent of the 191-run total. His first nine runs took 10 balls before he scored nine off his next two deliveries, having gained a five thanks to four runs from overthrows. McCullum raised his half-century in 29 balls, before registering his ton in 51 balls. He was dropped on 92 from the first ball of the 19th over, and

AFGHANISTAN
alanic

Shane Watson (Australia)

Matches	Innings	Not outs	Runs	Highest score	Average	50s	100s	Catches
6	6	1	249	72	49.80	3	-	3

Overs	Maidens	Runs	Wickets	Average	Best figures
24	-	176	11	16.00	3-26

then back-to-back fours and a six took him to 107 in the same over. He was caught from the final ball of the last over, having amassed 11 fours and seven sixes. One of McCullum's sixes came as he charged the bowler who pitched short and outside off-stump, before the batter struck the ball over long-off with a shot that resembled a tennis forehand.

Luke Wright 99 not out off 55 balls: England v Afghanistan at R. Premadasa Stadium (Colombo), 21 September

England was 1-0 after one over against Afghanistan, before Luke Wright's onslaught set up a match-winning total of 5-196. In the 10th over, a drive from Wright was touched by the bowler just before the ball hit the non-striker's stumps to dismiss an unlucky Alex Hales.

Undeterred, Wright reached 50 in 34 balls before going from 58 to 72 in three balls. On 75, he gave a chance to short third man. Wright creamed three successive sixes in the 19th over, which miraculously featured 32 runs and a wicket. Wright needed three runs from the final ball of the innings for a century, but managed only two from a low full-toss. Wright's first 50 runs included five fours and two sixes, before his last 49 runs included three fours and four sixes.

Harbhajan Singh 4-12 off four overs: India v England at R. Premadasa Stadium (Colombo), 23 September

England was skittled for 80 in reply to India's 4-170, following Harbhajan Singh's excellent four-over spell. Introduced for the sixth over, Harbhajan broke through with his second delivery as an arm ball uprooted Eoin Morgan's middle-stump. Following a wicket maiden, Harbhajan's second over cost nine runs before his third featured three singles and the wicket of Tim Bresnan to a miscued sweep. Harbhajan's final over was a double-wicket maiden, with Jos Buttler bowled before Graeme Swann was stumped.

Shakib Al Hasan 84 off 54 balls: Bangladesh v Pakistan at Pallekele International Cricket Stadium (Pallekele), 25 September

Shakib Al Hasan's 84 at number three helped Bangladesh to 6-175 against Pakistan. After scoring four runs from seven balls, Al Hasan hit three fours in a row and then slowed down briefly before hitting the accelerator. A six over mid-wicket took him to 52 off 33 balls, before he went from 63 to 77 in the 18th over. Having amassed 11 fours and two sixes, Al Hasan fell from the third ball of the final over as he was caught at long-off from a full-toss.

Al Hasan later conceded just 23 runs in four overs as Pakistan won by eight wickets. Dropped on one, opener Imran Nazir cashed in with 72 off 36 balls.

Lasith Malinga 5-31 off four overs: Sri Lanka v England at Pallekele International Cricket Stadium (Pallekele), 1 October

England was restricted to 9-150 when chasing 170 against Sri Lanka, following a five-wicket haul from Lasith Malinga. He struck with the third, fifth and sixth balls of his first over to reduce England to 3-18 after three overs. A slashing cut was caught behind point, and then a slower delivery was skied to mid-off before an lbw appeal was upheld when it appeared the ball may have missed leg-stump. Malinga's second over was the 14th, which featured a top-edged catch to deep backward square leg. His next over cost 15 runs, before the fifth ball of his final over produced his fifth wicket when a full-toss removed the off-peg.

Afghanistan's Shapoor Zadran is ecstatic after claiming a wicket.

PLAYER OF THE TOURNAMENT

Australia's opening batter Shane Watson was the leading run-scorer and second highest wicket-taker

The West Indians enjoy the spoils of victory after comfortably defending their total against Sri Lanka in the final.

in the competition, making him an easy choice for player of the tournament. He won player of the match honours in Australia's first four matches, all resulting in victories. Alas, Watson was ineffective as Australia lost its next two matches and missed out on a berth in the decider.

Watson took a wicket with the opening delivery of Australia's first match, as Ireland captain William Porterfield top-edged a hook shot. Bizarrely, Watson's remaining overs were the ninth, 15th and 20th of the innings. He captured 2-5 in the 15th over, before the final over cost 12 runs. Watson followed up his 3-26 with 51 off 30 balls, having hit five fours and three sixes before being run out. Australia won by seven wickets, chasing 124. In Australia's next match, Watson bowled the first, 11th, 15th and 18th overs. He dropped Chris Gayle on four, before holding a caught-and-bowled to dismiss the West Indian opener for 54. Watson nabbed 2-29 as West Indies amassed 8-191, before he hit 41 not out off 24 balls. At one stage he smacked 20 runs in four balls, with one of the sixes coming from a dropped catch. Australia won by 17 runs, having reached 1-100 in 9.1 overs when rain caused an early finish and spoilt a potentially thrilling game.

Shane Watson was the leading run-scorer and second highest wicket-taker in the competition, making him an easy choice for player of the tournament.

Watson bowled the fifth, 11th, 14th and 20th overs against India, and captured 3-34 before hammering seven sixes and only two fours in his 72 off 42 balls. Watson was the only casualty as Australia overhauled India's 7-140 with 31 balls remaining. Against South Africa, Watson took 2-29 for the second time in three games, this time as he delivered the sixth, ninth, 15th and 18th overs. Dropped on 52, Watson went on to score 70 off 47 as Australia coasted to an eight-wicket victory when the target was 147. Pakistan subsequently tallied 6-149 against Australia, with Watson taking 1-23 after bowling the third, sixth, 13th and 18th overs. However, he made only eight as

Australia tumbled to a 32-run defeat, before the semi-final against West Indies was a bigger disappointment. His figures were 4-0-35-0 after bowling the second, fifth, 13th and 17th overs, with West Indies topping 200 before Watson fell for seven in a 74-run defeat.

FIRST SEMI-FINAL

Sri Lanka v Pakistan at R. Premadasa Stadium (Colombo), 4 October

It was telling that Sri Lanka's total of 4-139 included 16 runs from the final over, before Pakistan lost by 16 runs. Sri Lanka was 0-62 after 10 overs before losing wickets in the 11th, 13th, 18th and 19th overs. Sri Lanka's openers tallied 77 runs, and the following four batters made scores between 10 and 18.

Pakistan was 1-55 after nine overs before losing 3-9 in two overs. Nineteen runs came in the following two overs, with Sri Lanka ruing a simple dropped catch. Rangana Herath snared two wickets in two balls with the total on 91 in the 15th over, including Shahid Afridi for a first-ball duck. The second-last over featured just four runs, and then the first two balls of the 20th over featured no runs as 23 were needed from the final six balls.

Sri Lanka 4-139 (Mahela Jayawardene 42, Tillakaratne Dilshan 35; Mohammad Hafeez 1-12) beat Pakistan 7-123 (Mohammad Hafeez 42, Umar Akmal 29 not out; Rangana Herath 3-25, Angelo Mathews and Ajantha Mendis 2-27) by 16 runs.

SECOND SEMI-FINAL

West Indies v Australia at R. Premadasa Stadium (Colombo), 5 October

West Indies ultimately outplayed Australia in all facets. A turning point came as West Indies was 1-33, when Marlon Samuels was lucky not to be adjudged lbw for eight. He went on to score a quick 26. Gayle faced just 24 balls in the first 14 overs, before hammering 16 runs in the 15th over which cost 19 runs to take the total to 2-132. The final three overs went for 13, 17 and 25, with Gayle hitting a six before Kieron Pollard hit a hat-trick of sixes in the final over and then fell for 38 off 15 balls. Gayle faced only 41 balls in his usual role of opener, and scored 56 of his 75 runs in boundaries. After Australia plunged to 6-43 in the eighth over, a 68-run partnership included 25 runs in the 11th over before the final four wickets fell for 20 runs. Australia's captain George Bailey played a lone hand as he blasted six fours and four sixes in his 63 off 29 balls.

West Indies 4-205 (Chris Gayle 75 not out; Pat Cummins 2-36) beat Australia 131 (George Bailey 63; Ravi Rampaul 3-16, Kieron Pollard 2-6) by 74 runs.

FINAL

West Indies v Sri Lanka at R. Premadasa Stadium (Colombo), 7 October

Only three batters from each team made double figures while there were plenty of failures. In the end, Samuels's 78 was the main difference between the teams as Sri Lanka's top score was 33.

Sri Lanka's Angelo Mathews began with a wicket maiden, before the first run off the bat came from the fifth ball of the third over. Gayle made a miserable three off 16 balls, and West Indies was a measly 2-32 after 10 overs. Samuels hammered three sixes off Malinga in the 13th over, before Dwayne Bravo was unluckily ruled lbw with six overs remaining. Mendis was on a hat-trick in the 16th over, before the next over cost 19 runs. Samuels departed from the first ball of the 18th over, before 15 runs in the final over boosted the total to 137.

Having lost an early wicket, Sri Lanka advanced to 1-48 in the 10th over before crumbling to 7-69 five overs later, with the collapse including two run-outs. Nuwan Kulasekara smacked 26 off 13 balls at number eight, but resistance was short-lived as Sri Lanka was all out with eight balls to spare while 37 runs shy of the target.

West Indies 6-137 (Marlon Samuels 78; Ajantha Mendis 4-12) beat Sri Lanka 101 (Mahela Jayawardene 33; Sunil Narine 3-9, Daren Sammy 2-6) by 36 runs.

2014

Indians fire until Sri Lanka steals the glory

With Bangladesh as the host, the 2014 tournament expanded to 16 teams while the format underwent major changes. The same nations from the previous two tournaments stayed put, and the Netherlands returned while Nepal, Hong Kong and United Arab Emirates (UAE) made their World Cup T20 debut.

Eight teams contested the first round, with only two moving to the next round. Bangladesh edged out Nepal on net run rate as these two teams finished ahead of Afghanistan and Hong Kong in Group A, while the Netherlands finished ahead of Zimbabwe and Ireland on net run rate as they were level on points in Group B. The ensuing Super 10 stage had two groups of five, with Sri Lanka and South Africa progressing from Group 1 while New Zealand, England and the Netherlands missed the cut. India and West Indies progressed from Group 2 while Pakistan, Australia and Bangladesh didn't.

For the third time, an all-Asian decider took place. India versus Sri Lanka was the third different combination of teams from the sub-continent, after the first World Cup T20 decider involved India and Pakistan before the second one involved Pakistan and Sri Lanka. India was the team to beat after winning all four of its Super 10s matches and its semi-final, but Sri Lanka was simply too good in the match that counted the most.

A HAT-TRICK OF CLASSICS: Three great contests

Zimbabwe v Ireland at Sylhet Divisional Stadium (Sylhet), 17 March

Ireland eyed an easy win, before a stutter led to the game going down to the final ball.

Brendan Taylor top-scored for Zimbabwe with 59 off 46 balls, while the other dismissed batters made between 10 and 21 as decent starts were wasted. Having been 1-56 after six overs, Zimbabwe stumbled to 4-111 midway through the 15th over before 17 runs in the final over boosted the total beyond 160.

Paul Stirling hit four successive fours in the sixth over of the run chase, before the ninth over yielded 1-10 to take Ireland to 1-89. Stirling's exit for 60 left the Irish

Forty-three-year-old Australian all-rounder Brad Hogg appeals unsuccessfully for a wicket against Pakistan.

The Indians were simply outbowled, outbatted and outclassed, after being undefeated until the decider.

2-100 in the 11th over, before a double breakthrough from Tinashe Panyangara made the score 4-129 with five overs left. The 18th over contained 16 runs from five balls and then a wicket, before three runs in the penultimate over meant only four were needed from the last over as five wickets remained. Following two singles, Ed Joyce was yorked before Max Sorensen was run out amid a collision with the bowler. An ensuing single levelled the score from the fifth ball, before the batters scrambled a winning bye from the final ball as the wicketkeeper's throw missed the stumps when a direct hit would have forced a tie and a Super Over.

Ireland 7-164 (Paul Stirling 60, William Porterfield 31; Tinashe Panyangara 4-37) beat Zimbabwe 5-163 (Brendan Taylor 59; George Dockrell 2-18, Andy McBrine 2-26) by three wickets.

South Africa v Sri Lanka at Zahur Ahmed Chowdhury Stadium (Chittagong), 22 March

South Africa needed 19 runs from the final two overs, before Sri Lankan duo Nuwan Kulasekara and Lasith Malinga came to the fore with brilliant death bowling.

The first over of the game featured 17 runs and a wicket. Kusal Perera thumped two fours and a six, and there were also two wides before Tillakaratne Dilshan lost his off-stump. Sri Lanka was 2-42 after 4.2 overs when Mahela Jayawardene fell, and then 3-83 in the 10th over when Kumar Sangakkara departed. Kulasekara hit the final ball for four to set up a competitive but not huge target of 166.

South Africa's first over yielded only four runs, before Quinton de Kock hammered 14 in three balls in the third over. De Kock was yorked in the fifth over, before 28 runs in two overs lifted the Proteas to 1-75 at the 10-over mark. The vital wicket of AB de Villiers left South Africa needing 56 off six overs with seven wickets in hand. Albie Morkel hit back-to-back sixes in the 17th over, but was caught in the deep next ball off a low full-toss. Kulasekara took a wicket and conceded only four runs in the 19th over, before the first two balls of the final over featured run-outs. Twelve runs were needed from two balls, with a match-sealing dot ball followed by a belated six.

Sri Lanka 7-165 (Kusal Perera 61, Angelo Mathews 43; Imran Tahir 3-26) beat South Africa 8-160 (JP Duminy 39; Sachithra Senanayake 2-22) by five runs.

South Africa v New Zealand at Zahur Ahmed Chowdhury Stadium (Chittagong), 24 March

The game was there for New Zealand's taking, before three wickets in the final six balls cost the Kiwis a certain victory.

The Proteas were merely 3-67 after 11 overs, before JP Duminy turned the tide. After scoring only 11 runs from 14 deliveries, he clubbed 10 fours and three sixes as he sped to 86 not out off 43 balls. Hashim Amla was bizarrely caught-and-bowled after his drive struck Duminy's bat at the non-striker's end. Unfazed, Duminy blasted 53 runs in the final six overs as the total raced from 4-97 to 6-170.

New Zealand was 0-57 after seven overs before faltering to 2-66. Kane Williamson reached 50 in the 12th over before Ross Taylor struck three sixes in a row, and then Williamson's dismissal left the Kiwis requiring 54 off 39 balls. Twenty runs in two overs were followed by two wickets and only 10 runs in the next two overs, before 14 runs came in the 19th over. A wicket and two dot balls were followed by a boundary in the final over, meaning New Zealand needed three runs from two balls. The fifth ball was loose but Nathan McCullum lobbed a catch, with Taylor crucially regaining the strike as the batters crossed. Taylor had 62 off 36 balls before Dale Steyn's final delivery was pitched up, and Taylor could only steer it back to Steyn who broke the stumps at the bowler's end to seal South Africa's triumph.

Pakistan's Umar Akmal plays a drive against Australia.

South Africa 6-170 (JP Duminy 86 not out, Hashim Amla 41; Corey Anderson 2-28) beat New Zealand 8-168 (Ross Taylor 62, Kane Williamson 51; Dale Steyn 4-17, Imran Tahir 2-27) by two runs.

SIX OF THE BEST: Individual performances

(excluding player of the tournament, and the finals)

Stephan Myburgh 63 off 23 balls: Netherlands v Ireland at Sylhet Divisional Stadium (Sylhet), 21 March

In response to Ireland's imposing 4-189, Netherlands opener Stephan Myburgh set up a six-wicket win with 6.1 overs to spare. He recorded four fours and seven sixes as he faced only 23 balls. He slogged three successive sixes over mid-wicket in the second over, and also blasted the first three balls of the fourth over beyond the rope to take the total to 0-64. Two successive fours took him to 56 off 18 balls, and in the seventh over he again cleared the mid-wicket boundary before being caught in that same region next ball. Amazingly, Tom Cooper later hit four consecutive sixes as his 15-ball knock of 45 included six sixes.

Umar Akmal 94 off 54 balls: Pakistan v Australia at Sher-e-Bangla National Cricket Stadium (Dhaka), 23 March

Pakistan was 2-25 before Umar Akmal set up a match-winning total of 5-191. He could have been dismissed for 22 off 16 balls, as a grassed catch at deep square leg made the score 2-56 instead of 3-55 after eight overs. Umar smacked 16 runs in four balls in the 12th over to reach his 50 off 28 balls, before he progressed to 94. With the first ball of the final over, he miscued a full-toss and was caught at long-on. His innings contained nine fours and four sixes.

Ahsan Malik 5-19 off four overs: Netherlands v South Africa at Zahur Ahmed Chowdhury Stadium (Chittagong), 27 March

Imran Tahir was the hero with 4-21 as the Proteas pipped the Netherlands by six runs, but the best bowling figures in the match went to Ahsan Malik. He had 0-6 after two balls as the Proteas reached 1-45 in 4.2 overs, before his third ball had Hashim Amla

KOOKABURRA
LG
LG

Virat Kohli (India)

Matches	Innings	Not outs	Runs	Highest score	Average	50s	100s	Catches
6	6	3	319	77	106.33	4	-	5

caught behind. His remaining overs were the 13th, 17th and 19th of the innings, with the 13th featuring a skied catch before the 17th contained an edge to the wicketkeeper. Ahsan's final over yielded two wickets, with Beuran Hendricks caught at cover before David Miller was bowled.

Alex Hales 116 not out off 64 balls: England v Sri Lanka at Zahur Ahmed Chowdhury Stadium (Chittagong), 27 March

England was 2-0 after one over in reply to Sri Lanka's 4-189, before a scintillating unbeaten century from opener Alex Hales set up a six-wicket triumph. He drove his first two deliveries for four, and also registered two fours in the third over before his seventh four took him to 50 off 38 balls. His eighth and ninth fours occurred in the same over that he reached 50, with his ninth boundary coming from a vital dropped catch at deep square leg. This left England 2-108 rather than 3-104 with seven overs remaining. In the 15th over, Hales hit a six and a two before striking back-to-back sixes and a four. A six over cover took Hales to 103 off 60 balls, and he also cleared the rope next ball to reduce England's task to just nine runs from nine balls. Hales's sixth six sealed the result with four balls to spare.

Ravi Ashwin 4-11 off 3.2 overs: India v Australia at Sher-e-Bangla National Cricket Stadium (Dhaka), 30 March

Australia had no answers to Ravi Ashwin, as India thrashed the Australians by 73 runs after setting a 160-run target. Introduced in the fourth over, Ashwin broke through with his second ball as Aaron Finch skied an attempted slog. David Warner lofted Ashwin's fifth delivery for six, before another attempted big hit from Warner produced his downfall in Ashwin's next over. Ashwin's next wicket was freakish, as he came around the wicket and bowled the threatening Glenn Maxwell who exposed all three stumps as he sought a reverse sweep.

Having delivered the fourth, eighth and 10th overs, Ashwin returned for the 17th and soon ended the match as James Muirhead edged behind.

Rangana Herath 5-3 off 3.3 overs: Sri Lanka v New Zealand at Zahur Ahmed Chowdhury Stadium (Chittagong), 31 March

Sri Lanka made only 119 before routing New Zealand for a miserable 60, which included 42 from opener Kane Williamson! Rangana Herath was chiefly responsible for the outcome. His first ball featured a run-out, before his sixth ball was flighted beautifully and produced a stumping to leave the Kiwis 2-18 after four overs. Herath's second over also featured two wickets for no runs, with Ross Taylor lbw and James Neesham bowled first ball. Herath missed out on a hat-trick in his next over, but two balls later he won another lbw appeal. With 4-2 in three overs, Herath was removed from the attack before returning for the 16th over which, like his first over, began with a run-out (Williamson this time). Two balls later the match was over, as Trent Boult was caught at slip.

PLAYER OF THE TOURNAMENT

Virat Kohli scored prolifically at number three in nearly all of India's matches, with his team winning every time apart from the game that counted the most! The finale must have grated on Kohli, after this contest yielded his highest score of the tournament.

India's first three matches had a similar theme, with India losing only two or three wickets before achieving targets between 130 and 139. Kohli contributed 36 not out against Pakistan, 54 against West Indies and 57 not out against Bangladesh. Next, Kohli made 23 in India's 7-159 before Australia succumbed for 86.

In the second semi-final, Kohli earned player of the match honours for his 72 not out from 44 balls in India's six-wicket triumph against South Africa. His innings featured five fours and two sixes, including the winning boundary. Kohli also led the way in the decider with 77 off 58 balls, but India's total of 4-130 proved too small as Sri Lanka coasted to a convincing victory.

Australia's Glenn Maxwell plays a cut shot.

FIRST SEMI-FINAL

Sri Lanka v West Indies at Sher-e-Bangla National Cricket Stadium (Dhaka), 3 April

A hailstorm forced the match to end early, with the Sri Lankans declared winners as West Indies needed 81 runs off 37 balls with six wickets in hand.

Sri Lanka raced to 0-41 in 3.5 overs before losing two wickets in three balls, including Mahela Jayawardene for a diamond duck. The total was a modest 3-65 after 10 overs, before Lahiru Thirimanne lifted the run rate. Tillakaratne Dilshan exited in the 14th over, before Thirimanne was dismissed with three overs remaining. Angelo Mathews produced a late onslaught as 39 runs were added in the final three overs, with Mathews caught from the final ball after scoring 10 in the previous two balls.

Dwayne Smith struck the first ball of the run chase for four and then whacked the next ball for six. The score was 0-17 after three legitimate balls, following a wide that went to the boundary. Crazily, only 17 more runs were scored for the loss of three wickets in the next 40 balls! Dwayne Bravo then struck 30 runs in 19 balls before exiting, and only three more balls were bowled before the players were forced from the field. It was hard to think the West Indians were hard done by, after three of their top-order batters had scored slowly.

Sri Lanka 6-160 (Lahiru Thirimanne 44, Angelo Mathews 40; Krishmar Santokie 2-46) beat West Indies 4-80 (Dwayne Bravo 30; Lasith Malinga 2-5) by 27 runs under the DL method.

SECOND SEMI-FINAL

South Africa v India at Sher-e-Bangla National Cricket Stadium (Dhaka), 4 April

South Africa appeared a good chance of winning after topping 170, but India triumphed with five balls to spare. An action-packed game began with nine runs after three legitimate deliveries, and then the wicket of de Kock. Seventeen runs came from the fourth over, but the Proteas went more than four overs without a boundary before reaching a modest 2-66 after 10 overs. The next five overs cost 61 runs before there was another lull, followed by 26 runs from the final 10 balls.

India had a flying start with 14 runs in the first over, before the first wicket fell in the fourth over as the total neared 40. Following a six from the last ball of the fifth over, there were no further boundaries until a six from the first ball of the 11th over took the score to 2-86. The 16th over contained 11 runs and the wicket of Yuvraj Singh, leaving India needing 40 off four overs with seven wickets in hand. Suresh Raina creamed 21 runs in 10 balls before Kohli finished the job.

India 4-176 (Virat Kohli 72 not out, Ajinkya Rahane 32; Beuran Hendricks 2-31) beat South Africa 4-172 (Faf du Plessis 58, JP Duminy 45 not out; Ravi Ashwin 3-22) by six wickets.

FINAL

India v Sri Lanka at Sher-e-Bangla National Cricket Stadium (Dhaka), 6 April

The Indians were simply outbowled, outbatted and outclassed, after being undefeated until the decider. They lost a wicket in the second over, before the number '11' seemed to keep haunting them. Kohli kept the runs flowing after being reprieved on 11, but the rest of India's batting was insufficient after Rohit Sharma's dismissal made the score 2-64 in the 11th over. Kohli smashed 14 runs in three balls at one point, but Yuvraj Singh was unusually bogged down as he limped to 11 off 21 balls before being caught off a full-toss with 11 balls remaining. Only 11 more runs were added before Kohli was run out from the final ball of the innings.

Chasing only 131, Sri Lanka lost an early wicket before Dilshan and Jayawardene struck multiple boundaries. Neither went on with the job, and Sri Lanka was 3-65 when Jayawardene was well caught. Thirimanne edged his first delivery for four, meaning only 62 runs were needed in the final 10 overs. Thirimanne fell with the total at 78, but there were no further worries for Sri Lanka. Two streaky fours off successive balls took Sangakkara to 51, before a six to Thisara Perera sealed the result with 13 balls to spare. It was a fitting way for Sangakkara and Jayawardene to sign off from the T20 international circuit.

Sri Lanka 4-134 (Kumar Sangakkara 52 not out; Mohit Sharma 1-18) beat India 4-130 (Virat Kohli 77, Rangana Herath 1-23) by six wickets.

Umar Gul (middle) is congratulated by teammates after capturing a wicket for Pakistan against Australia.

2016

Breathtaking Brathwaite onslaught seals deal for Windies

India had its first turn at hosting the T20 World Cup while there were two changes to the list of 16 competing teams. Scotland returned while Oman made its first appearance in a T20 World Cup as Nepal and United Arab Emirates were omitted. Again the first round involved eight teams, split into two groups. Bangladesh topped the Group A ladder as the Netherlands, Oman and Ireland occupied the next three spots, while Afghanistan finished on top in Group B and was followed by Zimbabwe, Scotland and Hong Kong.

West Indies and England finished equal on points in Group 1 of the Super 10s while South Africa, Sri Lanka and Afghanistan were third, fourth and fifth respectively. New Zealand was unbeaten in Group 2 while India was next best as Australia, Pakistan and Bangladesh failed to qualify for the semi-finals.

New Zealand faltered in the semi-finals, and India also fell short of a spot in the decider. With West Indies and England aiming to become T20 World Cup champions for the second time, the team from the Caribbean stole the spoils in a decider sure to be long remembered for explosive hitting in the final over.

A HAT-TRICK OF CLASSICS: Three great contests

South Africa v England at Wankhede Stadium (Mumbai), 18 March

After the first over cost two runs, a run glut followed as virtually every bowler was punished severely. Perhaps the most telling aspect was England conceding only four sundries compared to South Africa conceding 26, including 20 from wides.

South Africa was 0-96 after seven overs, before Quinton de Kock fell for 52 off 24 balls. He was one of three South Africans to post a half-century. The Proteas were 2-125 after 10 overs, and then there were no boundaries for the next 21 balls which yielded only 18 runs and a wicket. The final two overs cost 18 runs each to leave England a target of 230, before the first two overs of the run chase yielded 21 and 23 runs. The first ball of the second over featured a dropped catch which went for four, before the remainder of the over included another three fours and a six.

A six to Ben Stokes took England to 2-85 after just 5.1 overs, before the next boundary was a six to Joe Root to make the score 4-118 after 10 overs. Fifteen runs came from each of the next two overs, before 14 in the 17th over and 17 in the 18th meant only 11 were needed from the final two overs with five wickets in hand. Root's wonderful 83 ended as he was well caught off a full-toss, before 10 runs in the next four balls brought the scores level. Remarkably, the first two balls of the final over featured a great catch and a run-out, before the winning run came from the fourth ball.

Sri Lanka's Tillakaratne Dilshan attacks the Afghanistan bowling.

The team from the Caribbean stole the spoils in a decider sure to be long remembered for explosive hitting in the final over.

Bangladesh's Sabbir Rahman is bowled by Pakistan's Shahid Afridi.

England 8-230 (Joe Root 83, Jason Roy 43; Kyle Abbott 3-41) beat South Africa 4-229 (Hashim Amla 58, JP Duminy 54 not out, Quinton de Kock 52; Moeen Ali 2-34) by two wickets.

India v Bangladesh at M. Chinnaswamy Stadium (Bengaluru), 23 March

While only one run separated the teams, it was astonishing that there were no standout performances. Nobody scored more than 35, nor did anyone take more than two wickets. In the end, there were many turning points including dropped catches.

India's first six batters made scores between 13 and 30. After being 3-112 with five overs left, India lost wickets with successive balls and made only 34 more runs. Bangladesh was well-placed at 3-87 with nine overs left, before stumbling to 5-95. A wicket and a boundary from the final two balls of the 18th over were followed by seven successive singles, meaning 10 runs were needed from five balls. Two fours reduced the task to two runs from three balls, but then Mushfiqur Rahim and Mahmudullah paid dearly for rash shots as they were caught from successive balls. Shuvagata Hom failed to make contact with the final delivery, and Indian wicketkeeper MS Dhoni sealed the game as he scurried to break the stumps and run out Mustafizur Rahman for a diamond duck.

India 7-146 (Suresh Raina 30; Mustafizur Rahman 2-34, Al-Amin Hossain 2-37) beat Bangladesh 9-145 (Tamim Iqbal 35; Ravi Ashwin 2-20, Ravindra Jadeja 2-22) by one run.

Afghanistan v West Indies at Vidarbha Cricket Association Stadium (Nagpur), 27 March

A low-scoring thriller unfolded between the top and bottom teams in Group 1 of the Super 10s, with Afghanistan recording a surprise victory after being on the back foot for the most part against West Indies.

Afghanistan struggled as Samuel Badree bowled four brilliant overs, before a wicket each to Sulieman Benn and Daren Sammy made the score 5-56 in the 12th over. Najibullah Zadran made 48 not out off 40 balls at number six, having scored 11 in the final over after Rashid Khan struck the final ball of the 19th over for six. But the target of 124 didn't appear big enough, as West Indies lost its fourth wicket at 79 with six overs left. The West Indians scored only 20 runs for the loss of two wickets in the next four overs, before an entertaining 19th over featured a single, a six, a leg bye, a wicket, another six and another single.

Having hit both sixes in the 19th over, Carlos Brathwaite took strike for the final over as 10 runs were needed. Brathwaite twice swung and missed before he was superbly caught from a skier, and then the final three balls yielded only singles despite two full-tosses from Mohammad Nabi. Afghanistan's opening bowler Amir Hamza, meanwhile, was an unsung hero with figures of 4-0-9-1.

Afghanistan 7-123 (Najibullah Zadran 48 not out; Samuel Badree 3-14, Andre Russell 2-23) beat West Indies 8-117 (Dwayne Bravo 28; Mohammad Nabi and Rashid Khan 2-26) by six runs.

NISSAN

SIX OF THE BEST: Individual performances

(excluding player of the tournament, and the finals)

Pakistan opener Sharjeel Khan.

Mitchell Santner: 18 off 17 balls and 4-11 off four overs: New Zealand v India at Vidarbha Cricket Association Stadium (Nagpur), 15 March

After coming to the crease at 4-61 in the 12th over, Mitchell Santner made 18 before falling in the 17th over with New Zealand's total at 98. The eventual total of 126 appeared sub-standard, until Santner struck with his second and fifth deliveries. Rohit Sharma was stumped, before Suresh Raina was caught off a leading edge to leave India 3-12 in the third over.

The fourth ball of Santner's second over produced an lbw which left India 6-42 in the 10th over. His final over was the 18th of the innings, and featured the wicket of Dhoni who was superbly caught at long-on to leave India on the brink of defeat at 9-79.

Chris Gayle 100 not out off 48 balls: West Indies v England at Wankhede Stadium (Mumbai), 16 March

Chris Gayle made England's total of 6-182 appear small as he piloted West Indies to a six-wicket win, with 11 balls remaining. He recorded five fours and 11 sixes, with several of his sixes between long-on and long-off.

Astonishingly, Gayle produced only two scoring shots while facing just six deliveries in the first 5.2 overs. He crunched his third delivery for four, before thumping the next one for a straight six. He creamed back-to-back sixes in the ninth and 11th overs, before two singles in the 12th over brought up his 50 from 27 balls. A hat-trick of sixes in the 14th over took Gayle to 79 off 36, before he went from 80 to 96 in four balls in the 16th over. With victory imminent, Gayle helped himself to four singles from the final six balls he faced.

Tamim Iqbal 103 not out off 63 balls: Bangladesh v Oman at Himachal Pradesh Cricket Association Stadium (Dharamshala), 13 March

Bangladesh opener Tamim Iqbal made the highest score of the tournament, following a slow start against Oman. He faced the first five balls of the match, with four dots followed by a single. Iqbal's seventh four took him to 52 off 35 deliveries, before he clubbed the next ball for six. Iqbal finished with 10 fours

Virat Kohli (India)

Matches	Innings	Not outs	Runs	Highest score	Average	50s	100s	Catches
5	5	3	273	89*	136.50	3	-	3
Overs	**Maidens**	**Runs**	**Wickets**	**Average**	**Best figures**			
1.4	-	15	1	15	1-15			

and five sixes, with his final boundary taking him to triple figures from 60 balls. Bangladesh finished with 2-180, before Oman fell well short in a rain-reduced run chase.

Joe Root 83 off 44 balls: England v South Africa at Wankhede Stadium (Mumbai), 18 March

England was 2-71 after just 4.3 overs when Joe Root arrived, in reply to South Africa's 4-229. After reaching 12 runs off 11 balls without a boundary, Root struck the next two balls he faced for six and was virtually unstoppable thereafter. He showed his class as he mixed boundaries with plenty of singles. A reverse sweep for six off a full-toss raised his half-century in 29 balls, before a spate of boundaries ensued. He finished with six fours and four sixes, before departing as victory loomed.

James Faulkner 5-28 off four overs: Australia v Pakistan at Punjab Cricket Association IS Bindra Stadium (Mohali), 25 March

Pakistan fell 22 runs shy of its 194-run target, as James Faulkner's five-wicket haul included four from his back-of-the-hand slower ball in the death overs. Sharjeel Khan whipped Faulkner's first ball to the boundary, before bottom-edging the bowler's third delivery into the leg-stump to leave Pakistan 2-40 in the sixth over. Faulkner's second over cost 11 runs including a six and a bye, before he returned with three overs to spare as Pakistan required 49 runs. Faulkner was twice on a hat-trick as he claimed 4-3 in six balls. Khalid Latif and Imad Wasim swung desperately, with the former bowled and the latter skying a catch. Sarfaraz Ahmed reverse-swept a catch to backward point, before a miscued slog from Wahab Riaz went to third man.

Mustafizur Rahman 5-22 off four overs: Bangladesh v New Zealand at Eden Gardens (Kolkata), 26 March

Mustafizur Rahman's bowling against New Zealand should not be ignored, even if the Kiwis won by 75 runs. Rahman's off-cutters brought the Kiwis undone, as the left-armer struck in the fourth, ninth and 18th overs of New Zealand's innings, before striking twice in the final over.

The left-handed Henry Nicholls lost his off-stump as a drive failed to connect, and the right-handed Kane Williamson suffered the same fate as he attempted a lap sweep. Another right-hander, Grant Elliott, lobbed a legside flick and was brilliantly caught at mid-wicket.

Rahman rattled the left-handed Santner's off-stump with the fourth ball of the final over, before the next ball struck the off-stump of the right-handed Nathan McCullum. A hat-trick was denied, as Mitchell McClenaghan sent the final delivery over the boundary.

PLAYER OF THE TOURNAMENT

Virat Kohli won back-to-back player of the tournament awards in the T20 format, but again finished on a disappointing note. This time, India bowed out in the semi-finals.

The Indians began the tournament poorly as they were skittled for 79 in reply to New Zealand's 7-126, with Kohli making 23 off 27 balls. Kohli was player of the match against Pakistan for his 55 not out off 37 balls, as India cruised to the 119-run target for the loss of four wickets. In India's heart-stopping one-run win against Bangladesh, Kohli scored a run-a-ball 24.

Kohli's final two knocks were simply outstanding, with India beating Australia by six wickets before losing the semi-final to West Indies by seven wickets. With India chasing 161 against Australia, Kohli earned another player of the match award as his 82 not out off 51 balls included nine fours and two sixes. Against West Indies, Kohli luckily avoided being run out twice in a matter of seconds when he was on one. A run-out chance also went begging from the next ball.

Kohli's 89 not out came off 47 balls and included 11 fours and a six. Also called upon with the ball, Kohli took 1-4 in his first over to leave West Indies needing 73 runs from six overs. His first delivery resulted in a catch at long-off, before he returned for the final over as West Indies needed only eight runs. Kohli conceded just one run from two balls, before Andre Russell heaved the third ball for four and then sent the next one into the crowd.

The second semi-final was one of the best games of the tournament as there were 388 runs and only five wickets.

FIRST SEMI-FINAL

New Zealand v England at Feroz Shah Kotla (Delhi), 30 March

The second half of New Zealand's innings and the performance of England opener Jason Roy were particularly decisive. Martin Guptill cracked the first and fifth balls of the match to the fence, before Colin Munro hit three successive fours in the sixth over. New Zealand was 1-89 after 10 overs, but subsequently lost momentum. Twelve runs in the 16th over were followed by three quick wickets, including two off successive full-tosses. The last over contained a further two wickets and only three runs, including a bye and a leg bye.

With England chasing 154, the first over of the run chase proved crucial. Roy rode his luck as he hit four fours, including one off an inside edge and another off a top-edge. Alex Hales made just 20 in an 82-run opening stand, before Roy raced to 78 which included 11 fours and two sixes. Two wickets in successive balls left England 3-110 with 46 balls left, before 22 runs in the 17th over brought the scores level. Jos Buttler promptly smacked his third six in four balls to complete the demolition.

England 3-159 (Jason Roy 78, Jos Buttler 32 not out; Ish Sodhi 2-42) beat New Zealand 8-153 (Colin Munro 46; Ben Stokes 3-26) by seven wickets.

SECOND SEMI-FINAL

India v West Indies at Wankhede Stadium (Mumbai), 31 March

This was one of the best games of the tournament as there were 388 runs and only five wickets.

India was just 0-6 after two overs, before Rohit Sharma doubled the total with one shot. In the sixth over, Sharma hit a no-ball for six and then smashed the free hit for another maximum. Soon after Sharma fell for 43, Kohli was vitally reprieved in consecutive balls before the next delivery was edged wide of the wicketkeeper for four.

The 100 came up in 12.2 overs, before India scored at two runs per ball for the remainder of the innings. Following the second wicket, Kohli slammed 48 runs from his final 18 balls while Dhoni hit an undefeated 15 off nine.

The West Indians were 2-19 after Chris Gayle and Marlon Samuels were dismissed in the first three overs. Johnson Charles hit the next two balls for four, before Lendl Simmons was caught off a no-ball in the seventh over. Thirty-eight runs in three overs took the score to 2-97 with nine overs left, before Charles's dismissal left the West Indians needing 77 runs off 41 balls with seven wickets remaining. The 15th over proved a massive turning point as 18 runs were scored. Incredibly, Simmons was again caught off a no-ball, and this time he creamed the free hit for six.

With West Indies needing 32 runs from three overs, three dot balls were followed by a six, a two and a four. The six occurred as the fielder vitally stepped on the boundary before throwing the ball to a teammate as a dismissal beckoned. With 18 runs needed off eight balls, Andre Russell blazed a six and a four off successive balls before following up in the next over with another four and another six to seal the result with two balls to spare.

West Indies 3-196 (Lendl Simmons 82 not out, Johnson Charles 52) beat India 2-192 (Virat Kohli 89 not out, Rohit Sharma 43) by seven wickets.

FINAL

England v West Indies at Eden Gardens (Kolkata), 3 April

A miraculous finale unfolded, as West Indies needed 19 runs off the final over and surpassed it with two balls to spare. In defence of the bowler, Ben Stokes, the final over wasn't the only vital factor in the outcome.

England lost a wicket second ball, before faltering to 3-23 during a wicket maiden. Root and Buttler took the total to 3-67 after 10 overs, before Buttler struck successive sixes and then perished in the following over. Three wickets in five balls, including Root for 54 off 36, left England 7-111 with 35 balls remaining. A potentially crucial unbroken last-wicket stand of 13 unfolded, before West Indies' pursuit of 156 began disastrously as Charles, Gayle and Simmons exited in the first 2.3 overs.

Samuels moved the score along but Dwayne Bravo was tied down, before he registered a critical four from a dropped catch. Bravo hit a six in the next over, but departed three balls later to leave West Indies needing 70 runs from six overs. The 15th over cost 18 runs after Samuels hit the last two balls for six, but then two wickets fell in the 16th over. Thirty-one runs were needed from 13 balls, before a four to each batter was followed by four singles and a dot ball.

Having scored 10 runs off six balls, Carlos Brathwaite faced up for the final over. In a miraculous display under enormous pressure, Brathwaite slammed three successive sixes to level the scores before his fourth successive six clinched the victory.

West Indies 6-161 (Marlon Samuels 85 not out, Carlos Brathwaite 34 not out; David Willey 3-20, Joe Root 2-9) beat England 9-155 (Joe Root 54, Jos Buttler 36; Carlos Brathwaite 3-23, Dwayne Bravo 3-37) by four wickets.

India's Yuvraj Singh.

2021

Déjà vu as Aussies dismantle Kiwis

A Cricket World Cup was held entirely outside Test cricket-playing nations for the first time, as Oman and United Arab Emirates were joint hosts in 2021. The event was originally scheduled for Australia in late 2020, but this plan and subsequent revised plans were thrown into disarray due to the global COVID-19 pandemic in 2020 and 2021. Papua New Guinea and Namibia were World Cup T20 newcomers in 2021, as Hong Kong and Zimbabwe missed out.

The format somewhat changed, as the first round was followed by Super 12s rather than Super 8s or 10s. Group A teams Sri Lanka and Namibia progressed to the Super 12s after being too good for Ireland and the Netherlands, while Scotland and Bangladesh were the best of the Group B teams after defeating Oman and Papua New Guinea. England, Australia and South Africa had four wins and one loss each in Group 1 of the Super 12s, with the Proteas missing the semi-finals on net run rate. In Group 2, Pakistan won all five of its fixtures while New Zealand was next best with one defeat. Both semi-finals involved snatching victory from the jaws of defeat (and vice versa), with the Trans-Tasman rivals ultimately battling out the decider.

Having been a dominant force in the 50 overs per side World Cup since 1987, Australia finally reigned supreme in the shorter format after being runner-up once in the first six T20 World Cups.

A HAT-TRICK OF CLASSICS: Three great contests

Scotland v Bangladesh at Oman Cricket Academy Ground (Muscat), 17 October

Scotland's Chris Greaves played a vital role with bat and ball in this close game. George Munsey's bright 29 helped Scotland to 1-45, before five wickets fell for only eight runs. Following a 51-run seventh wicket partnership, Greaves raced from 28 to 42 in three balls. Greaves and teammate Josh Davey departed from successive balls in the final over, before Safyaan Sharif struck the final two balls for six and two to lift the total to 140.

Bangladesh's openers failed, and then Mushfiqur Rahim and Shakib Al Hasan took the total to 65 at the 11-over mark before Greaves dismissed them both to leave Bangladesh 4-74 with 41 balls left. Thirty-two runs were added for the fifth wicket, but then the loss of 3-10 in nine balls left Bangladesh needing 25 off seven. Needing to hit the last three balls for six, Mahedi Hasan managed one maximum before a four from the penultimate ball enabled Scotland to breathe a sigh of relief.

Scotland 9-140 (Chris Greaves 45; Mahedi Hasan 3-19, Shakib Al Hasan 2-17) beat Bangladesh 7-134 (Mushfiqur Rahim 38; Brad Wheal 3-24, Chris Greaves 2-19) by six runs.

Sri Lanka's Pathum Nissanka executes a fancy stroke.

West Indies v Bangladesh at Sharjah Cricket Stadium (Sharjah), 29 October

Poor fielding was costly, with both sides dropping catches while there were also missed run-outs and a missed stumping. It was also telling that West Indies scored 19 runs from its final five balls, before Bangladesh failed to score the required 16 runs from the final 11 balls.

West Indies fell to 3-32 in the seventh over after a catch was dropped from the previous delivery. In the 13th over, Kieron Pollard retired hurt before Andre Russell was unluckily run out without facing. Roston Chase and Nicholas Pooran hit a four each in the 15th over before Pooran struck successive sixes in the following over. Pooran also hit two sixes in the 18th over, before he and Chase departed in the next over. Jason Holder survived a chance later in the 19th over before hitting back-to-back sixes in the final over, followed by a last-ball six from Pollard.

Chasing 143, Bangladesh stumbled to 2-29 before recovering. A wicket fell for 25 runs in two overs, making the score 3-80 with eight overs left. A risky shot cost Mushfiqur Rahim in the 14th over, before 11 runs in the 16th over were followed by only three in the 17th. Mahmudullah creamed the first ball of the 19th over for six, but the next five balls featured just three runs and a vital wicket as a possible six turned into a catch. With Bangladesh needing 13 runs in the final over, a two was followed by a bye and three successive twos before Mahmudullah missed the final ball when he needed to hit a four. Russell bowled well in the frantic final over, which featured a dropped catch from the fourth ball and a misfield from the fifth ball.

West Indies 7-142 (Nicholas Pooran 40, Roston Chase 39; Shoriful Islam 2-20, Mahedi Hasan 2-27) beat Bangladesh 5-139 (Litton Das 44, Mahmudullah 31 not out) by three runs.

Sri Lanka v South Africa at Sharjah Cricket Stadium (Sharjah), 30 October

Sri Lanka was 1-46 after eight overs before two sixes were hit in the next three balls. The fifth ball of the over turned the game, as Charith Asalanka was brilliantly run out as he chanced a second run. Wickets fell regularly thereafter, while opener Pathum Nissanka did his best to keep the innings afloat. He hit 15 runs in the 18th over, before his dismissal for 72 with eight balls remaining left Sri Lanka 8-131. Another 11 runs were added before the final two wickets fell from the final two balls.

The Proteas were 2-26 after the openers fell in quick succession, before a run-out from a direct hit made the score 3-49 after eight overs. The next wicket came with five overs remaining, before Wanindu Hasaranga completed a hat-trick which left South Africa needing 31 runs from 16 balls with four wickets in hand. A six from Kagiso Rabada reduced the task to 16 runs from eight balls, before 15 were needed from the final over. David Miller smashed two huge sixes in succession before levelling the scores with a single, and then Rabada edged a match-sealing four from the fifth ball.

South Africa 6-146 (Temba Bavuma 46; Wanindu Hasaranga 3-20, Dushmantha Chameera 2-27) beat Sri Lanka 142 (Pathum Nissanka 72; Tabraiz Shamsi and Dwaine Pretorius 3-17) by four wickets.

SIX OF THE BEST: Individual performances

(excluding player of the tournament, and the finals)

Mujeeb Ur Rahman 5-20 off four overs: Afghanistan v Scotland at Sharjah Cricket Stadium (Sharjah), 25 October

After Afghanistan tallied 4-190, Scotland was 7-46 after eight overs as off-spinner Mujeeb Ur Rahman completed his spell. He struck with the second, third and sixth balls of his second over, with his first victim bowled before the next two were lbw. In Mujeeb's third over, the left-handed George Munsey hit a six before having his off-peg rattled next ball. From his third-last delivery, Mujeeb unluckily conceded five runs due to four from overthrows. Immediately afterwards he claimed his fifth scalp as another left-hander, Mark Watt, had his stumps splayed.

Haris Rauf 4-22 off four overs: Pakistan v New Zealand at Sharjah Cricket Stadium (Sharjah), 26 October

With Haris Rauf's second delivery, Martin Guptill backed away and was bowled from a ball that ricocheted off his thigh. This left New Zealand 1-36 in the sixth over, before Rauf's remaining overs were the 15th, 18th and 20th of the innings. The 18th was his best as he had two batters caught in the space of three balls. After conceding nine runs in the final over, Rauf finished with a wicket as Mitchell Santner swung unsuccessfully and heard the death rattle. Pakistan eventually won by five wickets, chasing 135.

Curtis Campher 4-26 off four overs (including four wickets in four balls): Ireland v Netherlands at Sheikh Zayed Cricket Stadium (Abu Dhabi), 18 October

Of the three hat-tricks in this tournament, Ireland's Curtis Campher's was the standout as he claimed four wickets in four balls. He had Colin Ackerman caught behind before having two successive lbw appeals upheld, although the first and third victims were given not out before the decisions were overturned upon review. Campher's fourth victim was Roelof van der Merwe, who dragged a widish delivery onto his off-stump. The Netherlands had gone from 2-51 to 6-51, before being all out for 106 and going on to lose by seven wickets. The final three balls of the Netherlands' innings also featured wickets – albeit one was a run-out – before Campher hit the winning run.

Sri Lanka's Wanindu Hasaranga claimed the second hat-trick, but was in a beaten side. He bowled Aiden Markram with the final ball of an over, and then dismissed Temba Bavuma and Dwaine Pretorius with the first two balls of his next over. Bavuma was well caught at deep mid-wicket, before Pretorius slogged a catch to long-on. This left the Proteas 6-112, before they passed the 143-run target in the final over.

South Africa's Kagiso Rabada also took three wickets in three balls, ironically after he had 0-45 from three overs and was entrusted with the final over as England needed 14 runs with five wickets in hand. Rabada had two batters caught in the deep on the on side before Chris Jordan holed out to long-off, and the Proteas held on to win by 10 runs.

Scotland's Chris Greaves scurries to make his ground while India's Ravindra Jadeja prepares to receive a throw from the outfield.

England was 3-47 after 10 overs, following nearly five overs without a boundary. Buttler hit the first ball of the 11th over for four, before going from 35 to 45 in two balls in the 13th over. His 50 took him 45 balls, before he slammed 51 runs from the remaining 22 balls he faced. In the 18th over, Buttler smashed two sixes in two balls and then clipped a four. He began the final over on 87, and then scooped the first ball for four. Two twos followed, with a catch going begging on the second occasion. Two dot balls kept Buttler on 95, before he clouted a leg-stump full-toss over the boundary from the final delivery to crack triple figures.

Adam Zampa 5-19 off four overs: Australia v Bangladesh at Dubai International Cricket Stadium (Dubai), 4 November

Bangladesh was 4-33 after six overs, before leg-spinner Adam Zampa bagged five wickets to help rout the batting side for only 73. Incidentally, Zampa's third victim was the only right-hander.

Zampa's first ball to Afif Hossain was edged to first slip for an easy catch. His next two scalps were from the final two balls of his third over, with Shamim Hossain caught behind before Mahedi Hasan was lbw. Oddly, Zampa was replaced for one over before returning for the 15th over. He was desperately unlucky not to take a hat-trick as Taskin Ahmed edged the ball to the wicketkeeper who failed to hold it. Zampa nonetheless struck with the fourth and sixth balls of the over, with a catch at long-on followed by another catch at first slip.

Rassie van der Dussen 94 not out off 60 balls: South Africa v England at Sharjah Cricket Stadium (Sharjah), 6 November

After arriving in the third over at 1-15, Rassie van der Dussen was largely responsible for South Africa's match-winning total of 2-189 against England. His innings included five fours and six sixes.

From his second delivery, van der Dussen shuffled across his stumps and scooped the ball over fine leg for four. On 29, he survived a very close call for lbw and then flicked the next ball to the boundary. He reached 50 off 37 balls, before hooking a six to raise South Africa's 100 on the 13-over mark. Van der Dussen whacked back-to-back sixes in the 16th over,

Of the three hat-tricks in this tournament, Ireland's Curtis Campher's was the standout as he claimed four wickets in four balls.

Daryl Mitchell played a starring role for the Kiwis in their semi-final victory against England.

Jos Buttler 101 not out off 67 balls: England v Sri Lanka at Sharjah Cricket Stadium (Sharjah), 1 November

With England tallying 4-163 and beating Sri Lanka by 26 runs, Jos Buttler's unconquered ton stood out. His innings included six fours and six sixes.

David Warner (Australia)

Matches	Innings	Not outs	Runs	Highest score	Average	50s	100s	Catches
7	7	1	289	89*	48.17	3	-	3

before a reverse-scoop brought him a four in the 18th over. He was on 82 with two overs remaining but faced only three of the next 10 balls, and a century was beyond reach as he struck the second-last ball for six and then finished with a single.

PLAYER OF THE TOURNAMENT

David Warner was the tournament's second highest run-scorer, despite patchy form. He scored 14 fewer runs from one more innings than Pakistan's Babar Azam.

In Australia's first outing, Warner hit three fours in a quick 14 before slicing a catch to backward point. This left the Australians 2-20, before they overhauled South Africa's 9-118 with just two balls to spare. Sri Lanka made a more competitive 6-154, before Warner set up a comfortable seven-wicket win. He blazed 10 fours in his 65 off 42 balls, having survived a chance on 18 as the wicketkeeper fumbled a sitter. Against England, Warner was not so fortunate. He scored a single from the first ball of the match before edging the next ball he faced to the wicketkeeper, and Australia fell to an eight-wicket loss after tallying 125.

Australia won its next two matches by eight wickets, having overhauled Bangladesh's 73 in just 6.2 overs before overtaking West Indies' 7-157 in 16.2 overs. After scoring 18 off 14 balls against Bangladesh, Warner earned player of the match honours against West Indies as he struck nine fours and four sixes in his 89 not out off 56 balls. Warner reached his half-century off 29 balls, before Mitchell Marsh reached 50 in 28 balls. Warner went from 69 to 79 in two balls, with a switch-hit going for four before he lifted a more conventional six over square leg. A stumping chance was botched with Warner on 80, and soon Marsh exited before Warner clipped a winning four.

With Australia achieving targets of 177 and 173 in the finals series, Warner played a vital role without registering a big score. In the semi-final against Pakistan, he slammed three fours and three sixes in his 49 off 30 balls before his dismissal left Australia 4-89 after 10.1 overs. In the final against New Zealand, Warner's 53 off 38 balls included four fours and three sixes before his exit left Australia needing 66 runs from 46 balls.

FIRST SEMI-FINAL

New Zealand v England at Sheikh Zayed Cricket Stadium (Abu Dhabi), 10 November

England appeared on top as New Zealand needed 57 runs in the final four overs, before a sizzling onslaught enabled the Kiwis to steal a shock victory with six balls remaining.

England was 0-13 after three overs before the fourth over cost 16 runs. The score was 2-53 after 8.1 overs, and then the next partnership produced 63 runs off 43 balls. Forty runs were added in the next four overs, and then a wicket was followed by 10 runs from the final four balls. Moeen Ali reached 50 in the final over before the last ball yielded two runs for captain Eoin Morgan from a dropped catch.

Guptill hit a first-ball boundary in the run chase, before the Kiwis fell to 2-13. The score was only 2-58 at the halfway stage, before the 11th over contained 15 runs. The Kiwis needed 72 runs from 38 balls when Devon Conway was stumped, before the pendulum changed in the 17th over which featured 19 runs to James Neesham and four sundries. The 18th over featured 14 runs from five balls including two sixes, before Neesham exited. After England scored 20 runs in its final two overs, New Zealand needed to do likewise but only required one over. Successive sixes from Daryl Mitchell reduced the equation to six runs from nine balls, before he slammed the winning four. Mitchell's undefeated 72 off 47 balls included 26 off his final seven deliveries.

New Zealand 5-167 (Daryl Mitchell 72 not out, Devon Conway 46; Liam Livingstone 2-22) beat England 4-166 (Moeen Ali 51 not out, Dawid Malan 41; James Neesham 1-18) by five wickets.

Australian duo Glenn Maxwell and Mitchell Marsh celebrate winning the decider.

SECOND SEMI-FINAL

Australia v Pakistan at Dubai International Cricket Stadium (Dubai), 11 November

For the second time in two days, the margin was five wickets with one over to spare. After New Zealand smashed its final 57 runs in three overs, Australia clubbed 50 runs in the same period.

Pakistan's openers were perhaps a little conservative at times, as they put on 71 runs in 10 overs. The 17th over cost 21 runs, before Mohammad Rizwan's dismissal in the next over made the score 2-143. The remainder of the 18th over cost 15 runs, before the 19th featured just three runs and a wicket. The first half of the final over featured two singles and a wicket, before Fakhar Zaman struck consecutive sixes and then finished with a single.

Australia's quest for 177 began disastrously as captain Aaron Finch was lbw with the third ball of the innings, before Marsh survived a close call for lbw next ball. Warner and Marsh added 51 runs which included 35 in 13 balls at one stage, before Shadab Khan took a wicket in each of his four overs to leave Australia 5-96 after 12.2 overs. Marcus Stoinis hit the next ball for six, but the task became stiff when a mere six runs in the 15th over meant 62 were needed in five overs. However, a chance to run out Stoinis went begging in the 15th over. Twelve runs came in the 16th over, including two from a free hit. Stoinis struck 13 runs in the 17th over despite two dot balls, before Matthew Wade hit 13 runs to Stoinis's two in the 18th over. The game virtually slipped from Pakistan's grasp with the third ball of the 19th over as two runs came from a dropped catch. Wade clubbed the next three balls over the boundary, and suddenly the game was over. Wade's 41 not out took just 17 balls.

Australia 5-177 (David Warner 49, Matthew Wade 41 not out, Marcus Stoinis 40 not out; Shadab Khan 4-26) beat Pakistan 4-176 (Mohammad Rizwan 67, Fakhar Zaman 55 not out; Mitchell Starc 2-38) by five wickets.

FINAL

Australia v New Zealand at Dubai International Cricket Stadium (Dubai), 14 November

The contest somewhat resembled the 2015 ODI World Cup, as the Kiwis could not prevent the Australians from reaching a target with plenty of wickets in hand.

The Kiwis were only 1-57 after 10 overs, having gone 32 balls without a boundary at one stage. The 11th over cost 19 runs, with the first of three successive boundaries coming from a dropped catch to reprieve Williamson. Guptill fell from the first ball of the 12th over, before Williamson whacked successive sixes in the next over to reach a 32-ball half-century. Twelve runs came in the 15th over before Williamson rode his luck as he slammed 22 in the following over. Two wickets fell in the 18th over, including Williamson for a 48-ball knock of 85, before 23 runs were added in the final two overs.

Australia was 1-15 when Finch exited, before Marsh struck his first delivery for six and followed up with back-to-back fours. Warner hammered 16 runs in the ninth over, before Australia's 100 came up in 11.3 overs. Warner fell for 53 in the 13th over, before 16 runs in the next over reduced the equation to 48 from six overs. Half of those runs came in the next two overs, and from there the result was inevitable. Marsh finished unbeaten on 77 from 50 balls, while Glenn Maxwell's reverse-swipe for the winning boundary took him to 28 not out from 18 balls.

Australia 2-173 (Mitchell Marsh 77 not out, David Warner 53; Trent Boult 2-18) beat New Zealand 4-172 (Kane Williamson 85; Josh Hazlewood 3-16) by eight wickets.

MAXWELL
32
AUSTRALIA

2022

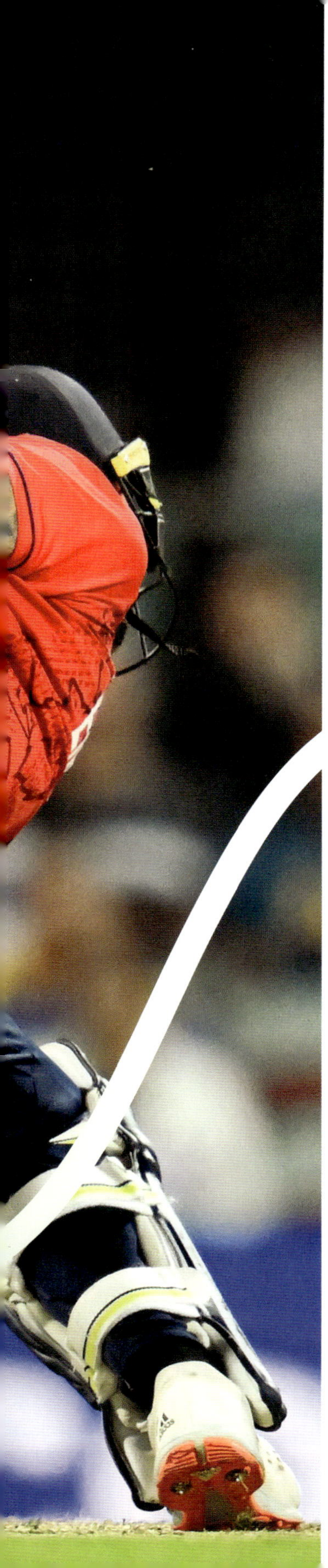

England completes the double

The COVID-19 pandemic prompted the eighth T20 World Cup to be postponed from 2020 to 2022, with reigning champion Australia ultimately becoming the host nation. Zimbabwe and United Arab Emirates (UAE) returned to the competition, in place of Oman and Papua New Guinea.

Sri Lanka and the Netherlands finished ahead of Namibia and UAE in Group A, while Zimbabwe and Ireland finished ahead of Scotland and West Indies in Group B. There was little point speculating what might have been, after three Group 1 matches and one Group 2 match were abandoned in the Super 12s. New Zealand, England and Australia were level on points after having one no-result each in Group 1, with Australia missing the semi-finals on net run rate. India and Pakistan were outright first and second in Group 2.

After Pakistan was too good for the Kiwis in one semi-final before England decimated India in the other, England became the second nation to win the tournament a second time.

A HAT-TRICK OF CLASSICS: Three great contests

Pakistan v India at Melbourne Cricket Ground (Melbourne), 23 October

This contest was beyond breathtaking. Indeed, cricket was the real winner.

Pakistan was 2-15 after four overs, and then progressed steadily before Iftikhar Ahmed cleared the boundary four times in six balls. But his exit for 51 sparked a collapse, as Pakistan fell to 7-120 in the 17th over. Thirty-four runs were added for the loss of one wicket in the final three overs as Shan Masood reached a half-century while Shaheen Shah Afridi and Haris Rauf hit a six each.

The run-out of Axar Patel left India 4-31 after 6.1 overs, before the 12th over yielded 20 runs including three sixes to take the total to 4-74. India needed 48 runs in the final three overs with Virat Kohli and Hardik Pandya settled at the crease, and then Kohli struck three fours in the 18th over which cost 17 runs. Twenty-eight were needed off eight balls, before Kohli produced back-to-back sixes in marvellous style.

India lost momentum as the wicket of Pandya from the first ball of the final over was followed by a single and a two. With India needing 13 runs off three balls, Mohammad Nawaz bowled a fatal no-ball full-toss which Kohli dispatched

England's Alex Hales is stumped by New Zealand's Devon Conway at the Gabba.

for six. An ensuing wide meant Kohli still had a free hit and, although he was bowled, the batters were able to scramble three byes. A messy stumping from the next ball, incredibly, left Ravi Ashwin needing two runs from the final ball for victory. Nawaz faltered again as he bowled a wide, before Ashwin managed a single to cap off a miraculous victory. Kohli finished unbeaten on 82 off 53 balls.

India 6-160 (Virat Kohli 82 not out, Hardik Pandya 40; Haris Rauf 2-36) beat Pakistan 8-159 (Shan Masood 52 not out, Iftikhar Ahmed 51; Hardik Pandya 3-30, Arshdeep Singh 3-32) by four wickets.

Zimbabwe's Sikandar Raza hammers the ball through the off side.

Zimbabwe v Pakistan at Perth Stadium (Perth), 27 October

This thriller involved modest scoring rates. After Zimbabwe raced to 0-22 in the first eight balls, things quietened down. The Africans went from 0-42 to 2-43, and would have been 3-60 in the ninth over had Sean Williams not been reprieved. Milton Shumba exited in the following over, before Williams gained a four as a tough catch went begging. Nevertheless, Zimbabwe soon slumped from 3-95 to 7-95 in six balls as Shadab Khan and Mohammad Wasim each took two wickets in consecutive balls. Shadab's latter wicket came as Babar Azam held a magnificent one-handed slips catch.

Zimbabwe managed 35 runs in the final 5.2 overs, while a dropped catch and a missed run-out didn't help Pakistan in the 19th over. Brad Evans hit a six in the final over, but was bowled next ball.

Chasing 131, Pakistan faltered to 3-36 before a 52-run stand was followed by two wickets from successive deliveries. When the sixth wicket fell, Pakistan needed 37 runs from 29 balls. A six from Mohammad Nawaz reduced the task to 12 from eight, before it became 11 from six. A three to Nawaz and a four to Wasim meant only four runs were needed from four balls, before a single was followed by a dot ball. Nawaz then skewed a catch to deep mid-off, before Shaheen Shah Afridi hit the final ball to long-on. He pursued a second run to tie the game but was run out, despite a fumble from the wicketkeeper who recovered just in time.

Zimbabwe 8-130 (Sean Williams 31; Mohammad Wasim 4-24, Shadab Khan 3-23) beat Pakistan 8-129 (Shan Masood 44, Mohammad Nawaz 22; Sikandar Raza 3-25, Brad Evans 2-25) by one run.

Netherlands v South Africa at Adelaide Oval (Adelaide), 6 November

This shock result was enough to end South Africa's finals hopes. Somewhat strangely, five Netherlands batters made scores between 12 and 41 before seven South African scores ranged from 13 to 25.

The Netherlands openers put on 58 runs before Tom Cooper struck 35 off 19 balls at number three. Cooper's dismissal made the score 3-112 with five overs left, before the 16th over contained only a single. Thirty-one runs came in the final two overs, including a six from the final ball to boost the total to 4-158. Anrich Nortje had wonderful figures of 1-10 from four overs.

South Africa's first six batters made starts but none faced more than 20 balls. Fourteen runs in the ninth over took the score to 2-63, and then Rilee Rossouw holed out to deep square leg in the next over as he looked threatening. Aiden Markram was brilliantly caught when he too looked ominous, before 12 runs in the 15th over meant 48 were needed from the final five. The Proteas were rocked in the 16th over as two wickets fell, with former Proteas player Roelof van der Merwe holding a spectacular catch to dismiss David Miller before Wayne Parnell edged behind. The next boundary came in the 19th over when Keshav Maharaj's six reduced the requirement to 27 from eight balls. The final three balls yielded a single, a wicket and a four after three sixes were needed for a tied result.

Netherlands 4-158 (Colin Ackermann 41 not out; Keshav Maharaj 2-27) beat South Africa 8-145 (Rilee Rossouw 25; Brandon Glover 3-9, Fred Klaassen 2-20) by 13 runs.

SIX OF THE BEST: Individual performances

(excluding player of the tournament, and the finals)

Curtis Campher 72 not out off 32 balls: Ireland v Scotland at Bellerive Oval (Hobart), 19 October

After Scotland opener Michael Jones clubbed 86 off 55 balls to set up a total of 5-176, Ireland was 4-61 after 9.3 overs. Miraculously, Curtis Campher and George Dockrell added 119 runs in the next 9.3 overs to give Ireland a six-wicket victory. The acceleration began in the 12th over, as eight successive overs cost anything from 11 to 18 runs each.

With 39 not out from 27 balls, Dockrell was the perfect foil for Campher who had arrived in the ninth over at 3-57. Campher advanced to seven off six before the boundaries began to flow. He reached his half-century in 25 balls after hitting three fours and two sixes. His next four took him to 60 off 29, before he crunched three successive fours through the off side to end the game. For good measure, Campher earlier took 2-9 from two overs.

Devon Conway 92 not out off 58 balls: New Zealand v Australia at Sydney Cricket Ground (Sydney), 22 October

Devon Conway remained unbeaten but couldn't quite reach a ton as the Kiwis made 3-200, before thrashing Australia by 89 runs. The opening stand brought 56 runs in four overs, before Finn Allen departed for 42 off 16 balls. At this stage, Conway had 14 off 9. He clipped his first delivery to the fine leg boundary, and drove his third delivery for another four.

Conway's second six took him to 55 off 36 balls, before his seventh four took him to 89 off 57 with one over remaining. He faced only one ball in the final over, scoring three runs.

Rilee Rossouw 109 off 56 balls: South Africa v Bangladesh at Sydney Cricket Ground (Sydney), 27 October

Rilee Rossouw struck seven fours and eight sixes as he faced 56 balls and scored at nearly two runs per ball. The Proteas were 1-2 after one over when he arrived, before he exited at 4-197 in the 19th over. South Africa finished with 5-205, before trouncing Bangladesh by 104 runs.

Rossouw had seven runs off seven balls before racing to 35 off 17, and then rain caused a stoppage. Rossouw settled back in quietly before hitting a six, and then two singles took him to 50 off 30 balls. In the next over he slammed a four and then back-to-back sixes, with the latter six off a high no-ball. Rossouw hammered back-to-back fours in another over, and then went from 88 to 90 as a catch was dropped before the next ball cost four more runs. The over cost 23. Rossouw raised his ton from his 52nd delivery and then whacked his next delivery for six; his final boundary.

Sam Curran (England)

Matches	Innings	Not outs	Runs	Highest score	Average	50s	100s	Catches
6	2	1	12	6	12.00	-	-	5
Overs	**Maidens**	**Runs**	**Wickets**	**Average**	**Best figures**			
22.4	-	148	13	11.38	5-10			

England became the first nation to hold both men's World Cups at the same time.

Anrich Nortje 4-10 off 3.3 overs: South Africa v Bangladesh at Sydney Cricket Ground (Sydney), 27 October

Bangladesh was 0-26 after two overs in reply to South Africa's 5-205, before Anrich Nortje's first over changed everything as the openers paid for swinging across the line. Nortje's first ball had Soumya Sarkar caught behind, before his fourth ball cleaned up Najmul Hossain Shanto's stumps. Nortje won an lbw shout in his next over, before having a break until the 15th over. Nortje's third over featured six runs and a run-out, before he ended the match in his next over as he rattled the left-handed Taskin Ahmed's leg-stump.

Glenn Phillips 104 off 64 balls: New Zealand v Sri Lanka at Sydney Cricket Ground (Sydney), 29 October

Rarely has one batter dominated a T20 innings as much as Glenn Phillips did in this fixture. While he made 104, the rest of New Zealand's innings contained just 53 runs off the bat as well as 10 sundries. The outcome could easily have been much different had Phillips not been reprieved on 12 when he hit a catch straight to long-off.

Colin Ackermann plays a ramp shot for the Netherlands.

The Kiwis were 2-7 when Phillips arrived, and then he crunched his second delivery to the boundary. New Zealand would have been 4-29 had Phillips not been dropped, and soon he had another close shave as he gloved the ball past the diving wicketkeeper.

Phillips raced from 41 to 58 in the 14th over, before hammering successive sixes in the 17th over. A four took him to his ton off 61 balls, before he departed with two balls remaining. Phillips had struck 10 fours and four sixes.

Trent Boult 4-13 off four overs: New Zealand v Sri Lanka at Sydney Cricket Ground (Sydney), 29 October

Following a wicket maiden from Tim Southee, Trent Boult's first delivery against Sri Lanka was hit for four before he struck twice in the same over. Kusal Mendis edged a catch behind, before Dhananjaya de Silva chopped the ball onto the stumps. When Charith Asalanka was caught behind point in Boult's next over, the left-arm paceman had 3-7 while Sri Lanka was 4-8 in pursuit of 168.

Boult's three-over spell yielded 3-11, before he delivered the 17th over and had Dasun Shanaka caught at deep square leg from his last ball to leave Sri Lanka 9-93 and facing a heavy defeat.

PLAYER OF THE TOURNAMENT

The player of the tournament was also the player of the match in the final, and in his team's first outing. Sam Curran was the equal-second highest wicket-taker, having played two fewer matches and taken two fewer wickets than Sri Lanka's Wanindu Hasaranga.

Curran was England's second change bowler in the round-robin fixtures, before being used as first change in the finals. In England's first fixture, Curran captured 5-10 after delivering the eighth, 12th, 18th and 20th overs. He struck with the first ball of his second over, the final two balls of his third over, and the second and fourth balls of his final over. All of his victims were caught in the field, with Afghanistan faltering from 2-62 to 112 all out before England won by five wickets.

Player of the tournament Sam Curran holds the ball aloft after taking a five-wicket haul against Afghanistan.

Against Ireland, Curran delivered three overs in three spells and was hit for 14 and 11 in his first two overs before finishing with 2-31. Curran bowled two tail-enders as Ireland managed 157, before winning narrowly as England had a revised target of 111 in 14.3 overs. Following a washout against Australia, England made 6-179 and restricted New Zealand to 6-159. Curran made six not out from three balls, having hit a six and then escaped injury from a beamer. He then captured 2-26, having delivered the fifth and 13th overs before bowling at the death. Curran's sixth delivery had Finn Allen caught from a sucker ball, before he began the 18th over as the Kiwis needed 49 runs. He had Glenn Phillips caught in the deep as the over cost nine runs, before the final over cost just five.

Against Sri Lanka, Curran delivered the fifth and ninth overs before returning for the 17th and 19th. His first over cost 13 runs before he finished with 1-27, after his second over included a catch at deep mid-wicket. Curran later scored six in a sixth-wicket stand of 18, before England passed the 142-run target with two balls left.

In the semi-final, Curran had 0-11 as he delivered two of the first five overs before he finished with 0-42 after his final over cost 20. In the final, Curran again bowled two of the first five overs and this time made the breakthrough in a spell of 1-5. He did even better as he bowled two of the final four overs and nabbed 2-7, with both victims caught after the first one was bowled off an inside edge.

FIRST SEMI-FINAL

New Zealand v Pakistan at Sydney Cricket Ground (Sydney), 9 November

A clinical all-round display enabled Pakistan to be the first team to enter the decider. The first ball of the match could have been an omen as New Zealand's Finn Allen belted it for four. But the third ball made an even bigger impact, as a brilliant Shaheen Shah Afridi delivery trapped Allen lbw. Another turning point arose in the sixth over when a direct hit ran out Conway, before the dismissal of Phillips left the Kiwis 3-49 after eight overs.

Having been 3-59 at the halfway stage, the Kiwis scored 57 runs in the next six overs before Kane Williamson exited in the 17th over. New Zealand passed 150, despite only two boundaries in the final five overs.

Pakistan's innings also began with a four, and then the fourth ball proved match-turning as Conway spilled a catch which would have dismissed Babar Azam for a golden duck. The third and fifth overs cost 15 runs each, and the partnership reached 105 before Azam fell in the 13th over. Pakistan was just 31 runs shy of victory when Mohammad Haris was reprieved from the first ball of the 16th over, before opener Mohammad Rizwan's exit left Pakistan needing 21 runs from three overs. Haris eased the pressure with a four and a six from consecutive balls, and then he was dropped at 2-145. Haris fell from the final ball of the 19th over, before a wide and a single enabled Pakistan to win with five balls remaining.

Pakistan 3-153 (Mohammad Rizwan 57, Babar Azam 53; Trent Boult 2-33) beat New Zealand 4-152 (Daryl Mitchell 53 not out, Kane Williamson 46; Shaheen Shah Afridi 2-24) by seven wickets.

SECOND SEMI-FINAL

England v India at Adelaide Oval (Adelaide), 10 November

India made a competitive 6-168 following a late onslaught, but the run chase turned out to be a cakewalk.

Yet again a semi-final began with a hit to the boundary. After losing wickets in the second and ninth overs, India was 2-62 at the 10-over mark. Suryakumar Yadav hit the final two balls of the 11th over for six and four, but then fell from the second ball of the 12th over. India was merely 3-80 after 13 overs, before 10 runs came in each of the next three overs. The 17th cost 11 runs, and then the next two cost 15 and 20 before the final over contained 12. Kohli fell with two overs remaining – straight after reaching 50 – and Pandya was bizarrely dismissed from the final ball. Having hit four fours and five sixes, Pandya found the boundary again but trod on his wicket and was out for 63 off 33 balls instead of being 67 not out.

The run chase began with a wide before Jos Buttler struck the first, third and sixth legitimate deliveries to the fence. From there, the openers were unstoppable as England romped to a 10-wicket victory with four overs remaining. A six took the total to 0-104 after 10.1 overs before the following three overs went for 15, 17 and 14. Buttler finished proceedings with his third six, having also hit nine fours in his 80 not out off 49 balls. Alex Hales's undefeated 86 off 47 included four fours and seven sixes.

England 0-170 (Alex Hales 86 not out, Jos Buttler 80 not out) beat India 6-168 (Hardik Pandya 63, Virat Kohli 50; Chris Jordan 3-43) by 10 wickets.

FINAL

England v Pakistan at Melbourne Cricket Ground (Melbourne), 13 November

England became the first nation to hold both men's World Cups at the same time, having overhauled Pakistan's modest 8-137 with an over to spare. Interestingly, it was the second time that these two nations had contested a World Cup decider at the Melbourne Cricket Ground; one in each format.

Ben Stokes began with a no-ball and a wide, before the first boundary came at the start of the fourth over when Mohammad Rizwan cleared the fence. Curran dismissed Rizwan in the following over, before Adil Rashid's first ball accounted for Mohammad Haris. Sixteen runs in the 11th over took Pakistan to 2-84, and then Rashid held a return catch to dismiss Azam. Stokes struck in the 13th over before the 16th cost 13 runs, but then Curran and Jordan took wickets and restricted Pakistan to only 18 runs in the final four overs.

Shaheen Shah Afridi dismissed Hales in England's first over, before the next over cost 14 runs. The fourth over contained a wicket, before Naseem Shah beat the bat repeatedly in the fifth over and was unlucky to concede 11 runs, via five wides and a scoop for six. Haris Rauf found the edge in the next over to leave England 3-45, before the boundaries dried up. Naseem again beat the bat multiple times without taking a wicket, before Shaheen injured himself as he caught Harry Brook off Shadab Khan. Only two runs came from the 14th over, before the next over contained a precious boundary from the final ball to lift England to 4-97. Shaheen delivered the first ball of the 16th over, but then succumbed to his injury. Iftikhar Ahmed completed the over, and conceded three singles before a four and a six turned the tide. Moeen Ali then crunched successive fours to reduce the task to just 20 runs from 22 balls. Ali departed with six runs needed, before Stokes passed 50 as he levelled the scores with eight balls remaining, and soon scored the winning single.

England 5-138 (Ben Stokes 52 not out, Jos Buttler 26; Haris Rauf 2-23) beat Pakistan 8-137 (Shan Masood 38, Babar Azam 32; Sam Curran 3-12, Adil Rashid 2-22) by five wickets.

DREAM11
2024

World Cup cricket hits the United States

The ninth edition of the T20 World Cup was historic for at least three reasons. It was the first time a major ICC tournament took place in the United States (US), which was a co-host along with West Indies. It was also the first time the competition contained 20 teams, after there had been 12 from 2007 to 2012 and 16 from 2014 to 2022. It was also the first time South Africa reached a World Cup final in any format.

US, Canada, Nepal, Oman, Papua New Guinea (PNG) and Uganda came on board, while Zimbabwe and United Arab Emirates (UAE) missed the cut after playing in 2022. The 2024 tournament was the first time US, Canada and Uganda featured in a T20 World Cup. The US team was coached by Stuart Law, who had played for Australia in the 1996 World Cup.

The format reverted to four groups, a Super 8 series and then the finals. It was notable that US, Afghanistan and Bangladesh progressed to the Super 8s while Pakistan, New Zealand and Sri Lanka failed to do so. With four group games having a no-result due to wet weather, Scotland was very unlucky to miss the Super 8s after being level on points with England in Group B. England finished second while Scotland was third on net run rate, after Scotland had been 0-90 at the 10-over mark against England when the contest featuring these two teams was rained off. Pakistan also narrowly missed reaching the Super 8s, having lost to US in Super Over before losing to India by just six runs.

Australia crashed out in the Super 8s with losses to Afghanistan and India, while Bangladesh and the host nations also faltered in the Super 8s. Afghanistan and England were heavily beaten in the semi-finals, before the Proteas appeared destined to win their first World Cup title. Alas it was not to be, as India became the third nation to win the T20 World Cup for the second time.

The player of the tournament, Jasprit Bumrah, savours winning the T20 World Cup.

A HAT-TRICK OF CLASSICS: Three great contests

Oman v Namibia at Kensington Oval (Bridgetown), 2 June

With Oman losing wickets from the first and second balls of this match, little did anyone know what an amazing spectacle would follow!

Oman was 3-10 in the third over before reaching 4-60 at the halfway stage, but then the momentum stalled again. A six in the 18th over was followed by two wickets in three balls, and the score became 9-99 in the 19th over before the final over featured two fours and the final wicket.

The Namibians were 1-0 after two balls before steady batting had them on course for victory. Four byes from one ball reduced the task to just 14 runs from 17 balls, with seven wickets in hand. The task became 14 off 12 with six wickets in hand, before David Wiese cleared the boundary to make it seven off nine. Five runs were needed in the final over, which was a thriller as Mehran Khan took two wickets in the first three balls. A single and a two were followed by a bye, which meant a Super Over was needed.

Wiese took strike for the first of the two overs, and started with a four and a six before hitting a two and a single. Successive fours to Gerhard Erasmus took the total to an imposing 21, before Wiese removed his batting gear and rolled the arm over. A two from the first ball was followed by a dot ball and then the wicket of Naseem Khushi, who edged the ball onto his stumps. Suddenly the Super Over aspect turned anti-climactic, as two singles were followed by a belated six.

Oman 109 (Khalid Kail 34; Ruben Trumpelmann 4-21, David Wiese 3-28) tied with Namibia 6-109 (Jan Frylinck 45; Mehran Khan 3-7) before Namibia won the Super Over.

United States v Pakistan at Grand Prairie Stadium (Grand Prairie), 6 June

Although the losing team in any match involving Super Over could consider itself unlucky, US richly deserved this hugely surprising victory against Pakistan.

Mohammad Rizwan struck the third ball of the match for six, before two quick wickets were followed by Fakhar Zaman hitting his first ball for six. An errant paddle stroke from Zaman left Pakistan 3-26, before a 72-run stand included 20 runs in the 10th over and 19 in the 12th. Two wickets in two balls in the 13th over left Pakistan 5-98, and the momentum swings continued as the 16th over yielded 13 runs and a wicket. None of the final four overs cost more than 10 runs despite a couple of sixes, as the Pakistanis fell just shy of 160.

US was 0-36 after five overs before the sixth over featured a wicket and two boundaries. Monank Patel went from 40 to 50 in two balls and reduced the task to 56 runs from 45 balls with nine wickets in hand, but the momentum stalled despite three wides from one ball and a streaky boundary to Aaron Jones. US had seven wickets in hand with one over remaining, but 15 runs was a tough ask. Three singles made the task even tougher, although the second ball of the 20th over featured a dropped catch. Jones hoicked the fourth ball for six and then squeezed a single, before Nitish Kumar chipped a low full-toss for four to level the score and ensure a Super Over.

Jones slashed the first ball of US's over for four before a series of twos, singles and wides enabled US to tally 18 runs despite a run-out from the final ball. The US batters crucially stole a bye or two with each of the wides. Pakistan's reply began with a dot ball, followed by a four, a wide, a great catch and another wide. The fourth legitimate ball went for four leg byes, before a two and a single enabled the Americans to win by five runs.

Pakistan 7-159 (Babar Azam 44, Shadab Khan 40; Nosthush Kenjige 3-30, Saurabh Netravalkar 2-18) tied with United States 3-159 (Monank Patel 50) before United States won the Super Over.

Scotland's Brad Currie celebrates a wicket.

Pat Cummins claimed two hat-tricks in three days during the Super 8 series.

South Africa v Nepal at Arnos Vale Stadium (Kingstown), 14 June

Both teams batted out the overs and scored at less than six runs per over, while the margin was the tightest possible. South Africa's innings contained 10 fours and two sixes, before Nepal's innings contained nine fours and four sixes while each team lost seven wickets. Only one South African and three Nepalis had a strike rate of 100 or more, while there was good spin bowling from each side. Both teams had a spinner with figures of 4-0-19-4.

Sent in, South Africa was merely 1-57 after 10 overs. The 11th over contained 10 runs including a four from a dropped catch, but the next five overs featured three wickets and no boundaries. Tristan Stubbs hit the first ball of the final over for six, before wickets fell from the final two deliveries.

A catch went begging as Nepal progressed to 0-35, before losing two wickets in three deliveries. Nepal advanced to 2-85 and needed 31 runs from 39 balls, but then lost momentum. Two wickets fell for two runs in the 18th over, and then the 19th over contained a wicket and three dot balls before a six and a two meant eight runs were needed from six balls. Two dot balls were followed by a four and a two, and then Ottneil Baartman prevented any runs from the final two balls. The last delivery also included a run-out, as Nepal fell heartbreakingly short of what would have been a well-deserved victory.

South Africa 7-115 (Reeza Hendricks 43, Tristan Stubbs 27 not out; Kushal Bhurtel 4-19, Dipendra Singh Airee 3-21) beat Nepal 7-114 (Aasif Sheikh 42, Anil Sah 27; Tabraiz Shamsi 4-19) by one run.

Namibia's Ruben Trumpelmann fires down a delivery.

SIX OF THE BEST: Individual performances

(excluding player of the tournament, and the finals)

Aaron Jones 94 not out off 40 balls: United States v Canada at Grand Prairie Stadium (Grand Prairie), 1 June

US was 2-42 in the seventh over when chasing 195 against Canada, and then the arrival of Aaron Jones changed the game as he overcame a scratchy start. He smashed 10 sixes and four fours as he helped US to a seven-wicket triumph.

Jones tentatively pushed at his first delivery and nearly edged it, before the next ball struck him on the pads. He opened his account from his fifth delivery, and his next scoring stroke was a six. Jones's first four came from a reverse sweep, before he cleared the boundary with amazing frequency. He reached 50 in 22 balls after hitting monstrous sixes from his 20th and 21st deliveries. Andries Gous did most of the damage as 33 runs came in the 14th over, and soon Jones rode his luck again as he scored two from a dropped catch and then edged a four. A century was out of reach as US needed 14 runs in three overs, with Jones settling the issue in four balls as another reverse sweep for four was followed by a six, a dot ball and another six.

Fazalhaq Farooqi 5-9 off four overs: Afghanistan v Uganda at Providence Stadium (Guyana), 3 June

Afghanistan's left-arm opening bowler Fazalhaq Farooqi had the best figures of the tournament, as Uganda succumbed for 58 in response to 5-183. Farooqi's first ball was driven for four, before the next two balls produced wickets from inswinging deliveries. The first one knocked the leg-stump back, and the second one produced an lbw. After bowling a two-over spell, Farooqi returned for the 13th and 15th overs. He struck with the first, second and sixth balls of the 13th over, as one victim was bowled before the last two were caught behind.

Akeal Hosein 5-11 off four overs: West Indies v Uganda at Providence Stadium (Guyana), 8 June

West Indian opening bowler Akeal Hosein claimed the second and final five-wicket haul of the tournament, as Uganda was dismissed for just 39 after West Indies compiled 5-173.

Uganda was 7-23 after seven overs when the left-arm orthodox spinner finished his spell. Roger Mukasa was lbw as he attempted to reverse sweep the second ball of the innings, before the left-handed Alpesh Ramjani was lbw as he tried to slog-sweep the final ball of Hosein's second over. Hosein's third and fourth victims were bowled, before he claimed another lbw.

Lockie Ferguson 3-0 off four overs: New Zealand v Papua New Guinea at Brian Lara Cricket Academy (San Fernando), 17 June

It was virtually unheard of for anyone to not concede a run while bowling their full quota of overs. For good measure, Lockie Ferguson also nabbed three wickets.

The Kiwi fast bowler delivered the fifth, seventh, 12th and 14th overs against PNG. His first delivery produced an edged catch to slip which made the score 2-14. The second ball of Ferguson's second spell produced an lbw, and the second ball of his final over hit the stumps off an inside edge. Two runs were scored from the following delivery but they were leg byes, before a further three dot balls ensured no runs were scored off the bat during Ferguson's four overs. PNG folded for 78, and the Kiwis won by seven wickets.

Pat Cummins 3-29 off four overs: Australia v Bangladesh at Sir Vivian Richards Stadium (North Sound), 20 June

Pat Cummins claimed two hat-tricks in three days during the Super 8 series, with both achievements spread across the 18th and 20th overs.

On the first occasion, Cummins struck with the final two balls of his third over and the first ball of his fourth over. Mahmudullah bottom-edged a pull onto his wicket before Mahedi Hasan guided a catch to third man, and the third victim was Towhid Hridoy who scooped a slower ball to short fine leg. Bangladesh finished on 8-140, and Australia won by 28 runs after being set a rain-revised target.

Emirates
aramco
Emirates
aramco
aramco
DP WORLD
aramco

It was the first time a major ICC tournament took place in the United States.

Jasprit Bumrah (India)

Matches	Innings	Not outs	Runs	Highest score	Average	50s	100s	Catches
8	1	-	0	0	0	-	-	2

Overs	Maidens	Runs	Wickets	Average	Best figures
29.4	2	124	15	8.27	3-7

Cummins nabbed 3-29 against Bangladesh and 3-28 against Afghanistan, having struck with the final ball of his third over and the first two balls of his fourth over on the latter occasion. The first two victims were caught at long-on, before Gulbadin Naib swatted a catch to deep mid-wicket. Afghanistan finished on 6-148, and ended Australia's campaign as the favourites were dismissed for 127.

Rohit Sharma 92 off 41 balls: India v Australia at Daren Sammy Cricket Ground (Gros Islet), 24 June

Indian skipper and opener Rohit Sharma was eight runs short of a century when he exited in the 12th over in the Super 8 clash with Australia. He hit seven fours and eight sixes in his breathtaking 41-ball knock, which set up India's match-winning total of 5-205.

India was 1-6 after two overs, before Sharma struck four sixes and a four off Mitchell Starc in the third over which cost 29 runs. Sharma also sent Cummins's first ball over the boundary, before a shower caused a brief stoppage. Afterwards, Sharma reached 50 off just 19 balls while taking the total to 1-52. After slog-sweeping Adam Zampa for six, Sharma clouted Marcus Stoinis for a four and two sixes in three balls.

The return of Starc paid off as he bowled Sharma with a yorker from around the wicket, before India tallied 78 runs in the final 8.4 overs.

PLAYER OF THE TOURNAMENT

The player of the tournament was the equal-third highest wicket-taker, while he conceded just 4.18 runs per over. Jasprit Bumrah was used as the first change bowler in India's round-robin matches, before being the team's second opening bowler in the Super 8s and finals series.

Bumrah was named player of the match in India's first two fixtures, which were against Ireland and Pakistan. In his first outing, Bumrah began with a maiden before finishing with 3-1-6-2. His first wicket came from a short ball before his second came from a full ball, as Ireland fell shy of 100 and lost by eight wickets.

Bumrah claimed 3-14 against Pakistan after delivering the third, fifth, 15th and 19th overs, as India won by six runs after defending a disappointing 119-run total. With Pakistan needing 21 runs in the last two overs, Bumrah conceded only three singles (including a leg bye) before his final ball yielded a wicket from a full-toss.

After taking 0-25 in a big win against US before India had a washout against Canada, Bumrah achieved terrific figures of 4-1-7-3 in a 47-run victory against Afghanistan as only four of his deliveries contained runs off the bat. After India made 5-196 in its second Super 8 match, Bumrah took 2-13 in his four overs as Bangladesh was restricted to 8-146. Next, Bumrah claimed 1-29 as Australia fell 24 runs short of India's 5-205. Bumrah dismissed Australia's top-scorer, Travis Head, who skewed a slower ball in the 17th over to leave Australia 5-150.

In the second semi-final, Bumrah took 2-12 in 2.4 overs as England fell well short of India's 7-171. Bumrah delivered the second, fifth and 17th overs. A fine delivery from Bumrah rattled Phil Salt's leg-stump to leave England 2-34, before the same bowler ended the match with an lbw. In the final, Bumrah claimed a vital wicket in his first two-over spell which cost 12 runs (plus a leg bye), before his remaining two overs were decisive in the final five overs. His third over cost only four runs before his final six balls featured a crucial wicket and only two runs, as he helped slow the run rate when the Proteas appeared certain to win.

David Wiese played a key role for Namibia in the 2024 T20 World Cup.

FIRST SEMI-FINAL

Afghanistan v South Africa at Brian Lara Cricket Academy (San Fernando), 26 June

Winning the toss was about the only thing to go right for the Afghans, who slumped to 6-28 in the seventh over. Twenty-two runs were added for the seventh wicket, and then three wickets fell without a run scored before the final wicket partnership produced six runs. Sundries top-scored with 13 while the highest batting score was 10, and half of the 56-run total came from boundaries as the innings lasted 11.5 overs. South Africa was 1-5 before Reeza Hendricks and captain Aiden Markram took the Proteas to victory with 67 balls to spare. Hendricks levelled the scores with a six, and punched the next ball for four.

South Africa 1-60 (Reeza Hendricks 29 not out, Aiden Markram 23 not out) beat Afghanistan 56 (Tabraiz Shamsi 3-6, Marco Jansen 3-16) by nine wickets.

SECOND SEMI-FINAL

India v England at Providence Stadium (Georgetown), 27 June

Following a late start due to rain, India reached 2-65 after eight overs before another rain interruption took place. Sharma passed 50 as he and Suryakumar Yadav combined to take 19 runs off the 13th over, but then Sharma departed in the next over before Yadav fell in the 16th. The 18th over featured a two, followed by back-to-back sixes, a double breakthrough and a single. The final two overs cost 12 runs each, to lift the total above 170.

England was 0-26 after three overs as Jos Buttler raced to 23, before he succumbed to Axar Patel's first delivery. The run chase crumbled from that point on, as wickets fell with alarming frequency while no partnerships developed. England was 69 runs shy of the target when the final wicket fell with 20 balls remaining.

India 7-171 (Rohit Sharma 57, Suryakumar Yadav 47; Chris Jordan 3-37) beat England 103 (Harry Brook 25; Kuldeep Yadav 3-19, Axar Patel 3-23) by 68 runs.

FINAL

India v South Africa at Kensington Oval (Bridgetown), 29 June

Although the Proteas finally reached a World Cup final, they again found a way to fall short when victory was within reach.

Dramatic momentum swings began early, as India was 0-23 after eight balls and then 2-23 after two overs. The third wicket fell at 34, before partnerships of 72 and 57 ensured a strong total as Virat Kohli, Axar Patel and Shivam Dube made the bulk of the runs. Sixteen runs in the 18th over were followed by 17 and a wicket in the 19th, before the final over yielded 2-9.

Needing nearly nine runs per over, South Africa fell to 2-12 before Quinton de Kock and Stubbs led a recovery. The Proteas were 4-106 in the 13th over when de Kock holed out, after hitting the previous ball for four. After David Miller hit 10 runs in two balls, Heinrich Klaasen smashed 22 runs in the next over which also included two wides. With only 30 runs needed from 30 balls with six wickets in hand, South Africa appeared home and hosed.

Incredibly, no boundaries were hit in the next four overs as the Proteas lost two wickets for just 14 runs while Bumrah, Hardik Pandya and Arshdeep Singh bowled well. The first ball of the final over was a sliding doors moment as Suryakumar Yadav took a spectacular catch at long-off, having released the ball and stepped over the boundary before returning to the field of play. Kagiso Rabada edged the next ball for four before a bye was followed by a leg bye and a wide. A catch at deep mid-off from the fifth ball sealed India's win as South Africa needed nine runs.

India 7-176 (Virat Kohli 76, Axar Patel 47; Keshav Maharaj 2-23, Anrich Nortje 2-26) beat South Africa 8-169 (Heinrich Klaasen 52, Quinton de Kock 39; Hardik Pandya 3-20, Jasprit Bumrah 2-18, Arshdeep Singh 2-20) by seven runs.

Emirates
aramco
DP WORLD
DSC

STATISTICS

ODI World Cup (60 and 50 overs)

ODI World Cup (60 and 50 overs)

Year	Host(s)	Winner	Runner-up	No. of teams
1975	England	West Indies	Australia	8
1979	England	West Indies	England	8
1983	England/Wales	India	West Indies	8
1987	India/Pakistan	Australia	England	8
1992	Australia/New Zealand	Pakistan	England	9
1996	India/Pakistan/Sri Lanka	Sri Lanka	Australia	12
1999	England/Ireland/Wales/ Scotland/Netherlands	Australia	Pakistan	12
2003	South Africa/Kenya/Zimbabwe	Australia	India	14
2007	West Indies	Australia	Sri Lanka	16
2011	India/Sri Lanka/Bangladesh	India	Sri Lanka	14
2015	Australia/New Zealand	Australia	New Zealand	14
2019	England/Wales	England*	New Zealand	10
2023	India	Australia	India	10

*** Match tied: England won on boundaries countback**

HIGHEST TOTALS

Team	Score	Overs	Opponent	Venue	Date
South Africa	5-428	50	Sri Lanka	Delhi	7 Oct 2023
Australia	6-417	50	Afghanistan	Perth	4 Mar 2015
India	5-413	50	Bermuda	Port of Spain	19 Mar 2007
South Africa	4-411	50	Ireland	Canberra	3 Mar 2015
India	4-410	50	Netherlands	Bengaluru	12 Nov 2023
South Africa	5-408	50	West Indies	Sydney	27 Feb 2015
New Zealand	6-401	50	Pakistan	Bengaluru	4 Nov 2023
South Africa	7-399	50	England	Wankhede	21 Oct 2023
Australia	8-399	50	Netherlands	Delhi	25 Oct 2023
Sri Lanka	5-398	50	Kenya	Kandy	6 Mar 1996
England	6-397	50	Afghanistan	Manchester	18 Jun 2019
India	4-397	50	New Zealand	Wankhede	15 Nov 2023
New Zealand	6-393	50	West Indies	Wellington	21 Mar 2015
Australia	388	49.2	New Zealand	Dharamsala	28 Oct 2023
England	6-386	50	Bangladesh	Cardiff	8 Jun 2019
New Zealand	9-383	50	Australia	Dharamsala	28 Oct 2023
South Africa	5-382	50	Bangladesh	Wankhede	24 Oct 2023
Australia	5-381	50	Bangladesh	Nottingham	20 Jun 2019
Australia	6-377	50	South Africa	Basseterre	24 Mar 2007
Australia	9-376	50	Sri Lanka	Sydney	8 Mar 2015
India	6-373	50	Sri Lanka	Taunton	26 May 1999
West Indies	2-372	50	Zimbabwe	Canberra	24 Feb 2015
India	4-370	50	Bangladesh	Mirpur	19 Feb 2011

LOWEST TOTALS

Team	Score	Overs	Opponent	Venue	Date
Canada	36	18.4	Sri Lanka	Paarl	19 Feb 2003
Canada	45	40.3	England	Manchester	13 Jun 1979
Namibia	45	14.0	Australia	Potchefstroom	27 Feb 2003
Sri Lanka	55	19.4	India	Wankhede	2 Nov 2023
Bangladesh	58	18.5	West Indies	Mirpur	4 Mar 2011
Scotland	68	31.3	West Indies	Leicester	27 May 1999
Kenya	69	23.5	New Zealand	Chennai	20 Feb 2011
Pakistan	74	40.2	England	Adelaide	1 Mar 1992
Ireland	77	27.4	Sri Lanka	St George's	18 Apr 2007
Bangladesh	78	28.0	South Africa	Mirpur	19 Mar 2011
Bermuda	78	24.4	Sri Lanka	Port of Spain	15 Mar 2007
South Africa	83	27.1	India	Eden Gardens	5 Nov 2023
Namibia	84	17.4	Pakistan	Kimberley	16 Feb 2003
Sri Lanka	86	37.2	West Indies	Manchester	7 Jun 1975
Netherlands	90	21.0	Australia	Delhi	25 Oct 2023
Ireland	91	30.0	Australia	Bridgetown	13 Apr 2007
England	93	36.2	Australia	Leeds	18 Jun 1975
West Indies	93	35.2	Kenya	Pune	29 Feb 1996
East Africa	94	52.3	England	Birmingham	14 Jun 1975
Zimbabwe	99	19.1	Pakistan	Kingston	21 Mar 2007

BIGGEST VICTORIES (BY RUNS)

Winner	Margin	Opponent	Venue	Date
Australia	309 runs	Netherlands	Delhi	25 Oct 2023
India	302 runs	Sri Lanka	Wankhede	2 Nov 2023
Australia	275 runs	Afghanistan	Perth	4 Mar 2015
India	257 runs	Bermuda	Port of Spain	19 Mar 2007
South Africa	257 runs	West Indies	Sydney	27 Feb 2015
Australia	256 runs	Namibia	Potchefstroom	27 Feb 2003
Sri Lanka	243 runs	Bermuda	Port of Spain	15 Mar 2007
India	243 runs	South Africa	Eden Gardens	5 Nov 2023
South Africa	231 runs	Netherlands	Mohali	3 Mar 2011
Australia	229 runs	Netherlands	Basseterre	18 Mar 2007
South Africa	229 runs	England	Wankhede	21 Oct 2023
South Africa	221 runs	Netherlands	Basseterre	16 Mar 2007
Australia	215 runs	New Zealand	St George's	20 Apr 2007
West Indies	215 runs	Netherlands	Delhi	28 Feb 2011
Sri Lanka	210 runs	Canada	Hambantota	20 Feb 2011
South Africa	206 runs	Bangladesh	Mirpur	19 Mar 2011

BIGGEST VICTORIES (BY RUNS)

Winner	Margin	Opponent	Venue	Date
Pakistan	205 runs	Kenya	Hambantota	23 Feb 2011
Australia	203 runs	Scotland	Basseterre	14 Mar 2007
England	202 runs	India	Lord's	7 Jun 1975
South Africa	201 runs	Ireland	Canberra	3 Mar 2015

BIGGEST VICTORIES (BY WICKETS)

Winner	Margin	Opponent	Venue	Date
India	10 wickets	East Africa	Leeds	11 Jun 1975
West Indies	10 wickets	Zimbabwe	Birmingham	20 Jun 1983
West Indies	10 wickets	Pakistan	Melbourne	23 Feb 1992
South Africa	10 wickets	Kenya	Potchefstroom	12 Feb 2003
Sri Lanka	10 wickets	Bangladesh	Pietermaritzburg	14 Feb 2003
South Africa	10 wickets	Bangladesh	Bloemfontein	22 Feb 2003
Australia	10 wickets	Bangladesh	North Sound	31 Mar 2007
New Zealand	10 wickets	Kenya	Chennai	20 Feb 2011
New Zealand	10 wickets	Zimbabwe	Ahmedabad	4 Mar 2011
Pakistan	10 wickets	West Indies	Mirpur	23 Mar 2011
Sri Lanka	10 wickets	England	Colombo (RPS)	26 Mar 2011
New Zealand	10 wickets	Sri Lanka	Cardiff	1 Jun 2019
West Indies	9 wickets	Sri Lanka	Manchester	7 Jun 1975
West Indies	9 wickets	India	Birmingham	9 Jun 1979
New Zealand	9 wickets	Sri Lanka	Nottingham	9 Jun 1979
England	9 wickets	Sri Lanka	Leeds	20 Jun 1983
India	9 wickets	New Zealand	Nagpur	31 Oct 1987
South Africa	9 wickets	Australia	Sydney	26 Feb 1992
Pakistan	9 wickets	UAE	Gujranwala	24 Feb 1996
England	9 wickets	Kenya	Canterbury	18 May 1999
Pakistan	9 wickets	New Zealand	Manchester	16 Jun 1999
Australia	9 wickets	India	Centurion	15 Feb 2003
New Zealand	9 wickets	South Africa	Johannesburg	16 Feb 2003
Sri Lanka	9 wickets	Canada	Paarl	19 Feb 2003
New Zealand	9 wickets	Bangladesh	North Sound	2 Apr 2007
Australia	9 wickets	Ireland	Bridgetown	13 Apr 2007
South Africa	9 wickets	England	Bridgetown	17 Apr 2007
Sri Lanka	9 wickets	Kenya	Colombo (RPS)	1 Mar 2011
West Indies	9 wickets	Bangladesh	Mirpur	4 Mar 2011
India	9 wickets	UAE	Perth	28 Feb 2015
Sri Lanka	9 wickets	England	Wellington	1 Mar 2015
England	9 wickets	Afghanistan	Sydney	13 Mar 2015

BIGGEST VICTORIES (BY WICKETS)

Winner	Margin	Opponent	Venue	Date
South Africa	9 wickets	Sri Lanka	Sydney	18 Mar 2015
South Africa	9 wickets	Afghanistan	Cardiff	15 Jun 2019
South Africa	9 wickets	Sri Lanka	Chester-le-Street	28 Jun 2019
New Zealand	9 wickets	England	Ahmedabad	5 Oct 2023

SMALLEST VICTORIES (BY RUNS)

Winner	Margin	Opponent	Venue	Date
Australia	1 run	India	Chennai	9 Oct 1987
Australia	1 run	India	Brisbane	1 Mar 1992
Sri Lanka	2 runs	England	North Sound	4 Apr 2007
New Zealand	3 runs	Zimbabwe	Hyderabad (Deccan)	10 Oct 1987
Australia	3 runs	New Zealand	Indore	18 Oct 1987
Zimbabwe	3 runs	India	Leicester	19 May 1999
West Indies	3 runs	South Africa	Cape Town	9 Feb 2003
Australia	5 runs	West Indies	Mohali	14 Mar 1996
Ireland	5 runs	Zimbabwe	Hobart	7 Mar 2015
New Zealand	5 runs	West Indies	Manchester	22 Jun 2019
Australia	5 runs	New Zealand	Dharamsala	28 Oct 2023
Sri Lanka	6 runs	West Indies	Cape Town	28 Feb 2003
England	6 runs	South Africa	Chennai	6 Mar 2011
Australia	7 runs	England	Eden Gardens	8 Nov 1987
England	9 runs	New Zealand	Manchester	20 Jun 1979
England	9 runs	India	Perth	22 Feb 1992
Zimbabwe	9 runs	England	Albury	18 Mar 1992
Pakistan	10 runs	Australia	Leeds	23 May 1999
South Africa	10 runs	Australia	Manchester	6 Jul 2019

SMALLEST VICTORIES (BY WICKETS)

Winner	Margin	Opponent	Venue	Date
West Indies	1 wicket	Pakistan	Birmingham	11 Jun 1975
Pakistan	1 wicket	West Indies	Lahore	16 Oct 1987
South Africa	1 wicket	Sri Lanka	Providence	28 Mar 2007
England	1 wicket	West Indies	Bridgetown	21 Apr 2007
Afghanistan	1 wicket	Scotland	Dunedin	26 Feb 2015
New Zealand	1 wicket	Australia	Auckland	28 Feb 2015
South Africa	1 wicket	Pakistan	Chennai	27 Oct 2023
New Zealand	2 wickets	England	Birmingham	15 Jun 1983

SMALLEST VICTORIES (BY WICKETS)

Winner	Margin	Opponent	Venue	Date
England	2 wickets	West Indies	Gujranwala	9 Oct 1987
Australia	2 wickets	England	Gqeberha	2 Mar 2003
Bangladesh	2 wickets	England	Chattogram	11 Mar 2011
Ireland	2 wickets	UAE	Brisbane	25 Feb 2015
New Zealand	2 wickets	Bangladesh	The Oval	5 Jun 2019

MOST RUNS

Player	Mat	Inns	NO	Runs	HS	Ave	100	50
SR Tendulkar (India)	45	44	4	2278	152	56.95	6	15
V Kohli (India)	37	37	7	1795	117	59.83	5	12
RT Ponting (Australia)	46	42	4	1743	140*	45.86	5	6
RG Sharma (India)	28	28	2	1575	140	60.57	7	6
KC Sangakkara (Sri Lanka)	37	35	8	1532	124	56.74	5	7
DA Warner (Australia)	29	29	2	1527	178	56.55	6	5
Shakib Al Hasan (Bangladesh)	36	36	4	1332	124*	41.62	2	11
BC Lara (West Indies)	34	33	4	1225	116	42.24	2	7
AB de Villiers (South Africa)	23	22	3	1207	162*	63.52	4	6

HIGHEST INDIVIDUAL SCORES

Player	Runs	Team	Opponent	Venue	Date
MJ Guptill	237*	New Zealand	West Indies	Wellington	21 Mar 2015
CH Gayle	215	West Indies	Zimbabwe	Canberra	24 Feb 2015
GJ Maxwell	201*	Australia	Afghanistan	Wankhede	7 Nov 2023
G Kirsten	188*	South Africa	UAE	Rawalpindi	16 Feb 1996
SC Ganguly	183	India	Sri Lanka	Taunton	26 May 1999
IVA Richards	181	West Indies	Sri Lanka	Karachi	13 Oct 1987
DA Warner	178	Australia	Afghanistan	Perth	4 Mar 2015
MR Marsh	177*	Australia	Bangladesh	Pune	11 Nov 2023
Kapil Dev	175*	India	Zimbabwe	Tunbridge Wells	18 Jun 1983
V Sehwag	175	India	Bangladesh	Mirpur	19 Feb 2011
Q de Kock	174	South Africa	Bangladesh	Wankhede	24 Oct 2023
CB Wishart	172*	Zimbabwe	Namibia	Harare	10 Feb 2003
GM Turner	171*	New Zealand	East Africa	Birmingham	7 Jun 1975

LEADING WICKET-TAKERS

GD McGrath (Australia)	71
M Muralidaran (Sri Lanka)	68
MA Starc (Australia)	65
SL Malinga (Sri Lanka)	56
Mohammed Shami (India)	55
Wasim Akram (Pakistan)	55
TA Boult (New Zealand)	53
WPUJC Vaas (Sri Lanka)	49
Z Khan (India)	44
J Srinath (India)	44
Shakib Al Hasan (Bangladesh)	43
TG Southee (New Zealand)	41
Imran Tahir (South Africa)	40

BEST BOWLING FIGURES

Player	O	M	R	W	Team	Opponent	Venue	Date
GD McGrath	7	4	15	7	Australia	Namibia	Potchefstroom	27 Feb 2003
AJ Bichel	10	-	20	7	Australia	England	Gqeberha	2 Mar 2003
TG Southee	9	-	33	7	New Zealand	England	Wellington	20 Feb 2015
WW Davis	10.3	-	51	7	West Indies	Australia	Leeds	11 Jun 1983
Mohammed Shami	9.5	-	57	7	India	New Zealand	Wankhede	15 Nov 2023
GJ Gilmour	12	6	14	6	Australia	England	Leeds	18 Jun 1975
A Nehra	10	2	23	6	India	England	Durban	26 Feb 2003
SE Bond	10	2	23	6	New Zealand	Australia	Gqeberha	11 Mar 2003
WPUJC Vaas	9.1	2	25	6	Sri Lanka	Bangladesh	Pietermaritzburg	14 Feb 2003
KAJ Roach	8.3	-	27	6	West Indies	Netherlands	Delhi	28 Feb 2011
MA Starc	9	-	28	6	Australia	New Zealand	Auckland	28 Feb 2015
Shaheen Shah Afridi	9.1	-	35	6	Pakistan	Bangladesh	Lord's	5 Jul 2019
SL Malinga	7.4	-	38	6	Sri Lanka	Kenya	Colombo (RPS)	1 Mar 2011
KH MacLeay	11.5	3	39	6	Australia	India	Nottingham	13 Jun 1983

MOST DISMISSALS BY A WICKETKEEPER

Player	Dismissals	Ct	St
KC Sangakkara (Sri Lanka)	54	41	13
AC Gilchrist (Australia)	52	45	7
MS Dhoni (India)	42	34	8
Q de Kock (South Africa)	39	37	2
JC Buttler (England)	33	29	4
Mushfiqur Rahim (Bangladesh)	33	25	8
BB McCullum (New Zealand)	32	30	2
MV Boucher (South Africa)	31	31	-
TWM Latham (New Zealand)	30	30	-
Moin Khan (Pakistan)	30	23	7

MOST CATCHES BY A FIELDER

RT Ponting (Australia)	28
JE Root (England)	25
V Kohli (India)	20
ST Jayasuriya (Sri Lanka)	18
DA Warner (Australia)	17
CH Gayle (West Indies)	17

MOST APPEARANCES

RT Ponting (Australia)	46
SC Tendulkar (India)	45
DMPD Jayawardene (Sri Lanka)	40
Muttiah Muralidaran (Sri Lanka)	40

T20 World Cup

T20 World Cup

Year	Host(s)	Winner	Runner-up	No. of teams
2007	South Africa	India	Pakistan	12
2009	England	Pakistan	Sri Lanka	12
2010	West Indies	England	Australia	12
2012	Sri Lanka	West Indies	Sri Lanka	12
2014	Bangladesh	Sri Lanka	India	16
2016	India	West Indies	England	16
2021	UAE/Oman	Australia	New Zealand	16
2022	Australia	England	Pakistan	16
2024	West Indies/USA	India	South Africa	20

HIGHEST TOTALS

Team	Score	Overs	Opponent	Venue	Date
Sri Lanka	6-260	20	Kenya	Johannesburg	14 Sep 2007
England	8-230	19.4	South Africa	Wankhede	18 Mar 2016
South Africa	4-229	20	England	Wankhede	18 Mar 2016
India	4-218	20	England	Durban	19 Sep 2007
West Indies	5-218	20	Afghanistan	Gros Islet	17 Jun 2024
South Africa	5-211	20	Scotland	The Oval	7 Jun 2009
India	2-210	20	Afghanistan	Abu Dhabi	3 Nov 2021
South Africa	5-209	20	Afghanistan	Wankhede	20 Mar 2016
South Africa	2-208	17.4	West Indies	Johannesburg	11 Sep 2007

LOWEST TOTALS

Team	Score	Overs	Opponent	Venue	Date
Uganda	39	12	West Indies	Providence	8 Jun 2024
Netherlands	39	10.3	Sri Lanka	Chattogram	24 Mar 2014
Uganda	40	18.4	New Zealand	Tarouba	14 Jun 2024
Netherlands	44	10	Sri Lanka	Sharjah	22 Oct 2021
Oman	47	13.2	England	North Sound	13 Jun 2024
West Indies	55	14.2	England	Dubai (DICS)	23 Oct 2021
Afghanistan	56	11.5	South Africa	Tarouba	26 Jun 2024
Uganda	58	16	Afghanistan	Providence	3 Jun 2024
New Zealand	60	15.3	Sri Lanka	Chattogram	31 Mar 2014
Scotland	60	10.2	Afghanistan	Sharjah	25 Oct 2021

BIGGEST VICTORIES (BY RUNS)

Winner	Margin	Opponent	Venue	Date
Sri Lanka	172 runs	Kenya	Johannesburg	14 Sep 2007
West Indies	134 runs	Uganda	Providence	8 Jun 2024
South Africa	130 runs	Scotland	The Oval	7 Jun 2009
Afghanistan	130 runs	Scotland	Sharjah	25 Oct 2021
Afghanistan	125 runs	Uganda	Providence	3 Jun 2024
England	116 runs	Afghanistan	Colombo (RPS)	21 Sep 2012
South Africa	104 runs	Bangladesh	Sydney	27 Oct 2022
West Indies	104 runs	Afghanistan	Gros Islet	17 Jun 2024

BIGGEST VICTORIES (BY WICKETS)

Winner	Margin	Opponent	Venue	Date
Australia	10 wickets	Sri Lanka	Cape Town	20 Sep 2007
South Africa	10 wickets	Zimbabwe	Hambantota	20 Sep 2012
Oman	10 wickets	PNG	Al Amerat	17 Oct 2021
Pakistan	10 wickets	India	Dubai (DICS)	24 Oct 2021
England	10 wickets	India	Adelaide	10 Nov 2022
England	10 wickets	USA	Bridgetown	23 Jun 2024

SMALLEST VICTORIES (BY RUNS)

Winner	Margin	Opponent	Venue	Date
South Africa	1 run	New Zealand	Lord's	9 Jun 2009
New Zealand	1 run	Pakistan	Bridgetown	8 May 2010
India	1 run	South Africa	Colombo (RPS)	2 Oct 2012
India	1 run	Bangladesh	Bengaluru	23 Mar 2016
Zimbabwe	1 run	Pakistan	Perth	27 Oct 2022
South Africa	1 run	Nepal	Kingstown	14 Jun 2024
South Africa	2 runs	New Zealand	Chattogram	24 Mar 2014

SMALLEST VICTORIES (BY WICKETS)

Winner	Margin	Opponent	Venue	Date
New Zealand	2 wickets	Sri Lanka	Providence	30 Apr 2010
Pakistan	2 wickets	South Africa	Colombo (RPS)	28 Sep 2012
Hong Kong	2 wickets	Bangladesh	Chattogram	20 Mar 2014
Oman	2 wickets	Ireland	Dharamsala	9 Mar 2016
England	2 wickets	South Africa	Wankhede	18 Mar 2016
Bangladesh	2 wickets	Sri Lanka	Dallas	7 Jun 2024

MOST RUNS

Player	Mat	Inns	NO	Runs	HS	Ave	100	50
V Kohli (IND)	35	33	11	1292	89*	58.72	-	15
RG Sharma (IND)	47	44	9	1220	92	34.85	-	12
DPMD Jayawardene (SL)	31	31	5	1016	100	39.07	1	6
JC Buttler (ENG)	35	34	10	1013	101*	42.20	1	5
DA Warner (AUS)	41	41	3	984	89*	25.89	-	8
CH Gayle (WI)	33	31	3	965	117	34.46	2	7
TM Dilshan (SL)	35	34	5	897	96*	30.93	-	6
Shakib Al Hasan (BAN)	43	43	6	853	84	23.05	-	4
KS Williamson (NZ)	29	27	4	727	85	31.60	-	3
AB de Villiers (SA)	30	29	5	717	79*	29.87	-	5

HIGHEST INDIVIDUAL SCORES

Player	Runs	Team	Opponent	Venue	Date
BB McCullum	123	New Zealand	Bangladesh	Pallekele	21 Sep 2012
CH Gayle	117	West Indies	South Africa	Johannesburg	11 Sep 2007
AD Hales	116*	England	Sri Lanka	Chattogram	27 Mar 2014
Ahmed Shehzad	111*	Pakistan	Bangladesh	Mirpur	30 Mar 2014
RR Rossouw	109	South Africa	Bangladesh	Sydney	27 Oct 2022
GD Phillips	104	New Zealand	Sri Lanka	Sydney	29 Oct 2022
Tamim Iqbal	103*	Bangladesh	Oman	Dharamsala	13 Mar 2016
JC Buttler	101*	England	Sri Lanka	Sharjah	1 Nov 2021
SK Raina	101	India	South Africa	Gros Islet	2 May 2010
CH Gayle	100*	West Indies	England	Wankhede	16 Mar 2016
DPMD Jayawardene	100	Sri Lanka	Zimbabwe	Providence	3 May 2010

LEADING WICKET-TAKERS

Shakib Al Hasan (Bangladesh)	50
Shahid Afridi (Pakistan)	39
SL Malinga (Sri Lanka)	38
PW Hasaranga (Sri Lanka)	37
Rashid Khan (Afghanistan)	37
A Zampa (Australia)	36
Saeed Ajmal (Pakistan)	36
TG Southee (New Zealand)	36

BEST BOWLING FIGURES

Player	O	M	R	W	Team	Opponent	Venue	Date
BAW Mendis	4	2	8	6	Sri Lanka	Zimbabwe	Hambantota	18 Sep 2012
HMRKB Herath	3.3	2	3	5	Sri Lanka	New Zealand	Chattogram	31 Mar 2014
Umar Gul	3	-	6	5	Pakistan	New Zealand	The Oval	13 Jun 2009
Fazalhaq Farooqi	4	-	9	5	Afghanistan	Uganda	Providence	3 Jun 2024
SM Curran	3.4	-	10	5	England	Afghanistan	Perth	22 Oct 2022
AJ Hosein	4	-	11	5	West Indies	Uganda	Providence	8 Jun 2024
Ahsan Malik	4	-	19	5	Netherlands	South Africa	Chattogram	27 Mar 2014
A Zampa	4	-	19	5	Australia	Bangladesh	Dubai (DICS)	4 Nov 2021

MOST DISMISSALS BY A WICKETKEEPER

Player	Dismissals	Ct	St
MS Dhoni (India)	32	21	11
Q de Kock (South Africa)	30	23	7
Kamran Akmal (Pakistan)	30	12	18
D Ramdin (West Indies)	27	18	9
KC Sangakkara (Sri Lanka)	26	12	14
JC Buttler (England)	25	21	4

Stats courtesy of *Cricinfo*

MOST CATCHES BY A FIELDER

DA Warner (Australia)	25
AB de Villiers (South Africa)	23
GJ Maxwell (Australia)	23
RG Sharma (India)	21
MJ Guptill (New Zealand)	19

MOST APPEARANCES

RG Sharma (India)	47
Shakib Al Hasan (Bangladesh)	43
DA Warner (Australia)	41
Mahmudullah (Bangladesh)	37
JC Buttler (England)	35
TM Dilshan (Sri Lanka)	35
V Kohli (India)	35

AUSTRALIA

BIBLIOGRAPHY

Arnold, Peter, *The Illustrated Encyclopedia of World Cricket,* Golden Press, 1987.

Bichel, Andy and Collins, Gerry, *No Bull,* ABC Books, 2009.

Border, Allan, *An autobiography,* Mandarin Australia, 1990.

Browning, Mark, *A Complete History Of World Cup Cricket,* Kangaroo Press, 1999.

Crowe, Martin, *Out on a Limb,* Reed Publishing, 1995.

Gilchrist, Adam, *True Colours,* Pan Macmillan Australia, 2008.

Imran Khan, *All Round View*, Chatto and Windus, 1988.

Johnson, Martin and Blofeld, Henry, *The Independent World Cup Cricket '87,* The Kingswood Press, 1987.

Miller, Allan, *Allan's Australian Cricket Annual*: 1987–88, 1991–92, 1996, 1999. Self-published.

Smith, Patrick (editor), *The Age World Cup Cricket 1992,* The Five Mile Press Pty Ltd, 1992.

Tendulkar, Sachin, *Playing It My Way,* Hodder & Stoughton, 2014.

Ward, Andrew, *Cricket's Strangest Matches,* Robson Books, 1994.

WEBSITES

espncricinfo.com

Cricket.com.au

Wikipedia

YouTube

Australia's Mitchell Johnson is airborne with joy after bowling India's Rohit Sharma during a 2015 semi-final at the Sydney Cricket Ground.

ABOUT THE AUTHOR

Liam Hauser is a sports journalist and author who has written about cricket, rugby league and other sports for more than 15 years. His previous books include *A Century of Cricket Tests* (New Holland, 2013), *A History of Test Cricket* (New Holland, 2016), *The Immortals of Australian Cricket* (Gelding Street Press, 2018), *State of Origin: 45 Years* (Gelding Street Press, 2025), *The Great Grand Finals: Rugby league's Greatest Contests* (New Holland, 2017, 2019 and 2022), *The Immortals of Australian Rugby League* (Gelding Street Press, 2019), and *The Immortals of State of Origin* (Gelding Street Press, 2023).

With a Bachelor of Journalism from Queensland University of Technology, Liam has worked as a reporter for regional newspapers in Queensland and NSW since 2007. Over the years he has written about many sports including cricket, rugby league, rugby union, oztag, touch football, soccer, gymnastics, swimming, athletics, campdrafting, equestrian, tennis, bowls, boxing, hockey, golf, rifle shooting, horse racing and archery.

He has been a guest on radio many times to speak about his in-depth knowledge of cricket.